JOSEPH PAPP, one of the most important forces in theater today, is the founder and producer of the New York Shakespeare Festival, America's largest and most prolific theatrical institution. Since 1954, Mr. Papp has produced or directed all but one of Shakespeare's plays, in Central Park, in schools, off and on Broadway, and at the Festival's permanent home, The Public Theater. He has also produced such award-winning plays and musical works as *Hair*, *A Chorus Line*, *For Colored Girls Who Have Considered Suicide When the Rainbow Is Enuf*, and *Runaways*, among many others.

ELIZABETH KIRKLAND graduated from Harvard-Radcliffe in Classics in 1983 and earned an advanced degree in English as a Rhodes Scholar at Oxford. She has been involved in the theater backstage as a producer, publicity manager, and stage manager, and onstage as a performer. She now works with Joseph Papp at the New York Shakespeare Festival.

SHAKESPEARE ALIVE!

JOSEPH PAPP
AND
ELIZABETH
KIRKLAND

BANTAM BOOKS

TORONTO · NEW YORK · LONDON · SYDNEY · AUCKLAND

SHAKESPEARE ALIVE!

A Bantam Book / February 1988

Cover photographs, clockwise from left corner are from New York Shakespeare Festival productions:

Othello, *with Raul Julia as Othello and Richard Dreyfuss as Iago, directed by Wilford Leach at the Delacorte Theater in Central Park, 1979.*

Photo © Martha Swope

Richard III, *with Kevin Kline as Richard III, directed by Jane Howell at the Delacorte Theater in Central Park, 1983.*

Photo © Martha Swope

A Midsummer Night's Dream, *with Kathleen Widdoes as Titania, Albert Quinton as Nick Bottom, and Ralph Hoffman and Herman Dalkieth Howell as fairies, directed by Joel J. Friedman in 1961 at the Wollman Memorial Rink in Central Park, 1961.*

Photo © George E. Joseph

King Lear, *with James Earl Jones as Lear and Tom Aldredge as the Fool, directed by Edwin Sherin at the Delacorte Theater in Central Park, 1973.*

Photo © George E. Joseph

Two Gentlemen of Verona, *with (l. to r.) Deborah Rush as Silvia, Dylan Baker as Launce, Thomas Gibson as Proteus, and Elizabeth McGovern as Julia, directed by Stuart Vaughan at the Delacorte Theater in Central Park, 1987.*

Photo © Martha Swope

Twelfth Night, *with F. Murray Abraham as Malvolio and Peter MacNicol as Sir Andre, directed by Wilford Leach at the Delacorte Theater in Central Park, 1986.*

Photo © Martha Swope

Henry IV, Part One, *with Stacy Keach as Sir John Falstaff, directed by Gerald Freedman at the Delacorte Theater in Central Park, 1968.*

Photo © George E. Joseph

ISBN 0-553-27081-8

Published simultaneously in the United States and Canada

Bantam Books are published by Bantam Books, a division of Bantam Doubleday Dell Publishing Group, Inc. Its trademark, consisting of the words "Bantam Books" and the portrayal of a rooster, is Registered in U.S. Patent and Trademark Office and in other countries. Marca Registrada, Bantam Books, 666 Fifth Avenue, New York, New York 10103

PRINTED IN THE UNITED STATES OF AMERICA

O   0 9 8 7 6 5 4 3 2 1

ACKNOWLEDGMENTS

THE IDEA FOR this book originated in the mind of my wife and colleague Gail Merrifield Papp. My thanks to her for her assistance and for those long nights we spent together reviewing Elizabeth Kirkland's completed manuscript. I also would like to thank Linda Grey, Bantam's publisher, and Kathy Robbins, my agent, for their support.

—Joseph Papp

I WOULD LIKE to thank the many who helped along the way, beginning with Peter Conrad, of Christ Church, Oxford, who not only taught but inspired. I am grateful to Jeremy Maule of Trinity College, Cambridge; Peter Holland of Trinity Hall, Cambridge; David Norbrook and Oliver Taplin, both of Magdalen College, Oxford; Emrys Jones of New College, Oxford; Julia Briggs of Hertford College, Oxford; Nigel Smith of Keble College, Oxford; and Christopher Butler of Christ Church, Oxford, all of whom provided helpful suggestions at the outset of this project. Dick McCaw of The Medieval Players in London offered hands-on advice from his perspective, as did Estelle Parsons and the company of Shakespeare on Broadway from theirs.

In addition to Martin Segal, whose early advice is still appreciated, special thanks go to the staff of the Archives Office and all others at the New York Shakespeare Festival who helped; and to Nessa Rapoport and Linda Loewenthal at Bantam Books. Daniel Benjamin made helpful comments and corrections on the first six chapters. Alan Fine gave hours of criticism and advice; my gratitude to him goes far beyond this. And finally, to my parents, deep thanks for making it all possible.

—Elizabeth Kirkland

CONTENTS

PART I

PROLOGUE

Autolycus, a peddler, gloats at the success of his business as he traverses the countryside selling trinkets and ballads. (Roscoe Lee Browne as Autolycus in the 1963 New York Shakespeare Festival production of *The Winter's Tale*.)
Photo: George E. Joseph

ONE DAY AT A TIME: WHAT DAILY LIFE WAS LIKE

GIVE US THIS DAY OUR DAILY BREAD

YOU ARE LIVING in England in the late years of the sixteenth century. Like most people, you live with your family in the countryside, eking out a meager existence as best you can. If you're lucky, your father is a yeoman farmer who owns enough land to support his family, or a "husband-man" who has less property but supplements his income by wage-earning.

The land you live in is full of contradictions. A woman, Queen Elizabeth, rules the nation, while within the family, men still rule women. A highly-educated elite enjoys the fruits of literature, while many people can't even read. The government invests huge sums of money in voyages of exploration and wars with other nations, while science and medicine remain in an appallingly primitive state. In London, the royal Court glitters with jewels and finery, while misery reigns in rural hovels. Rich young men wander around Europe for fun, while in England, thousands of homeless people wander from parish to parish, begging and stealing to survive.

The gap between the rich and the poor seems to have widened in the 1570s and 1580s; wealth and power are concentrated in the hands of the few, and many people can't even find a job.

You come from a family of laborers. You don't have any land at all, hardly even a vegetable garden you can call your own, and you are completely dependent on whatever wages you can get by harvesting other people's crops and doing odd jobs around the village. There is no money for such "extras" as education or nice clothes or red meat. In fact, your father's daily income, even when combined with yours, barely covers the cost of feeding you and your brothers and sisters; thank goodness your mother is able to bring in a few extra pennies from her spinning.

There's no doubt about it, life is a struggle even in the best of circumstances. Of course, usually circumstances aren't anywhere near the best. Disease, malnutrition, and tragic natural disasters are givens of your daily existence and keep you from taking anything you have for granted. Just a month ago, for example, an old widow's thatched roof caught on fire, and even though you were right there along with everyone else in the village, pulling the flaming thatch down with iron hooks, it was too late. Her cottage burned to the ground, and she, too, is now among the homeless—and hopeless.

Your dependent status as a tenant makes your perch in life still more precarious. To an unjust and unscrupulous landlord, profit is more important than principles, and yours feels no obligation to look out for your best interests. If he decides to "enclose" the land—to stop using it for farming and turn it into grazing pastures for sheep —he has endless means of forcing you out: he might make you give up your lease, or renew it only at great expense, or, most commonly, charge you exorbitant rent.

While your family has been struggling against these odds and worrying about how to make ends meet from day to day, larger forces have been at work that are going to affect you drastically. First, England has been undergoing a huge increase in population. The two-and-a-half million English people who were alive when your grandparents were born will practically have doubled by the time your grandchildren die. This unprecedented population growth is already being translated into inflated prices, as too many people chase after scarce resources. It also means that wages stay unacceptably low; with so many laborers on the job market, farmers and other employers can easily find people willing to work for the pathetically low wages they offer if you're not interested.

Getting and spending have been a constant battle, and staying on the winning side has depended on plentiful harvests, which bring the twofold benefit of jobs and low grain prices. But in recent years the battle has become a losing one: the heavy rains of the last two summers have ruined the harvests, the population has been growing faster than the crops, and famine has begun to cast its long, thin shadow across your life.

Grain—whether you eat the oatmeal cakes of northern England or the coarse wheat bread of the southerners— is a staple of your diet and, if you have no land and have to buy all your grain on the market, your single biggest expense. When prices shoot up, as they do in bad harvest years, it spells disaster for many a citizen; the Carriers in Shakespeare's *Henry IV Part 1* remember a comrade who "never joyed since the price of oats rose. It was the death of him." You try to find cheaper kinds of grain than your usual wheat, supplementing your diet with stomach-filling peas and beans—but even the prices of these are rising now, and you begin to realize, horrifying though it is, that there aren't many alternatives. Starvation seems inevitable.

You wonder how you and your family are going to cope with the steady advance of such hunger, the hair falling out and the skin turning gray and the bleak prospect of watching your fellow villagers "starving and dying in our streets and in the fields [because] of lack of bread," as a contemporary in the northern town of Newcastle writes.

Little do you know that the famine has darkened all of Europe, not just England. In Sweden, old women have reportedly been found dead in the fields with seeds and grass in their mouths, and in far-off Hungary, Tartar women are rumored to have eaten their own children!

To make matters worse, there has been an economic recession too, mainly because of a slump in the cloth trade that your mother had been depending on for her liveli- hood. Many people rely on the cloth and wool trades for their living, and now, "the deadness of that trade and want of money is such that they are for the most part without work, and know not how to live," as an official of one parish reports.

HITTING THE ROAD

CLEARLY, THE SITUATION is getting desperate. After a lot of agonizing, you decide that your only hope is to leave your family and village and migrate to London. "After all," you think, "it will be one less mouth for them to feed. And maybe I'll find an apprenticeship or something."

Anything would be better than staying here and slowly starving to death. And so you say goodbye to your parents, kiss your little sister on the head, punch your brother in the arm, and head off to the big city—not roaring down the interstate highway on a Greyhound bus, as future generations of teenagers will do, but trudging along a dirt track on foot. At least it's not winter, when the quagmires of mud and hundreds of ruts and holes make the roads impassable. They're not in good repair as it is, and progress is slow and uneven.

Once you've reached the slightly larger London road, you find yourself being passed by wealthier travelers who can afford to ride on horseback. They are traveling at a leisurely enough pace now, but no doubt as the afternoon wears on they will pick up speed in order to reach one of the fashionable inns for the rich before nightfall; as Shakespeare observes in *Macbeth*, "Now spurs the lated traveler apace To gain the timely inn."

You're surprised at how many people are on the road, especially given the discomfort of traveling. A few well-heeled young gents are headed for the university life at Oxford and Cambridge. Important-looking government officials gallop by on their swift post-horses. Most often, though, you see other pedestrians, for walking is the poor person's method of transportation, and there are lots of poor people on the move. Apparently you weren't the only one with the idea of going to London—the roads seem to be flooded with migrants like you.

As you strike up conversations with a few of your fellow

walkers, you realize that everyone has a different story to tell. You meet an unwed and very pregnant servant girl who was fired from her job and kicked out of her parish when her pregnancy could no longer be hidden; she's been wandering for several weeks, hoping to find a parish that will take her in without a husband. A middle-aged man is going to give evidence in court. A newly-married young couple are on their way to visit relatives.

You also run into a peddler who, like Autolycus in Shakespeare's play *The Winter's Tale*, travels around the countryside, stopping at fairs and markets to sell his assortment of wares: gloves, bracelets, perfumes, pins and needles, and ballads. "Come buy of me, come. Come buy, come buy," he cries persuasively. "Buy, lads, or else your lasses cry."

The most depressing sight on the road is the old people, sick, decrepit, and lame, who are "forced to walk the country from place to place" because there isn't any organized system of hospitals, shelters, or charitable institutions to take care of them. As a contemporary social critic writes, many of them, as they are driven from one parish to another, just die, "some in ditches, some in holes, some in caves and dens, some in fields . . . like dogs."

The majority of wanderers you run into, however, are solitary young men about your age who are traveling, like you, in the hope of finding work. Three amiable youths ask you to join up with them, but you decide that your chances of finding something are better if you're alone, so you thank them but turn down their invitation. If three is a crowd, four is an unemployment line.

At all times you keep an eye out for anyone who looks vaguely "official," for you don't have the required papers that state where and why you are traveling. If you're caught without them, you'll be in a lot of trouble; as an unofficial traveler, you are considered a vagrant, a vagabond—in short, an undesirable.

The prevailing opinion in government circles seems to be that vagrants are idle and lazy by choice, or even dangerous. From what you can tell, this is absurd. Of course there are a few pickpockets and petty thieves among the travelers, but most of them are like that old woman you saw picking the pocket of a sleeping man because she had no shoes for her feet—hardly a violent criminal! The fact

is, of course, that with the famine and the trade depression, the majority of these people couldn't find work if
they wanted to. And even if they could, their wages would
hardly be enough to live on. For most of the people you
meet, London is their only hope.

THE CITY THAT NEVER SLEEPS

ONE HUNDRED MILES and several days later, as the sun
comes up, London also rises above the green fields. As
you enter the city gates, you draw your breath in wonder.
The city you have come to—the largest in all of Europe
—is noisy and bustling. At its heart is the River Thames,
the center of trade and social life. You see the opulent
state barge of the queen moored on the bank and marvel
at how many "watermen," the taxi drivers of the river, are
rowing from one riverbank to the other. You get lost in
the narrow winding streets; as you stare up at the looming
Tower of London, you are nearly run over by one of the
many coaches that are causing perpetual gridlock in the
city. You hear vendors hawking "hot peas!" or "new brooms,
green brooms!"; their voices mix with the pitiful moans
and cries of the prisoners in the Tower to create a deaf-
ening and exhausting hubbub. It is hard to believe how
many people live here—well over 100,000.

Although you're slightly overwhelmed by it all, you
decide to do what you came here for and begin looking
for work. Unfortunately, everyone else is doing the same
—the market is saturated with laborers, and prospects are
not good. Most days you just sit around hoping something
will come your way. You wonder what will become of you.
There isn't any formal system of welfare to support the
unemployed, no food stamps, no soup kitchens.

Together with other migrants just like you, you huddle
in a cold attic and share memories of what each of you
has left behind. You yourself recall the small stone cottage
that you lived in all of your life. Although it was only one
room, and what little furniture you had was very rough,
although your bed was of straw and your sheets were of

canvas—still, it was home, and it was better than this smelly tenement where all of you are sleeping on the floor.

An old man in the room, once the servant of a prosperous farmer, describes the opulent house of his former employer—so many rooms, and carpets on the floor, woven tapestries on the walls, carved oak woodwork, lots of candles giving light, and the ultimate luxury—feather beds. He remembers serving his first Christmas dinner at the house, at the long table in the great hall, or dining room. He'd never *seen* so much meat on one table—beef, pork, veal, venison, game. There were oysters and eel, cabbage and carrots, some delicious finely-ground bread, dried fruit, and wines imported from the French or German countryside. As you listen to his description, you wonder how the rich aren't chronically constipated with all that meat.

In your own little cottage the fare was usually coarse brown bread, cheese and eggs, the occasional chicken or hunk of bacon. Everything used to be cheap—two loaves of bread for a penny—but in the last few wretched years, prices have risen enormously and food for the poor like you has become scarce. With the onset of famine you had to resort to eating bread (still a staple), peas and beans, and whatever else you could hunt up in the woods around the village.

Two would-be apprentices—fresh from the alehouse—tumble into the already crowded room, singing the praises of beer. Indeed, the constant friend of all of you during these times of tribulation is beer. Imported wines are too costly; tea and coffee are still luxuries; but beer is cheap to make and a regular feature of social life. Everyone drinks it, even your young brothers and sisters back in the village. Sometimes, admittedly, people go overboard—at local fairs and country markets, scores of people regularly end up lying dead drunk in the field.

And drinking seems to provide the same comfort here in London. The alehouses are always full; you can find one on nearly every corner. A Frenchman was provoked to remark that no business could be done in England without pots of beer. But the truth is that alcohol helps people forget the strains of life. It flows freely in the prisons and during outbreaks of the plague. At public executions the person condemned to death is always offered a drink. You can understand why. A beer or two eases the hardships of daily existence—the lack of jobs, the high prices, the scarcity of food, the awful diseases, and all the other things that make life so hard.

Indeed, sickness and death are regular features of life in this enormous city you've come to. Disease is even more prevalent here and in the squalid suburbs you passed on your way into London than in the impoverished village you left behind. The contagious bubonic plague is the number one killer. Coming in at a close second is small-pox, which blinds or disfigures the people it doesn't actually kill; your beautiful little sister has been left pock-marked for life. And tuberculosis takes lives daily.

The spread of infectious diseases is furthered by the total ignorance about personal and public hygiene. Rich and poor alike don't bathe very often; the poor can't afford the high price of soap and don't have the facilities. The toothbrush won't come on the scene for another seventy years. Most Elizabethans, and you are no exception, have bad breath, rotting teeth, constant stomach disorders, and scabs or running sores all over their skin.

Things are no better on a public scale. The city ditches are used as toilets. Butchers throw dead animal carcasses into the street to rot. Housewives nonchalantly toss putrid garbage into the river. Poor people are buried in mass graves, and the bodies of the rich, lying beneath the church building in burial vaults, force the congregation to evacuate because the stench of decomposition is so strong.

Not even trained doctors make a connection between these unhygienic conditions and the high incidence of disease. Medical care is not very advanced, and knowledge of the human body is still very primitive. The prevailing theory of illness is that it is a result of an imbalance in the four humors, the four chief fluids of the human body. Health requires a perfect balance of bile, phlegm, choler, and blood; when any one of these becomes excessive, a doctor tries to restore the balance by using leeches to suck out some of the sick person's blood. X rays and stethoscopes haven't yet been invented; the most common operation is amputation, performed *without* anesthesia. In the city of London there are two hospitals and one doctor for every five thousand people. Health insurance such as

Medicare or Medicaid doesn't exist, which means that doctors are pretty much only for the wealthy. In your opinion, doctors are more likely to kill than cure, and you're probably better off consulting a faith healer, good witch, or wise woman who uses techniques of white magic.

While medical knowledge remains in a fairly backward state, liberal arts education is expanding prodigiously. But you yourself only got as far as basic reading skills at the village school. You weren't able to go to grammar school, the lynchpin of the Elizabethan educational system, because your parents couldn't spare you from work in the fields. Although they had more schools to choose from, they couldn't afford the books, papers, and candles you'd have needed. To them, school seemed a luxury.

But what you can't experience, you can hear about from the down-at-the-heels scholar sitting next to you in the cold room, reminiscing fondly about his old schooldays. The morning session went from 6 A.M. to 11 A.M., with a two-hour lunch break; the afternoon session was from 1 P.M. to 6 P.M.—six days a week! Grammar school education made available to upper-class boys the wealth of Latin literature uncovered by Renaissance scholars—playwrights such as Plautus, Terence, Seneca; the poets Virgil and Horace; and prose writers such as Cicero and Caesar. A lot was demanded of the pupils; and if any boy was lazy or inattentive, he might be whipped, sometimes savagely, by the schoolmaster.

Status-conscious families felt compelled to send their sons to school in order to prepare them for a career in politics or the Church. Only in the highest reaches of the aristocracy was any money spent on educating girls. Your queen, Elizabeth, for example, is an extremely accomplished speaker of Latin, Greek, French, and Italian. But she is certainly the exception.

Still, you don't have to be a queen or a scholar to learn about the world around you. Recent developments in communications have made literature more accessible to those, like you, who can at least read. The printing press, brought to England in the late fifteenth century by a man named William Caxton, has enabled a lot of people to share in the riches of the Renaissance. Books, once the sole province of the wealthy, are now not only available but affordable. Translations of ancient classical and modern European writers are proliferating wildly.

There are also hundreds of devotional tracts on the market, and Bibles are everywhere—the most popular book in the nation. Of course, newspapers won't be invented until the eighteenth century, but topical pamphlets and broadside ballads are gobbled up by news-hungry Londoners.

News travels more slowly to the rest of the country. There are only four or five major roads in all of England. The roads connecting smaller towns and villages are just dirt tracks, frequented by bands of robbers. Even though the penalty for highway robbery is death, bandits continue to rob the rich (and leave the poor alone). The most famous highwayman in English legend is, of course, Robin Hood; you know the stories about him and his band of merry men and his love Maid Marian backward and forward.

If travel within England is limited, foreign travel is even more so, as it is almost exclusively for the rich. Gentlemen consider it necessary to their education and often aspire to study in a foreign university in Italy or France.

In order to go abroad, a license, similar to a passport, must first be obtained. Once a gentleman arrives in Europe, he speaks Latin, the universal language in educated circles.

But not everyone who travels abroad is in pursuit of higher education. Acting companies tour the Continent and are very popular there, even though they speak English. Merchants and traders are frequent travelers, too.

And as the ex-soldier across the room can attest, the fourth group that gets the chance to see foreign lands is the military. Although there isn't a permanent army that drafts and trains young men, English troops are constantly engaged in campaigns in Ireland, France, and elsewhere. This fellow spent some time—and lost an arm—on the battlefields of the Low Countries (or the Netherlands), in the Earl of Essex's campaign. There *is* a permanent navy, albeit a small one, whose expeditions make talk of foreign lands a part of Londoners' everyday conversation. Military service might seem like a good opportunity for unemployed men like you, but it is in fact extremely unpopular, and the grizzled veteran tells you why. The queen pays her soldiers only very grudgingly. And conditions are bad: the typical daily navy rations are a dry stale biscuit, some mouldy cheese, and sour beer. For all these reasons it is difficult to keep the military adequately manned. Often the ranks are filled with ex-convicts and disreputable sorts. And underhanded methods are used to press men into service. Just last Easter, when the church was more full than usual, army officers unexpectedly locked the church doors and walked through the aisles signing up every able-bodied man inside.

PLAYTIME

THE CONSTANT WARFARE conducted outside of England is matched by the constant violence within its borders. Fights, brawls, and riots erupt at the drop of a hat. On the London streets you've gotten used to hearing the cry "Clubs!" which means a fight is breaking out somewhere. Favorite weapons in these street fights are daggers, swords, and old reliable fists. The police force that would be controlling this violence today is all but non-existent; the London constables are petty and incompetent, utterly incapable of maintaining order. Even the activities you regard as "fun" are brutal by later standards. The leading national amusements are bearbaiting, in which several dogs are loosed on a bear tied to a stake, and cockfighting, gladiatorial contests between trained roosters that involve a good deal of blood.

Public executions are also popular. The convicted criminal often sits in a cart with a noose around his neck and is left hanging as it rides away; sometimes his friends pull at his legs to relieve him of his suffering. Death by the axe is even gorier, of course; it can often take two or three chops before the victim is dead. Then the executioner holds up the head for all to see. Witch-burnings are increasingly popular and always gruesome.

You prefer bearbaiting and spend many a Sunday afternoon across the river watching the dogs savagely bite and growl as the bear tosses and tugs in a rage. Recently, another activity has come to your notice, thanks to an attic mate who shares your floor—dramatic performances held in the public theater. He hopes to sign on with an acting company as a hired man and goes to the theater often. After talking with him for a while, you think you'll probably go along. With an admission price of a penny, it doesn't cost any more than the bearbaiting—and may be just as much fun. You once saw a band of traveling players in a nearby village, putting on a play about Noah and his wife, but a performance in one of these outdoor public theaters must be a different experience altogether. Maybe you'll even see a play by William Shakespeare, whose hometown of Stratford isn't too far from your old village.

You idly wonder if this Shakespeare is really as good as people say he is. Even if he's not, you think to yourself as you curl up on the floor in your crowded, wretched little attic, seeing a play may turn out to be a great way for you to forget about your worries for an hour or two. Certainly you have enough of them.

And yet, for all your troubles, you wouldn't go back to your village. You sense that a world your parents have never imagined is unfolding around you, and all you want is to be part of it.

PART II

THE ELIZABETHANS

King Henry V, with strategic diplomatic alliances and territorial gains on his mind, attempts to win over the Princess of France to their already-arranged marriage. (Meryl Streep and Paul Rudd as Katherine and Henry in the 1976 New York Shakespeare Festival production of *King Henry V*.)
Photo: George E. Joseph

CHAPTER 2

ORDER IN THE COURT: THE RENAISSANCE

TODAY WE USE the term "Renaissance" (meaning "rebirth") to describe the incredible flowering of art, scholarship, and literature that took place as fifteenth- and sixteenth-century Europe blossomed forth from the Middle Ages. The "Reformation" is the name given to the landmark religious movement that began when King Henry VIII split with the Pope and the Catholic Church of Rome and founded the Protestant Church of England. And we include the many exciting geographical and scientific discoveries and the expansion of trade and commerce of that era in the phrases "the Age of Exploration" or "the Age of Discovery."

But it didn't occur to the inhabitants of England in the late part of the sixteenth century that they were living in the Renaissance, the Reformation, the Age of Exploration, or any other such tidy historical period. From their close-up perspective, the developments and discoveries were specific to their lifetimes, not part of wider historical movements. All they knew was that when they looked around, things seemed to be changing at a bewildering pace.

The world was opening up, and the possibilities were wonderful, if a little overwhelming. The recently redis-covered Greek and Roman writings were taking the book market by storm, unleashing a new enthusiasm for edu-cation. Explorers were discovering worlds where everyone used to think nothing existed. And although the English were still deeply religious, the institution of the Church had been seesawing at a dizzying rate during the past decades. There were so many choices in learning and belief that it must have been tempting to brush them all aside with one impatient, anxious motion and stick to the old ways.

THE BESTSELLER LIST

THE INTELLECTUAL SPIRIT of the Renaissance was completely changing people's way of looking at life and at themselves. This movement began in the fourteenth century in Italy, then the intellectual center of Europe with major universities at Bologna and Padua; in *The Taming of the Shrew* Lucentio calls the city "fair Padua, nursery of the arts." When Italian scholars began to look into the long-buried works of ancient authors such as Homer and Hesiod, Plato and Aristotle, Virgil and Ovid, they were unknowingly releasing a vigorous life-force into the bloodstream of Western culture.

Throughout the Middle Ages, the Church had dominated civilization, and both literature and education had been considered servants of religion. In those days literary works were judged only by how "Christian" they were; not surprisingly, most "pagan" writings of the Greeks and Romans—the ancient classics of Plato, Sophocles, and the like—were forced out of circulation.

When scholars rediscovered them, it wasn't long before Italy was ablaze with interest in the classical culture that inspired these writers. Knowledge broke out of the cloisters to the freedom of an increasingly secular society. And the world of the human spirit that had been so long undervalued burst into flames, fanned by the rich colors and sensuous shapes of painters and sculptors such as Titian, Raphael, and Michelangelo, and the rich narratives and romantic epics of Boccaccio, Tasso, and Ariosto.

This cultural explosion eventually reverberated in England, although it took nearly a century to make itself heard. When it did, however, echoes of the new "humanism" reached the remotest parts of the nation. Education, formerly dominated by clergymen, became a prestigious possession of the upper classes and an indispensable qualification for the "good life." There was a rash of schools founded all across the nation, with the result that the riches of the Renaissance became available to more and more people. Translations of ancient Greco-Roman and contemporary Italian authors became bestsellers, aided by the arrival of the printing press from Europe. Of the many works on the market, the heroic epics of the Greek poet Homer (the *Odyssey* and the *Iliad*) and the Roman Virgil (the *Aeneid*) were considered the highest achievements of ancient literature for their combination of action-packed stories with instruction in Christian moral virtues such as courage, loyalty, and patience.

But contemporary Italian works weren't slighted by English printers and publishers either: the pastoral poems of Sannazarro, for example, influenced the courtier Sir Philip Sidney in his famous work *The Arcadia*. Handbooks of manners and self-help books for ambitious courtiers, such as Thomas Hoby's translation of *The Courtier* by Baldassare Castiglione, were well-thumbed by those in Court circles most anxious to get ahead. Many such books set forth the ideal of the "Renaissance man," as we call it: a widely-accomplished man who was statesman and athlete, scientist and poet, philosopher, courtier, and soldier all rolled into one.

WHICH WAY IS UP?

THESE HUNDREDS OF old books in new translations coupled with the explosion in education were certainly broadening the Elizabethans' literary horizons. Meanwhile, literal horizons were expanding with an almost frightening rapidity. European astronomers were challenging age-old beliefs about the universe. One of them, Copernicus, even went so far as to suggest that the Sun, and not the Earth, was the center of the universe; he further maintained that the Earth was actually in motion, not fixed in place. Although such theories sound elementary to us now, at the time they ran contrary to everything people had ever thought about the centrality of the Earth. Suddenly they were being told that instead of being the focus of God's attention, the Earth was just a small lonely planet orbiting the sun. Skeptics were numerous and loud. But as the telescope revolutionized astronomy and an Italian named Galileo discovered even more unsettling truths about the universe, the Elizabethans' old assumptions had to give way, even though it seemed that the sky above their heads was crumbling.

The ground beneath their feet was none too steady either, thanks to the crowd of explorers who were racing all over the globe propelled by better maps, new mathematical tables, and other advances in technology. As one writer enthusiastically crowed, "The sea yields to the world by this art of arts, navigation."

And the world was yielding to adventurous explorers of all the European nations as they sailed off in search of wealth and fame. The race was on to discover—and claim—sea-routes to the phenomenal storehouses of wealth in the East. The Portuguese won the first lap when Vasco da Gama sailed around the southern tip of Africa and discovered an eastern route to India. Other nations turned west instead to find a throughway to the East. After Amerigo Vespucci ran into Brazil in the southwest and John Cabot found Newfoundland in the northwest, it began to dawn on geographers that there was an entire continent in the way—which might prove valuable in itself. Spain wasted no time exploring and exploiting this possibility: explorers such as Francisco Vásquez de Coronado and Hernando de Soto traipsed up the Pacific coast and around the southern areas of the place they called America.

The English didn't just sit idly by while all this was taking place, but eagerly pursued their own avenues of discovery and trade. Such heroes as Martin Frobisher, Hugh Willoughby, the Cabot family, and John Davis tried repeatedly to establish a northeast and then a northwest passage to Asia. After encouraging starts, all of them were ultimately unsuccessful, defeated by storms and solid blocks of ice. But English explorers, who combined the roles of pirate, missionary, and adventurer, were planting the seeds of good trade relations in the Far East, seeds that eventually grew into a sprawling empire.

A whole new order of global economic activity was in

the making, promising lucre and glory. Upper-class gentlemen, well-to-do merchants, and the shrewd Queen Elizabeth herself were quick to sense the potentially enormous profits in foreign trade, and before long joint-stock companies were being formed to invest money in trade ventures. By the end of the century England would be trading with such far-off regions as Africa, Turkey, and India, and Shakespeare would be able to say that Owen Glendower, in *Henry IV Part 1* is "as bountiful As mines of India." Falstaff in *The Merry Wives of Windsor* describes his intended courtship of Mistress Page and Mistress Ford in terms more appropriate to a potential mercantile investor than a starry-eyed lover: he assesses Mistress Page as "a region in Guiana, all gold and bounty" and then plots his investment strategy, "I will be cheaters to them both, and they shall be exchequers to me. They shall be my East and West Indies, and I will trade to them both."

Such growing investment opportunities weren't within the reach of every Elizabethan's pocketbook. But if the wealth to be gained from the voyages of exploration and trade was not available to all, at least the information about world geography and cultures brought back by these world travelers was for everyone. Maps of the world more accurate than any ever drawn were arriving in England, a fact that the clever Maria uses to mock Malvolio in *Twelfth Night:* "He does smile his face into more lines than is in the new map with the augmentation of the Indies." And even a servant like Dromio of Syracuse in *The Comedy of Errors* is aware of the new dimensions of the world when he describes his master an impressive global tour when he describes the globular kitchen wench pursuing him: "she is spherical, like a globe. I could find out countries in her," he confides, and proceeds to compare the parts of her body to England's neighbors France, Spain, Scotland, and the Netherlands, as well as the remote and exotic America.

More spellbinding than the geographies were the sensational stories and amazing descriptions of the peoples and customs of these strange new worlds. Every day another mind-stretching tale of incredible creatures in foreign parts docked with the ships in London. Whether it was a description of the African "sciapod," a being with only one foot enormous enough to shade him from the glaring African sun, or a rumor of men with the heads of dogs—not unlike that "puppy-headed monster" Caliban who curses and drinks his way through Shakespeare's *The Tempest*—the streets of London were buzzing. Savvy Londoners weren't always sure whether or not to believe these fantastic stories. But if strange creatures such as elephants from Africa could clump around the animal yard at the Tower of London, they reasoned, why not man-eating savages and headless monsters? Ever curious, they didn't think twice about paying good money to gape at dead crocodiles brought back from abroad. In fact, these Londoners were just the kind of people Shakespeare is thinking of when he has Trinculo encounter Caliban on the island of *The Tempest:* "Were I in England now . . . and had but this fish painted, not a holiday fool but would give a piece of silver." In the same breath, Shakespeare makes a stinging comment about Londoners' social priorities: "When they will not give a doit to relieve a lame beggar, they will lay out ten to see a dead Indian."

Of course, the Elizabethans had always known about Europe and had grown up with tales of Turks, Moors, and other infidels. But suddenly seductive spices, strange clothes, and glittering jewels were jumping off the safe pages of travel accounts and into the markets of London, and accurate descriptions of exotic cultures were flooding the bookstalls. What was an Elizabethan to make of black Africans who, according to one explorer's account, wore heavy gold and ivory jewels over otherwise naked bodies? Or of the new luxury drink "coffee"? It must have been vaguely threatening to learn that the English way of doing things wasn't the only way.

A MIGHTY FORTRESS

NOR COULD THE church provide much stability. The religious changes set in motion decades before Elizabeth came to the throne were still affecting everyone. Politics and religion had long been familiar bedfellows in England, and had become even more intertwined in the early sixteenth century when Henry VIII decreed that the ruler of the nation would also be the formal head of the new Protestant

Church. In Elizabethan times this meant that there was rarely a religious issue that didn't have political implications.

Although Henry's split with the Catholic Church established the separate Church of England, it was still on shaky ground when he died. Following his reign, there was more than a decade of turmoil and uncertainty, as each of his successive heirs instituted a different religious policy. "Bloody" Queen Mary's return to Catholicism provoked widespread hostility and violence in the mid-1550s. When Queen Elizabeth came to the throne, she decided to settle the matter once and for all by freezing the status quo of her father, warning her subjects not to attempt "the breach, alteration, or change of any order or usage presently established within this realm." Elizabeth made the Protestant faith England's official national religion and instituted the Book of Common Prayer. She also passed a law that required every subject to go to church on Sunday.

At the same time, she declared that she had no interest in sifting the consciences of her people. In other words, as long as everyone looked and acted like Protestants, and as long as unauthorized forms of worship weren't perceived to threaten national security, she didn't care what was done in the privacy of her subjects' homes. Although such tolerance was exceptional at that time, it was a far cry from the religious freedom in modern democratic nations. Anyone who publicly professed atheism or criticized the Church would be taken to the nearest gallows.

As the Church of England became more established in the course of Elizabeth's reign, two groups of religious—and therefore political—nonconformists emerged. The first group were radical reformers who thought that the process of change begun by Henry VIII hadn't gone nearly far enough. These Puritans detested anything that smacked of Roman Catholic ritual and wanted a church that was purer, cleaner, and more austere than the Church of England's version. Their political-religious platform called for the dismissal of the bishops of the established Church, whose hierarchical authority was condemned by the more egalitarian Puritans. Puritan pamphlets urging these and other reforms circulated all around London.

The queen watched the zealots carefully, wary of those

who might make trouble and disturb the peace she was working so hard to bring to the realm. Although she kept her private views to herself, she was quick to pounce on anyone she perceived as a real threat. A Puritan separatist named Henry Barrow, for example, was hauled into court and put on trial for publishing subversive literature criticizing the Church of England and the queen's position as its head. He confessed, under questioning, that he considered the Church's Book of Common Prayer "false, superstitious, and popish"; although he acknowledged the queen as the supreme governor of the Church, he also asserted that she should make laws based only on the words of Jesus Christ himself, as quoted in the New Testament. The court made short shrift of Henry Barrow's argument, and he was publicly hanged soon after his trial.

If the Puritans thought that religious reform hadn't gone far enough, the English Roman Catholics thought that it had already gone much too far. Despite the laws requiring attendance at Protestant churches, some Catholic recusants—especially noblemen with large estates in the remote north—were faithful to the outlawed forms of worship. Elizabeth was generally content to leave them alone as long as she was sure they weren't being disruptive. And many English Catholics were just as happy to live and let live, attending Church of England services as required while still maintaining their allegiance to the Pope in Rome.

But gradually this precarious balancing act became impossible, and Catholic allegiances were dangerously split. When the Pope excommunicated the Protestant Queen Elizabeth from the Catholic Church—an act of great hostility—more than a decade after she had come to the throne, English Catholics were hopelessly torn between loyalty to their faith and loyalty to their nation. The Pope's action, intended to stir up Catholic revolt within England, had several consequences (although *not* a Catholic revolt). First, loyal subjects rushed to their queen's defense with a stream of anti-Catholic pamphlets, sermons, and ballads. Second, oppression of Catholics within England was stepped up.

One of Elizabeth's biggest fears was that the Spaniards, England's chief enemy, would try to infiltrate the community of English Catholics, stir them to rebellion, and restore Catholicism to England. The approach of the Spanish Armada in 1588 didn't do much to calm her or anyone else's fears, even after the would-be invaders suffered a resounding defeat. The queen became more and more willing to do whatever she felt she had to in order to protect her country's security, including outright persecution.

And so government officers would search the houses of known Catholic families, however harmless and law-abiding they might seem, tearing their homes apart until they found what they had been looking for: Catholic books, ornaments, and religious images often hidden in holes beneath the floor. There were several proclamations ordering parents of young men studying in Catholic European countries to bring them home to England within four months. Other decrees put Catholics under a virtual quarantine, declaring that no Catholic over the dangerous age of sixteen could go further than three miles from his home without special permission, "because the enemy [Spain] doth make accompt to have the assistance of evil affected subjects of this land."

While lay Catholics were generally let off with nothing more than a fine, Catholic priests—especially those who had come over from the Jesuit seminaries of Europe to drum up support for their cause—were arrested and often tortured hideously. The most dreaded fate was to be sent to the house of Richard Topcliffe, who had been given permission by Queen Elizabeth herself "to torment priests in his own house in such sort as he shall think good." The sort he thought good involved clamping a victim's wrists into iron bands above his head so that his toes just barely scraped the floor, leaving the weight of his body on his wrists. Topcliffe may also have thought it good to prolong torture well after the priest had broken down and confessed. Whether they had to suffer at the hands of Topcliffe or not, more than one priest was executed for high treason—not heresy; the English government nearly always claimed that Catholics were being executed as political traitors, not heretics or religious martyrs. For in a nation where being Protestant was equivalent to being patriotic, Catholics were by definition betraying the nation.

The position of most English Catholics was uncomfortable if not dangerous; they were regarded with suspicion by the Elizabethan on the street, who imagined them to be in league with the Spaniards, ready at any moment to undermine and overthrow Protestant England. And, as often happens with matters of conscience, the lives of many families were disrupted. When the husband of one upper-class woman discovered, after twenty years of marriage, that she had been a practicing Catholic all along, he walked out, refused to give her a living allowance, and denied her custody of their children.

In most cases, though, the result of religious differences was friction rather than fracture. One young man grumbled about his old-fashioned parents who were clinging to their Catholic ways: "My father is an old doting fool and will fast upon the Friday, and my mother goeth always mumbling on her [rosary] beads."

The generation gap wasn't just a religious one; it spread to all areas of a changing society. The invention of the printing press, for example, meant that word-of-mouth traditions passed down by older people—"time's doting chronicles," as Shakespeare calls them—were no longer the only means of finding out about the past. Those who resolutely held on to the old ways of learning, worshipping, and understanding their world were going to be left behind as the wave of progress carried everyone else forward.

The unsettling speed of change was creating panic within the aristocracy. Books—and knowledge—were no longer limited exclusively to the ruling class. The growing and profitable trade activities meant that merchants and financiers were for the first time becoming as wealthy as hereditary nobles and the landed gentry; in the new economic climate, the divisions between the social classes were dissolving. In addition, many Elizabethans thought that the abandonment of the medieval church and the celebration of the secular in art and literature were turning society into an ungodly and immoral place. Nothing seemed stable or reliable anymore; the old ways were disappearing fast, and the search for a fixed point of moral reference was a futile one—everything depended on your point of view, for as Hamlet says, "there is nothing either good or bad but thinking makes it so." Anxiety gripped individuals, families, and the entire society.

A MOST EXCELLENT AND
PERFECT ORDER?

WHAT DID THEY do about it? Many people clung tenaciously to past ways of understanding the world and making sense of their place in it. The more things seemed to be teetering on the brink of chaos, the more Elizabethan society emphasized old concepts of order. The more freedom and self-determination people gained from trade and education, the more Elizabethan society stressed rank, propriety, and obedience. And the fainter the distinctions of social status and class became, the more Elizabethan society insisted upon the validity of those distinctions.

The buzz-word of the age was "hierarchy." Hierarchy was the great bulwark of social inequality that Elizabethan society put up against the wolves of confusion and disorder that were howling at its walls. Each person, according to this scheme, had a fixed place along the rigid columns of the social order; and each place came with its own obligations to superiors and inferiors alike. "Every degree of people . . . hath appointed to them, their duty and order," Elizabethans heard in church on Sunday. "Some are in high degree, some in low, some kings and princes, some inferiors and subjects. . . ." The preachers insisted that such an ordered society was part of God's arrangement for the universe—"Almighty God hath created and appointed all things . . . in a most excellent and perfect order."

Nowhere was this principle clearer than in the rigid clothing laws, which detailed who could wear what. The idea that the poor and merchant classes might be able to dress as extravagantly as their social superiors sent shivers up and down the richly-clothed spines of the upper classes. Clothing Acts were designed expressly to put a stop to this "intolerable abuse and unmeasurable disorder," as the Act of Apparel labeled it. And so no one who ranked lower than a knight could legally parade around in velvet cloaks or silk stockings; only countesses and higher could drape their limbs in the elegance of purple silk; gold and silver cloth were for the use of hereditary nobles only.

If this plan had worked as it was supposed to, people would have worn their social standing on their backs. But for the most part everyone ignored the restrictions, much to the chagrin of the lawmakers. Puritan writers were equally annoyed, firing off pamphlets condemning disobedient citizens for wearing rich clothing, "notwithstanding that they be both base by birth, mean by estate, and servile by calling. This is a great confusion and a general disorder, God be merciful unto us."

Hierarchy was the guiding principle of all realms of existence. In the heavenly kingdom, for example, several levels of archangels and angels spread downward from God's throne, and each level knew its place. Wasn't Satan thrown out for offending the principle of heavenly order and trying to make himself equal with God? The universe was a hierarchy too, and each planet and star was assigned to a specific position. As Ulysses says in Shakespeare's *Troilus and Cressida*, "the heavens themselves, the planets, and this center Observe degree, priority, and place." The animal world was another very stratified society in which each species had its king: the eagle was the king of birds; the whale the king of fish; and the lion, of course, the king of beasts.

The Great Chain of Being, stretching from the lowliest creature in the natural world all the way up to God, connected these worlds to each other, and the hierarchy of one was mirrored in the others. And so humans could often justify or explain their way of doing things by pointing to the animal world. The ruler of England, for example, was analogous to the king of beasts, and was expected to display the lion's formidable power. The Queen in *Richard II* chides her deposed husband for his unlionlike behavior when she sees him conveyed to the Tower of London. "The lion dying thrusteth forth his paw And wounds the earth, if nothing else, with rage To be o'erpowered; and wilt thou, pupil-like, Take the correction, mildly kiss the rod, And fawn on rage with base humility, Which are a lion and the king of beasts?" Bees were one of the most popular models of good government; in *Henry V*, the Archbishop of Canterbury begins a long speech on this topic: ". . . for so work the honeybees, Creatures that by a rule in nature teach The act of order to a peopled kingdom."

Of course, humans were expected to surpass the examples of the animal world, since they were seen as superior to animals by the measure of their intellect. Luciana points this out to her married sister Adriana as she lectures her on the virtues of being submissive to men in *The Comedy of Errors:* "The beasts, the fishes, and the wingèd fowl, Are their males' subjects and at their controls. Man, more divine, the master of all these, Lord of the wide world and wild watery seas, Endued with intellectual sense and souls, Of more preeminence than fish and fowls, Are masters to their females, and their lords; Then let your will attend on their accords."

A feminist before her time, Adriana replies that "This servitude makes you to keep unwed," but in fact Luciana is right; Elizabethan attitudes toward the family reinforced the wider notions of proper order. The family was a miniature monarchy, as hierarchical as earthly and heavenly monarchies. A man's home was literally his castle, for he was king of the family, with complete authority over his wife and children. He expected them to be obedient, and they usually were. Whatever children didn't learn within their families would be learned soon enough at school, for the educational system was another tool used to enforce Elizabethan notions of order and obedience. One of its explicit aims was to educate pupils to be good, dutiful subjects in the commonwealth.

To transgress boundaries or shirk duties and obligations was an unforgivable offense against the social order. It's a theme that Shakespeare addresses again and again. In *Romeo and Juliet*, a young woman rejects her obligation to obey her family's wishes, instead marrying the son of their bitterest enemy. Duke Frederick violates a younger brother's duty by stealing the power from his older brother, Duke Senior, while Oliver neglects an older brother's responsibility to his younger brother, Orlando, in *As You Like It*. And Macbeth is one of the biggest transgressors of all; his murder of King Duncan violates two codes of honor at once, as he himself recognizes: "He's here in double trust: First, as I am his kinsman and his subject,

Strong both against the deed; then, as his host, Who should
against his murderer shut the door, Not bear the knife
myself."

As Macbeth discovers, the consequences of disregarding order are terrible. His violations plunge Scotland into
bloody civil war. Titus Andronicus fails to show the quality
of mercy to his pleading captive Tamora and brings personal catastrophe crashing down upon him and his family.
And Bolingbroke's usurpation of the rightful king, Richard
II, infects the kingdom with a disease that will fester for
years in the form of civil rebellion: as the fallen Richard
warns the king-maker Northumberland, "The time shall
not be many hours of age More than it is ere foul sin,
gathering head, Shall break into corruption."

Since all living things were linked by the Great Chain
of Being, violations of order in society were thought to set
off violent disturbances in the heavens or the world of
nature. "Take but degree away," Ulysses warns in *Troilus
and Cressida*, "untune that string, And hark what discord
follows." Anything out of the ordinary—floods, storms, unnatural behavior in animals—chilled Elizabethan hearts
with fear, for it signaled that the time was out of joint and
disaster imminent. In *King Lear*, Gloucester darkly pre-
dicts, "These late eclipses in the sun and moon portend
no good to us." In *Julius Caesar*, strange and terrible goings-
on are reported in Rome as the conspirators hatch the
assassination plot against the emperor: "A lioness hath
whelpèd in the streets, And graves have yawned and yielded
up their dead . . . Horses did neigh, and dying men did
groan, And ghosts did shriek and squeal about the streets."
Similar signs and omens in *Richard II* "forerun the death
or fall of kings." And Macbeth's treacherous murder of
Duncan triggers a horrifying chain reaction in nature, as
Lennox reports "Lamentings heard i' th' air, strange screams
of death, And prophesying with accents terrible Of dire
combustion and confused events New hatched to the woe-
ful time."

If these were the probable outcomes of disobedience,
small wonder that order was so highly prized and so repeatedly urged on all good citizens. Elizabethans were
reminded over and over that any violation of duty, any
rebelliousness, any tendency to disrespect the laws and

government of the land would have horrific consequences not only for the individual but for the state.

The irony of it all was that this elaborate view of a divinely ordered universe, the "party line" put forth by the upper classes, neither obscured nor prevented the transformations that were going on in society. Things were actually quite fluid, at least when compared with previous centuries. All the pamphlets and sermons and proclamations insisting on rigid obedience to a fixed system were, in the end, simply last-ditch efforts to fend off the tidal wave of change that threatened to overwhelm the social order.

And so, paradoxically, the age of great change was also the age of great conservatism. Ethically, spiritually, and personally unready to accommodate all the new discoveries and advances, many Elizabethans retreated to the traditional ideal of an unchanging "establishment." For the alternative—chaos and disorder—was too horrible to contemplate. "Take away order from all things," wrote a contemporary of Shakespeare's plaintively, "what should then remain?"

CHAPTER 3

ELIZABETHAN STAR WARS: SUPERSTITION AND THE SUPERNATURAL

DO YOU KNOW exactly why thirteen is an unlucky number? Or why it's a bad omen for a black cat to cross your path? Or why knocking on wood is supposed to protect you? If you stop to think about it, you might conclude that you don't have any explanation for these superstitions.

And yet they exert a mysteriously powerful influence on the way we behave. You'd have to look long and hard to find a skyscraper that has a floor numbered thirteen. Many people go to great lengths to avoid walking under ladders. And not long ago, a National League baseball team won a crucial victory after a black cat just "happened" to appear (some fans suspect it was planted) in front of the visiting team's dugout in the middle of the game; from that moment on, the players couldn't stop committing errors.

The Elizabethans were no different; in fact, in an age before computers had been invented, before medical science understood disease, before astronomy, meteorology, and geology had learned much about the heavens and the earth, magical beliefs played an even larger role in daily life than they do today. Most Elizabethan households were well stocked with peculiar superstitions and strange practices: there might be a horseshoe over the door to ward off evil spirits, an astrological almanac on the table, a bowl of cream set out for the fairies every night, and a stockpile of charms to ward off ghosts and witches should they come a-knocking.

Whether it was a magical cure for hiccups or a warning not to whistle after dark, few people questioned any of these beliefs or practices. The fact that their parents and grandparents had believed in them was good enough. "The superstitious idle-headed eld," Shakespeare says in *The Merry Wives of Windsor*, describing one tradition, "Received and did deliver to our age This tale of Herne the hunter for a truth." No one really needed to know much more than that.

Except, of course, the Church, which did its best to discourage black (or malevolent) witchcraft. Village priests and city bishops all over England preached that belief in witches, fairies, ghosts, and the influence of the stars was wicked and sinful, the work of the Devil. "Let us also learn and confess with the Prophet David," they might thunder, "that we ourselves are the causes of our afflictions; and not exclaim upon witches, when we should call upon God for mercy."

But they were preaching to deaf ears, and their efforts didn't meet with much success, especially among the people in the countryside. Despite the law requiring attendance at Protestant services on Sundays, some people didn't put too much stock in churchgoing. One defiant old woman declared that she could serve God as well in the fields as in the church. The behavior of the vast majority who did go usually left a lot to be desired. Children ran up and down the aisles while disruptive servants and apprentices climbed onto the church roof. More mature members of the congregation contented themselves with spitting, telling jokes, falling asleep, shouting back at the preacher, and sometimes even firing off guns (accidentally). One man was hauled up to the front of his church and publicly scolded for "his most loathsome farting." The service must have been quite a show, for one worried bishop sermonized at length on the common people's "heathenish contempt of religion and disdainful loathing of the ministers."

Indeed, priests hadn't always enjoyed good standing among the ordinary people, especially in the days before the Protestant Reformation. One man, for example, refused to confess to a priest about his sins with a certain woman because he was sure that "the priest would be as ready within two or three days to use her as he [had]." And the dismantling of the Catholic rituals begun by Protestant reformers set off an orgy of pillage and plunder, fueled by resentment of the clergy. Sacred objects were destroyed, priests' robes vandalized and priests themselves beatin up.

And yet, even after the period of Protestant reforms, many of the old habits and practices associated with the Catholic Church lingered on—and some seemed to lead a double life in the worlds of religion and magic. In pre-Reformation days, young women had prayed at saints' shrines for the blessing of blonde hair (Saint Urbane) or a boy baby (Saint Felicitas). People believed in those days that if they left church with the wafer of the Mass still in their mouths, they would have magical powers; others wore pages from the Scriptures as protective amulets against the Devil. One farmer even tried to cure his sick cow by reading it chapters from the Bible!

Were these things worship or wickedness? It wasn't always clear. If a farmer made the sign of the Cross to ward off evil spirits, was he engaging in religion or blasphemy? If a local folk healer advised a troubled customer to repeat the Lord's Prayer seven times each morning when he woke up, was she advising magic or religion? And if a whole congregation believed in the efficacy of touching priests' robes or ringing specially-consecrated bells during thunderstorms, were they being religious or superstitious? Shakespeare's Dr. Pinch, in *The Comedy of Errors*, demonstrates how easily the lines could be blurred as he tries to cure the supposedly possessed Antipholus of Ephesus with this charm: "I charge thee, Satan, housed within this man, To yield possession to my holy prayers," and with this triumphant conclusion, "I conjure thee by all the saints in heaven."

The Catholic Church seemed to leave the criteria for distinguishing between magic and religion unclear, deciding arbitrarily that one practice was worshipful and another sinful. But the Protestant reformers, as might be expected, had very definitive views on the subject. They insisted that there were no magical powers in any of the old rituals and practices. Saints' shrines, church bells, repetition of prayers, holy relics, special amulets—all were swept away in the flood of reform, as "Catholic" gradually came to be equated with "superstitious" and "ritual" with "necromancy." One zealous Protestant even called the sacraments "plain devilry, witchcraft . . . and all that naught is." Instead of spells, incantations, charms, and conjuring, Protestant preachers recommended prayer, penitence, fasting, and faith in God's inscrutable will.

Since this was not an easy exchange, it was one not often made by most people. Complicated and erudite theological debates didn't really interest them; their approach to religion was fairly elementary. The world was divided into good and evil; the good was to be embraced, the evil to be eschewed—by whatever means were at hand, including superstition and magic. And so they went right on making the sign of the Cross, using holy relics, and relying on a host of nonreligious superstitions to help them avoid or survive the slings and arrows of outrageous fortune.

There were many beliefs that guided day-to-day activities and gave great significance to the most ordinary occurrences. When an Elizabethan fell from his horse, for example, he would carefully note the day and hour of the fall as an unlucky time to ride. If a child or animal came between two friends as they strolled in the meadows, it was a sure sign that they would soon be going their separate ways. Putting a shirt on wrong side out in the morning usually foretold a bad day. Birds had their uses, too: chattering magpies announced the arrival of guests, while a croaking raven issued the more ominous warning that the dreaded bubonic plague was on its way.

Certain numbers, of course, were luckier than others; as Falstaff remarks in *The Merry Wives of Windsor*, "They say there is divinity in odd numbers." And particular days of the month were advisable for starting a journey, sowing crops, or even cutting fingernails! If paved sidewalks had been invented, Elizabethans would undoubtedly have taken great care to avoid stepping on the cracks.

STAR-STRUCK

THE ELIZABETHANS WERE great believers in the influence of the stars and the planets. How could they have been otherwise when the rhythms and routines of their daily lives were so dependent on the skies? The stars were not dimmed,

as one day they would be, by the lurid yellow glow of big-
city lights. And without street lights, desk lamps, and elec-
tric wiring, travel was undertaken only by the shine of the
full moon, study illuminated by the flickering light of the
candle, and plays put on in the daylight hours of the afternoon. The working day was longer in the summer, when
light lingered until ten or eleven o'clock at night.

The influence of the heavens on the environment was
equally inescapable; crops rose or rotted according to the
disposition of the sun, the moon, and the rain. The weather,
particularly the phases of the moon, also affected the balance of hot and cold, dry and moist in the human body
—the humors. And so it followed, as the night the day,
that the heavens influenced personal fortunes as well.

Given the arrangement of the universe, as it was then
understood, astrology made a good deal of sense. Despite
the recently-advanced theories of Copernicus, which took
a long time to catch on, most people probably still believed
that the Earth, not the Sun, was the center of the universe.
The "heavens themselves, the planets, and this center," as
Ulysses calls them in *Troilus and Cressida*, were seen as a
series of spheres within spheres—not unlike the little
wooden Russian dolls that keep opening up to reveal a
still smaller doll inside. The outermost sphere was called
by its Latin name, the primum mobile. Within it was the
"starry firmament," as one poetic-minded astrologer called
it—the sphere of stars, permanently in place. Next came
the seven planets—cold, dry Saturn, fair and bright Jupiter, fiery Mars, the Sun ("the well of pure light," said the
same astrologer), moist, chilly Venus, dimmer Mercury,
and the Moon. And finally, in dead center, hung the small,
motionless Earth, suspended from God's throne by a golden
chain—the primary object of His attention.

An elaborate system of belief unfolded quite naturally
from this picture of the universe. As the planets orbited
and the spheres revolved against the permanent backdrop
of the twelve signs of the zodiac, their influence was felt
on human life below. For example, the configuration of
the skies and stars at the exact moment of a person's
birth—which any half-competent astrologer could ascertain
—determined what kind of person he or she would be and
what kind of life, and death, would follow.

Romeo and Juliet may be the most famous pair of "star-crossed lovers," but other Shakespearean characters also reflect the influence of the stars. In *Henry VI Part 2*, as the Duke of Suffolk is about to be murdered on shipboard, he recalls, "A cunning man did calculate my birth And told me that by water I should die." And sometimes astrology has less tragic consequences: when Benedick is having trouble composing a love poem to Beatrice in *Much Ado About Nothing*, he consoles himself with the knowledge that "I was not born under a rhyming planet, nor I cannot woo in festival terms." Julia, in *The Two Gentlemen of Verona*, puts all her faith in astrology, confident that her particular gentleman of Verona will be as faithful as she, since "truer stars did govern Proteus' birth."

Consulting the stars—courtesy of the local stargazer in a village or a fancier private practitioner in London—helped confused Elizabethans determine what specific course of action to take. An astrologer who knew the position of the stars and planets at the exact moment a crucial question was asked could then provide answers to all sorts of personal queries—when to get married, when to look for a job, and even that rare dilemma of when to take a bath (never, was the usual answer!). Failing to act at the moment dictated by the heavens was invariably catastrophic. As Prospero acknowledges in *The Tempest*, "my zenith doth depend upon A most auspicious star, whose influence If now I court not, but omit, my fortunes Will ever after droop."

Many of Queen Elizabeth's courtiers shared Duke Prospero's affinity for stargazing; it had a huge following at Court. High-ranking government officials and famous men were avid enthusiasts, among them Sir Walter Raleigh and the queen's favorite, the Earl of Essex. Lord Burleigh, Elizabeth's right-hand minister, even invested some money in a corporation run by an astrologer/alchemist who promised to turn iron into copper, at huge profits to the investors. And the Earl of Leicester conferred at length with the well-known astrologer John Dee to ascertain the most auspicious day—and hour—for Queen Elizabeth's coronation.

Elizabeth herself, however, did not share her courtiers'

enthusiasm; her own skepticism of astrology was well known and, like everything else about her, celebrated. She astonished and impressed a group of her courtiers when a comet came hurtling near the Earth; unswayed by their pleas that it was highly dangerous to look at comets, she walked right up to the window and said daringly, "The die is cast." The fact that she continued to rule successfully for more than twenty years after this incident should have told her superstitious nobles something about astrology, but apparently it did not.

Astrology wasn't just the preserve of the glittering stars of the Court. If anything, it was even more popular in the workaday world. Landless laborers and gentlemen farmers alike could keep up with the latest astrological forecasts for just a few pennies by buying an almanac from a wandering bookseller. These almanacs were as widely circulated in Elizabethan times as gossipy grocery-stand newspapers are today. Although they didn't have daily horoscopes counseling a romantic rendezvous with a dark lady or predicting a profitable business deal, they were absolutely chock-full of interesting and relevant information.

For example, they had a helpful list of upcoming astronomical events, such as eclipses and full moons—events that could greatly influence schedules. No wonder Bottom calls for an almanac in *A Midsummer Night's Dream:* "A calendar, a calendar! Look in the almanac. Find out moonshine . . . " as he and his company of amateur actors try to decide what night they'll perform their play. The almanacs also had calendars listing the months, the days of the week, and fixed church holidays such as Christmas. The "prognostication" outlined unusual astrological occurrences likely to happen in the next year. And sprinkled throughout were gardening tips, notices of markets and fairs, and weather reports; Enobarbus in *Antony and Cleopatra* says sarcastically that Cleopatra's sighs and tears "are greater storms and tempests than almanacs can report." There was also helpful medical advice; one almanac prognosticator, Leonard Digges, warned his readers to undergo the operation of bloodletting only on "a fair, temperate day."

GHOST-BUSTED

MANY AN ELIZABETHAN bedside was haunted by fears of what one writer called "the terrors of the night." Chief among these night visitors were ghosts—souls of the dead who were making return trips to earth for very specific and rarely comforting reasons. They invariably limited their visiting hours to the hospitable darkness of the night, disappearing as dawn broke; as Puck points out to Oberon in *A Midsummer Night's Dream*, "yonder shines Aurora's harbinger, At whose approach, ghosts, wand'ring here and there, Troop home to churchyards."

Ghosts were terribly gruesome, nothing like the harmless white-sheeted Halloween figures that the word conjures up in the twentieth century. In fact, as revitalized corpses, they usually came back to earth looking as they did when they left it: the ghost of Hamlet's father wears "the very armor he had on When he the ambitious Norway combated." His beard, Horatio tells Hamlet, "was, as I have seen it in his life, A sable silvered," and his face is still pale from the poison that killed him. Banquo's ghost, stabbed to death by Macbeth's henchmen, appears at the banquet with bloodied countenance and still-oozing wounds, to Macbeth's horror—"Never shake Thy gory locks at me," he cries out. The ghost of Banquo, like many other ghosts, is only visible to the person he is haunting—which makes his visitation more terrifying still.

A ghost always had a mission when he came to earth —although it might vary considerably. Some came to ask for a proper burial, without which they were condemned to wander for an eternity; Puck speaks of "Damnèd [condemned] spirits all, That in crossways and floods have burial." Others saw into the future and wanted to warn the living, and still others intended to punish a promise-breaker. The ghosts who hover over the bed of Shakespeare's murderous Richard III have returned to avenge their deaths at his hands and to predict his imminent defeat in battle: "Despair and die" is their refrain, and, indeed, it is answered the very next day. Hamlet's father comes to expose Claudius' foul play, revealing to Hamlet that "The serpent that did sting thy father's life Now wears his crown." When Hamlet fails to act in revenge, the ghost appears again, lecturing his son that "this visitation Is but to whet thy almost blunted purpose."

Not only was a ghostly visitation unpleasant, but it also cast the visited into a state of spiritual confusion: the Church insisted that ghosts were really just devils in disguise. If a ghost told a young man to kill his uncle, how could he be sure that it wasn't Satan tempting him to sin? This is an essential part of Hamlet's dilemma: is the ghost of his father really who he says he is? "Angels and ministers of grace defend us! Be thou a spirit of health or goblin damned, Bring with thee airs from heaven or blasts from hell, Be thy intents wicked or charitable, Thou com'st in such a questionable shape That I will speak to thee." Horatio fears that the ghost is a devil who will lure Hamlet to his death: "What if it tempt you toward the flood, my lord, Or to the dreadful summit of the cliff . . . And there assume some other horrible form Which might deprive your sovereignty of reason And draw you into madness?" No doubt many Elizabethans felt caught in the middle: obeying a devil would cast them into hell, but ignoring a real ghost had equally dire consequences. Perhaps the safest tactic was to live an upright life—and hide beneath the bedcovers.

FAIRY-TAILED

IF WORRIES ABOUT ghosts weren't enough to guarantee sleepless nights, there were the fairies to think about, too. Those to be feared weren't the tiny sweet playful fairies that Shakespeare invented for *A Midsummer Night's Dream*—that mischief-making but good-hearted fairy tribe led by Oberon and Titania; nor were they the cute little animated figures who flit around Walt Disney Studios on their shimmering wings. No, these Elizabethan fairies were life-sized creatures, fiendish and malicious, who made the milk go sour and the livestock sick. *This* is the kind of fairy that Dromio of Syracuse means when he calls his churlish master in *The Comedy of Errors* "A fiend, a fairy, pitiless and rough."

Fairies came in several models: there were hostile river spirits and wily mermaids who lured unsuspecting sailors to their deaths; giants and hags; fairy aristocrats who, like their human counterparts, spent their time dancing, hunting, and feasting; and the ordinary everyday goblins. But not all fairies were malevolent. Best-known of all was the native English fairy Robin Good-fellow, or Puck, a "shrewd and knavish sprite," as Shakespeare calls him, who was the special guardian of home and hearth.

The fairies considered the workings of the household to be their special concern and inspected domestic operations during their nocturnal visits. They rewarded a well-kept house and a well-swept hearth by helping with the chores and bringing luck. Puck could make himself particularly useful to a family that treated him well; as a fellow-fairy points out in *A Midsummer Night's Dream*, "Those that 'Hobgoblin' call you, and 'Sweet Puck,' You do their work, and they shall have good luck."

The best strategy for an Elizabethan family to adopt with the fairies was one of preemptive obedience and flattery, which might work where charms and conjurations failed. They could also be won over by food and drink left out for them at night. As a contemporary wrote, women "were wont to set a bowl of milk before [the fairies] and Robin Good-fellow, for grinding of malt or mustard, and sweeping the house at midnight."

But woe to the housewife who neglected her chores! The fairies were enemies of untidiness, or "sluttery," and punished it wherever they found it, almost always by third-degree pinching during the night: "Where fires thou find'st unraked, and hearths unswept, There pinch the maids as blue as bilberry. Our radiant Queen hates sluts and sluttery," the make-believe fairies are reminded in *The Merry Wives of Windsor*.

Pinching wasn't reserved only for the slovenly housekeeper, however; the lustful and lecherous—or any other mortals judged offensive by the fairies—often found themselves similarly bruised when they woke up. This is why Mistress Ford and Mistress Page, the merry wives of Windsor, can punish the lustful (and superstitious) Falstaff by

dressing children up "fairylike, to pinch the unclean knight."
And Dromio of Syracuse, bewildered by the topsy-turvy
events of *The Comedy of Errors*, wonders if he and his
master have blundered into the wrong place: "This is the
fairy land. O spite of spites, We talk with goblins, elves,
and sprites! If we obey them not, this will ensue: They'll
suck our breath or pinch us black and blue."

One thing fairies enjoyed more than anything was
causing domestic confusion with their practical jokes—
which sometimes weren't so funny. They loved dairy tricks
—spilling the milk from the pail as the milkmaid carried
it back to the house, or keeping the cream from turning
to butter. Fairies put spells on animals, sometimes even
causing death. And they considered it great fun to lead
travelers astray: Caliban, in *The Tempest*, mutters that his
master Prospero will send fairies who will "lead me, like
a firebrand, in the dark Out of my way."

Fairies were most notorious and most feared for their
practice of abducting a human baby from its cradle and
replacing it with a fairy changeling, which was usually
hideous, deformed, or retarded. This was one of an Elizabethan mother's greatest fears. But King Henry IV, fed
up with his Plantagenet son's wild and riotous behavior
(in contrast to the honor and valor of the young Percy)
resorts to some wishful thinking about changelings: "O,
that it could be proved That some night-tripping fairy had
exchanged In cradle clothes our children where they lay,
And called mine Percy, his Plantagenet!"

Of course, no Elizabethan actually *saw* the fairies abducting a human baby; for that matter no Elizabethan
ever saw a fairy at all. In the first place, they came out
only during the night—Puck calls himself "that merry
wanderer of the night." In the second place, everyone knew
that mortals were expressly forbidden to see or speak to
fairies. They guarded their privacy fiercely and didn't take
at all kindly to being spied on, even accidentally. This is
the fear that grips Falstaff as the child-fairies dance around
him. Throwing his huge body down on the ground outside
Windsor Forest, he yelps, "They are fairies. He that speaks
to them shall die. I'll wink and couch; no man their works
must eye."

The fact that the Elizabethans never saw the fairies
didn't suggest to anyone that they weren't real. After all,

proof of their existence could be established in the over-turned milk pails, the diseased animals, the lost travelers, the housewives pinched black and blue. What more evidence did anyone need?

SPELL-BOUND

EVEN MORE SINISTER than fairies, in the minds of Elizabethans, were the old hags thought to be evil witches. The accused men and women were often ugly, poverty-stricken, disheveled, and diseased, or as a contemporary put it, "commonly old, lame, bleary-eyed, pale, foul, and full of wrinkles." A frequent scenario leading to charges of black witchcraft (as opposed to the helpful white magic of the local wise woman) was this: someone —usually a woman —living on the fringes of village life was offended by a neighbor or a passerby. She uttered a curse or some sort of malediction; when someone fell ill or something went wrong, her harsh words were remembered, and she was brought to trial as a witch.

Many Elizabethans were afraid that these "Soul-killing witches that deform the body," as Antipholus of Syracuse calls them in *The Comedy of Errors*, would overrun England unless they were hunted down and punished according to the law—which could require death. Even members of the queen's government were alarmed; the Lord Chief Justice declared that "The land is full of witches . . . they abound in all places. . . ." Out of these irrational fears came the massive witch-hunts of the sixteenth century in which hundreds of defenseless old people were burned to death for crimes they didn't commit.

It wasn't only England's problem; witches were feared all over Europe as well. The Europeans hated the witches for different reasons. They objected more on theological grounds, citing the supposed satanic beliefs of the witches and their heretical partnership with the Devil. Not too many of the ordinary people in England cared much about heretical beliefs—indeed, given the constant switching back and forth between the Catholic and the Protestant Church in the last few decades, what was "heretical" one day was "belief" the next. To most Elizabethans, witchcraft wasn't a matter of thought but of action; they went on the hunt only when there was actual damage done, either by witches or their Satanic sidekicks known as "familiars," evil spirits that became cats or other animals to carry out the witches' instructions.

Unlike the fairies' activities, black magic was always malevolent; the harm witches could do ranged from the merely annoying to the totally destructive. They kept the beer from fermenting and the butter from hardening. They caused men and women to commit adultery; they could prevent women from getting pregnant and cause miscarriages or stillbirths. A contemporary document had them "boil infants (after they have murdered them unbaptized)" and "eat the flesh and drink the blood of men and children openly." Witches also cast spells on animals and humans, causing sickness and death.

They had fearful powers over the elements; like "the foul witch Sycorax" of Shakespeare's *The Tempest*, they had the power to "control the moon, make flows and ebbs," manipulating the winds and rains to bring bad weather. Macbeth begs the witches, "Though you untie the winds and let them fight Against the churches . . . Though bladed corn be lodged and trees blown down . . . answer me To what I ask you."

Cursing and uttering evil charms were probably the most common ways these witches operated. Caliban and Prospero practically have a cursing contest in *The Tempest:* the monster cries, "All the charms Of Sycorax, toads, beetles, bats, light on you!" and Prospero, in turn, issues equally dire threats: "If thou neglect'st or dost unwillingly What I command, I'll rack thee with old cramps, Fill all thy bones with aches, make thee roar That beasts shall tremble at thy din."

The Elizabethans didn't have to rely on Shakespeare for evidence of witches' "mischiefs manifold and sorceries terrible" (as Prospero calls them) when there were plenty of real-life examples closer to home. There was the case in one village of a young man who simply insulted a foul-looking old woman in the alehouse after one beer too many. "Do you hear, witch," he called to her, "look tother ways, I cannot abide a nose of that fashion, or else turn your face the wrong side outward, it may look like raw flesh for flies to blow maggots in." She cursed him, he fell ill, and she "worthily suffered death."

In another village, Alice Trevisard knocked on her neighbor's door one afternoon and asked for a half-penny's worth of beer. The neighbor refused, Alice muttered ominously, "I will not leave you worth a groat," and two days later, one of the neighbor's precious beer barrels suddenly leaped in the air of its own accord, fell on the ground, and exploded. All the beer was lost—ruinous in times of high grain prices. Alice faced charges of witchcraft as a result.

There was more to witchcraft than ominous mutterings and curses—charms and magical methods were equally effective. Some witches concocted truly horrible mixtures of hair, saliva, blood, urine, and animal entrails—as stomach-turning as anything Macbeth's witches throw into their bubbling cauldron—"Eye of newt and toe of frog, Wool of bat and tongue of dog," "sow's blood, that hath eaten Her nine farrow; grease that's sweaten From the murderer's gibbet."

Image-magic was another technique in the witches' bag of tricks, though one less frequently used. The witch would make a likeness of her intended victim out of clay, wax, wood, or whatever material she could get her hands on, and then prick the part she wanted to hurt. When the Earl of Derby suddenly died there was rumor that a wax image with a hair through its heart had been found in his room, and an old woman was held for questioning. A surgeon in another parish was suspected of making a wax picture of his mother-in-law in order to get rid of her!

Most Elizabethans probably preferred a tactic of nonconfrontation with those they thought were witches. But when they did find themselves the victims of witchcraft, what could they do?

They could start by trying to identify which witch was the guilty one, with the considerable help of the village wizard. Burning a handful of thatch from a suspected witch's cottage, for example, usually brought about a confession. To find the witch who had bewitched his cattle, a farmer need only follow this charm: "Put a pair of breeches upon the cow's head, and beat her out of the pasture with a good cudgel upon a Friday, and she will run right to the witch's door, and strike thereat with her horns."

Once the witch's identity had been pinned down, there were various kinds of retaliatory magic that would reverse her spell, courtesy of the local wizard. Burying a bottle filled with thorns or pins or needles, adding fingernails or hair or urine for good measure, often did the trick. A truly foolproof method, which had the extra advantage of curing the victim of the spell, was to scratch the witch until she bled. And, of course, execution by burning was a fool-proof solution.

HOUSE CALLS

ONE COMFORT in the midst of all this anxiety about the supernatural was the local wise woman or cunning man, whose white magic provided remedies for the perplexed, injured, or beleaguered. Combining the roles of astrologer, physician, and psychologist, these white witches were enormously popular with the ordinary people and offered a range of useful services.

They could help their hapless customers recover stolen goods or escape arrest, win at cards or win at love. They could catch a thief using a contemporary version of a police lineup: writing the names of the suspects on scraps of paper, rolling them up in little clay balls, throwing them into a pail of water, and pronouncing the guilty party to be whichever ball unrolled first. They also advised on personal affairs. In *The Merry Wives of Windsor*, Slender seeks out a wise woman to find out "whether one Nym . . . that beguiled him of a chain, had the chain or no," while Simple inquires "if it were my master's fortune to have [Ann Page] or no."

The wizards also acted as local doctors, at much more affordable prices than real medical men. They had fistfuls of home remedies for stings, blisters, burns, running sores, cramps, and the "thousand natural shocks That flesh is heir to" (as Hamlet might say). They cured headaches—not by advising two aspirin and a call in the morning but by the more hands-on method of driving a nail into the skull of a dead man. If that failed, there was always this charm: "Tie a halter [noose] about your head, wherewith one hath been hanged." Were warts the problem? Relief was at hand, not in the form of Compound W, but in the more down-to-earth remedy of sprinkling dirt from a newly-dug grave over the offending growths. One shudders to think what their cure for pimples was.

Of course, sometimes these cunning folk ran afoul of the Church because of their prominence in the lives of their fellow villagers. Many Elizabethans would choose the instant gratification of a visit to a white witch over the longer-term Church treatment of prayer and fasting, much to the annoyance of the village clergy. Of course, the Church itself wasn't above using a little white magic; officials in one parish hired a wise woman to discover who ran off with their altar cloth!

Magical beliefs provided the Elizabethans with the comfort of explanations and the satisfaction of redress when random and inexplicable misfortunes occurred. The preachers of the day preferred to view such calamities as instances of God's wrath toward sinful mortals. But to many Elizabethans, it was much more consoling to believe that the cause of the disaster was something outside of them, that the fault lay not in themselves but in their stars, that a fairy was to blame for the spilled milk, or that a devil made them do it.

Witches, of course, were the best scapegoats of all. They were real people readily available to scream at, scratch, and even put to death. Because of their odd appearance and behavior, people suspected of being witches were easy targets. In fact, anyone perceived as deviating from the English norm might suffer this kind of "outrageous and barbarous cruelty." The need for a scapegoat was overwhelming; if witches weren't there to fulfill it, other groups—immigrants and foreigners, for example—might step in to take their place.

CHAPTER 4

DON'T TALK TO STRANGERS: FOREIGNERS AND IMMIGRANTS IN ENGLAND

TO MANY EUROPEANS hard-pressed by the events of the sixteenth century, England must have looked like the land of plenty—plenty of money, plenty of freedom, plenty of opportunity. For all was not well on the Continent. The sometimes brutal efforts of French and Spanish Catholics to destroy the forces of Protestant resistance were making life difficult for non-Catholic Dutch and French Huguenots. And England's expanding trade activity dangled the prospect of great wealth in front of profit-minded European traders and merchants.

For whatever reasons, foreigners were flooding England—or so it seemed to the provincial English. In fact, the influx was small by today's standards. But like modern immigrants, they were eager to find the freedom they lacked at home or to fulfill their dreams in this wonderful new land.

The attraction was not at all mutual, however, and these foreigners were not exactly welcomed with open arms after they had made the Channel crossing and landed at Dover. The English had a well-deserved reputation for hating "strangers," as they called foreigners. More than one European traveler returned from a tour of England to echo the words of the Antwerp merchant who remarked that the English are "very suspicious of foreigners, whom they despise." Even an Elizabethan would acknowledge this fault in his people when he wrote a history of the age:

many citizens, said John Stow, " (especially the more ordinary sort) had no great love for them [strangers] and were glad of an opportunity of oppressing them."

For England, unlike the American nation it eventually spawned, took no pride in becoming a melting pot for many cultures. Even though Elizabethans were living in an age when explorers, scholars, merchants, and writers were flinging open the doors to other cultures, most people preferred to hang back, tarrying on the well-trodden thresholds of ignorance and fear.

Except for the very rich or the very enterprising, the majority of Elizabethans never crossed the Channel to get to know Europe on its own terms. As one observant German summed it up, "because the greater part, especially the tradespeople, seldom go into other countries, but always remain in their houses in the city attending to their business, they care little for foreigners, but scoff and laugh at them." Aside from the thrown-together companies of traveling English "comedians" and the British troops— each group going for reasons other than tourism—not many bona-fide Elizabethan travelers ever graced the countries of Europe with their presence.

As far as their queen was concerned, this was all for the good. The government was chronically worried about the considerable dangers of Catholic infiltration. Since Europe was largely Catholic, Protestant England was deathly afraid that its impressionable young Protestants would be first taken in by foreign hosts and then taken over by Catholicism. Accordingly, the government made getting there no fun at all; an Elizabethan had to have a fairly intense desire to travel—and good connections in the government—to cut his way through the red tape. In order to leave England, testimonies to the good upstanding Protestantism of the prospective traveler often had to be given, a defense of the value of the trip might have to be advanced in the presence of opposing government officials, and a special license or passport had to be wangled. Even then the Elizabethan traveler couldn't rest easy; several times, when Catholic fears gripped the queen, she issued proclamations calling back any English subjects who were studying or traveling in Catholic countries.

Not only did foreign travel expose impressionable young men to the lurking forces of Catholicism, it also made them vulnerable to foreign fopperies and fripperies. According to this theory, people who went abroad as upstanding Elizabethans returned as pretentious snobs, mindlessly aping the trends, fashions, phrases, and manners of foreign lands—just the sort of affectation that Rosalind credits Jaques with in *As You Like It:* "Farewell, Monsieur Traveler. Look you lisp and wear strange suits, disable all the benefits of your own country, be out of love with your nativity, and almost chide God for making you that countenance you are; or I will scarce think you have swam in a gondola." Portia delivers a similarly withering criticism of her English suitor as she dismisses him before he ever makes it onto the stage of *The Merchant of Venice:* "I think he bought his doublet in Italy, his round hose in France, his bonnet in Germany, and his behavior everywhere."

Instead of going to all the unnecessary trouble and expense of travel, these practical English suggested, why not just read about it? Books written by others were far better—and much safer—sources of information about other lands. As one upper-class noblewoman advised her son: "The language to be learned with the sight of countries [can be learned] here at home by books with less danger than, in these days, by journey. The certain fruits daily found of young men's travel nowadays [are] nothing but pride, change, and vanity."

But in advocating such books, these armchair travelers were putting their trust in notoriously unreliable sources of information, full of what a critic called "sweet-sauc'd lies." The farther some travelers got from home, the taller their tales of other lands seemed to get. Rather than giving sympathetic and objective portraits of other countries and peoples, most of these travel accounts simply reinforced damaging—and marketable—stereotypes, perpetrating far-fetched and best-selling myths. And so it wasn't surprising that the English lacked a realistic understanding of other cultures.

Hand in hand with the Elizabethan people's provincial outlook went the certainty that they were better than everyone else. Once the English had more or less settled the religious question, built up a powerful navy, and established themselves as a power to be reckoned with in international politics, they experienced a wave of intense patriotism. This is the emotion that Shakespeare appeals to throughout *Henry V*, especially as the hero-king Henry leads his men against France with stirring words: "On, on, you noblest English, Whose blood is fet from fathers of warproof . . . And you, good yeomen Whose limbs were made in England, show us here The mettle of your pasture; let us swear that you are worth your breeding."

If the Elizabethans saw a good-looking but obviously foreign man on the street they pitied him for not being an Englishman—as if that were the pinnacle of existence. Stereotypes rose easily to their lips, and they were quick to pin pithy national characteristics on foreigners. Thumbing through the work of one popular prose-writer, an Elizabethan might come across statements such as "pride is the disease of the Spaniard"; the Italian is "a cunning proud fellow"; the Frenchman "for the most part loves none but himself and his pleasures"; and the Danes are "the most gross and senseless proud dolts."

On top of these traditional stereotypes and the instinctive English dislike of anything foreign was a pile of specific fears about church and pocketbook. There was a general prejudice, for example, one shared by all the Christian nations of Europe, against the so-called infidel races—Turks, Moors, and Jews. To an Elizabethan it was not shocking for the witches in *Macbeth* to toss "Liver of blaspheming Jew," "Nose of Turk and Tartar's lips" into their cauldron along with such delicacies as "Finger of birth-strangled babe" and "baboon's blood." There was a storehouse of concocted myths about ritual murders of Christian infants by Jews for religious purposes, myths that usually surfaced around the time of the Jewish Passover. And Turkish atrocities—the torturing, imprisoning, and impressing of children into the Turkish army—were chronicled in John Foxe's gory, gossipy, contrived bestseller, *The Book of Martyrs*.

Where infidels feared to tread, Catholics rushed in to pose another big threat to Elizabethans' sense of wellbeing. As acknowledged leaders in the free world of Protestantism, the Queen's English were implacably opposed to Catholicism in *any* form—especially its Spanish form.

But even the state of their Church wasn't as troubling as the state of their wallets, and many Elizabethans were worried about foreign bodies in their economic system. The inclination to shun homemade English products in favor of foreign imports raised a protest from protectionists and patriots in London: "many things thereof are not there [in London] made, but beyond the sea; whereby the artificers [craftsman] of our towns are idle." The trade imbalance was enough of a threat on its own, but when foreign workers kept popping up in the English labor force during the heavy unemployment of the late sixteenth century, the level of English anxiety about losing jobs to foreigners rose dramatically. Though Shylock might believe that "the trade and profit of the city Consisteth of all nations," the English preferred that profit to consist of one nation only—their own.

A would-be European immigrant on the eve of his departure for England might very well have second thoughts. He might realize that he just wouldn't win with the English, no matter who he was. If Turkish or Jewish, he'd be scorned as an infidel; if Dutch or French Protestant, he'd be resented as an economic rival; if Spanish, he'd most likely be drawn and quartered. With sinking spirits, he might wonder whether it was too late to change his mind about going—better to face a known enemy at home than an unknown one in a strange land. But then a cheery thought might strike him: these expectations were based on nothing more solid than rumor and hearsay. Perhaps things would be different once he arrived.

TURNING TURK

ALTHOUGH THEIR GOVERNMENT had recently established trade relations with the English nation, Turks didn't take the idea of going to England very seriously. In fact, the first Turkish official to visit London didn't arrive until after Elizabeth's death. But if they rarely appeared in the flesh, they were certainly there in spirit, a subject of endless fascination to Elizabethans, whose imaginations were fed by "true-to-life" accounts of travelers and merchants capitalizing on the newly-established trade relations between England and the Levant.

The relentless push of Turkish forces into eastern Europe and their political domination of the peoples they conquered were casting a shadow over the rest of Europe; the Ottoman Empire hung like a dark rain-cloud on the European skyline. The free world speculated endlessly about the "glorious empire of the Turks, the present terror of the World," as one historian christened them. The Elizabethan curiosity seemed unquenchable—they thirsted to know *why* the Turks were so successful. Was it their native hardiness? Stern discipline? Stamina on the battlefield? Was it Islamic unity? Everyone had an opinion. But whatever the secret of their success, one thing was for sure—the Turks were much admired from afar.

And yet the Elizabethans' admiration was tinged with both fear and scorn. They disdained Turks as infidels, unbaptized and unblessed by the Christian church. Elizabethan diplomatic documents and treaties with other European nations referred to the Turkish nation as the "ancient common enemy and adversary of our faith." The Turkish infidels were considered the stubborn antagonists of Christian Europe and were disparaged accordingly.

The infidels were seen as creatures of boundless cruelty, holding no act of violence too extreme. Stories of their atrocities sent shudders up and down Elizabethan spines—plunder, pillage, and barbaric executions, like that of the man who was buried waist-deep in the earth and pierced by hundreds of arrows of sharp-shooting Turkish archers. The legend of the Turkish sultan Amurath, who had his nineteen brothers (potential rivals for power) strangled as he looked on, was another widely-circulated story. When Prince Harry becomes King Henry in Shakespeare's *Henry IV Part 2*, he reassures his anxious brothers that "This is the English, not the Turkish court; Not Amurath an Amurath succeeds, But Harry Harry."

Several other characteristics that came under the label "Turk" included stubbornness, lustfulness, and general barbarism. "Stubborn Turks," declares the Duke in *The Merchant of Venice*, are "never trained To offices of tender courtesy." And in *As You Like It*, Rosalind's reaction to Phebe's supposedly antagonistic letter is this: "Why, she defies me, Like Turk to Christian." As Edgar plays the part of a lunatic in *King Lear*, he boasts of his lust by saying that he has "in woman out-paramoured the Turk."

"Turk" also served as a handy catch-all term of insult. An Elizabethan could vouch for his character or his word by swearing he was not a Turk. Iago in *Othello* declares to Desdemona that he means what he says, "or else I am a Turk"—that is, a liar. Turks were evil, shifty, not to be trusted; Hamlet speculates on his shifting luck as he wonders, "if the rest of my fortunes turn Turk with me . . ."

The less the English knew, the more they feared, and the readier they were to assume the worst. Islam was for pagans. The Turkish Empire, because it was a vague but frightening threat on the fringes of Europe, was peopled by supersoldiers of unearthly stamina and power. And the Turkish people, never seen on a London street, were lustful, cruel barbarians. Was it any wonder that Turks in the sixteenth century kept a safe distance from England?

OUT OF AFRICA

THE ELIZABETHANS ACTUALLY had a chance to scrutinize black Africans, unlike the Turks, and could ponder the mystery of their existence first-hand. Londoners saw their first black men in the 1550s, when a few natives of Guinea came out of Africa with an English explorer; all but one returned home—and that one married a white Englishwoman and fathered a black child. But by 1601, Elizabeth was so perturbed by the numbers of Africans "which are crept into the realm" that she employed another foreigner, a German merchant, to transport them out of England.

No one was quite sure what to make of the blacks who appeared in sixteenth-century London. Gawking, gaping, and rudely whispering as they glimpsed Africans on the streets of London, the Elizabethans were especially curious about the dark skin of this unfamiliar people. With their usual zest for argument and debate, they tackled the question over and over. Some advocated the "climatic theory"—Africans were black because they lived near the sun. The Prince of Morocco, recognizing this English prejudice, explains his dark skin to Portia on these grounds in *The Merchant of Venice:* "Mislike me not for my complexion, The shadowed livery of the burnished sun, To whom I am a neighbor and near bred." The religious narrow-mindedly interpreted it as evidence of God's curse.

Everyone was especially intrigued by the fact that black skin couldn't be washed off, no matter how much water and soap were vigorously applied. In fact, "to wash an Ethiop's skin" became a favorite metaphor for any pointless task. In *Love's Labor's Lost*, Berowne gives this a neat twist as he comments on the cosmetic-caked faces of Englishwomen; unlike his dark-skinned Rosaline, he declares to his friends, "Your mistresses dare never come in rain, For fear their colors should be washed away."

Though curious, the English were generally uninformed and xenophobic. They often lumped all dark-skinned peoples together under a single name, completely oblivious to, or uninterested in, geographical and physical differences. The terms "Moor," "blackamoor," "Ethiope," and "Negro" were interchangeable, despite the fact that these peoples spanned the African continent. In *The Merchant of Venice*, Lorenzo distastefully reveals this provincialism when he accuses the servant Launcelot Gobbo of "the getting up of the *Negro's* belly. The *Moor* is with child by you, Launcelot."

If to be nonwhite was to be black, then to be black, in the prejudiced Elizabethan mind, was to be ugly. English standards of beauty called for red cheeks and white skin; in Shakespeare's poem *Venus and Adonis*, the goddess of love praises her "rose-cheeked Adonis" for being "more white and red than doves or roses are." Black obviously didn't have much of a place in this two-dimensional rose-and-lily scheme. When Tamora, the Queen of the Goths, gives birth to a black baby fathered by Aaron the Moor in *Titus Andronicus*, the Nurse laments, "A joyless, dismal, black, and sorrowful issue! Here is the babe, as loathsome as a toad Amongst the fair-faced breeders of our clime."

Apparently it didn't occur to many Elizabethans that the pallid white flesh of the English might leave much to be desired in some people's eyes. But Shakespeare lets Aaron the Moor fiercely defend his dark-skinned baby: "is black so base a hue? Sweet blowse, you are a beauteous blossom, sure." And Berowne, whose beloved Rosaline is "black as ebony," is another exception when he chirps, "No face is fair that is not full so black." Yet most Elizabethans would probably agree with the King, who buys into the myth that black equals evil as he answers Berowne, "Black is the badge of hell, The hue of dungeons, and the school of night."

Since the Elizabethans firmly believed that outward appearance reflected inner reality, to them, a black skin mirrored a sinful soul. As one contemporary wrote, "A black soul may and doth take the shape of a blackmoor." Indeed, as the "irreligious Moor" Aaron exults in his savage crimes, he exclaims that he "will have his soul black like his face." In *As You Like It*, Rosalind calls Phebe's harsh words "Ethiope words, blacker in their effect Than in their countenance."

Since ancient times, evil spirits and demons, especially the Devil, had been portrayed with black skin. To the Elizabethans, the logic seemed impeccable: since Satan was black, it followed that black people were satanic. By this satanic reasoning, Africans were lustful, cruel savages who delighted in evil for evil's sake.

An Elizabethan only had to pick up any of the numerous travel accounts written by explorers to find a multitude of these stereotyped images of blacks. Alongside balanced and even impartial descriptions of the people of Guinea—"And albeit they go in manner all naked, yet are many of them and especially their women, laden with collars, bracelets, hoops and chains, either of gold, copper or ivory"—the Elizabethan reader could revel in stories of Ethiopians who were eight feet high, or had only one eye in the middle of their foreheads, or had the heads of dogs. The explorers were happy to provide their reading public with descriptions of wild lands and wilder monsters, such as the tales Othello tells Desdemona, "of antres vast and deserts idle, Rough quarries, rocks, and hills whose heads touch heaven . . . And of the Cannibals that each other eat, The Anthropophagi, and men whose heads Do grow beneath their shoulders."

More than one of these explorers saw only what they wanted to see. Prejudiced by centuries-old myths and childhood stories about strange African lands, a ship's captain might persuade himself that he really had encountered such monsters and savages walking about on

the deserted shore. And whatever his Elizabethan imagination couldn't supply, ancient volumes by such Greek
geographers as Herodotus and Pliny could, with fantastic
descriptions galore.

Rarely did the Elizabethans stretch their lively minds
beyond their own rigid preconceptions to try to understand black Africans for what they were; it was far easier
to reject them for what they were not—not Christian, not
white, and not English. Because African peoples embodied
a different kind of beauty and lived in a society built according to a different cultural, economic, and religious
standard, they were dismissed and disdained. Simplistic
and simplifying stereotypes of black Africans flourished in
the foggy, raw, and dull climate of Elizabethan England.

Despite such prejudices, Shakespeare was one of the
first playwrights to create a leading role for a black character. Even though he reflected the conditions of his time,
he was unique in producing two roles, one for a black and
one for a Jew—Othello and Shylock—that are among the
greatest and most challenging roles in English drama. Living as he did in the narrow-minded society of sixteenth-
century England, Shakespeare may not have intended
Othello to be portrayed by a black man. But it is a measure
of his genius that some of our greatest contemporary black
actors—including Paul Robeson and James Earl Jones—
have performed the role, giving it a modern resonance
that Shakespeare couldn't have imagined. Nowhere was
this clearer than in Johannesburg, where a black South
African actor played Othello in a recent production that
made a powerful statement against racial prejudice.

JOINING THE JEWS

A YOUNG JEW of Spanish or Portuguese descent, looking
around for a friendly country to live in after the horrors
of the Catholic Inquisition, would certainly think twice
about going to England, for every Jew knew about the
terrible suffering his people had endured in medieval England. In the Middle Ages, English Jews weren't allowed
to own land, master a craft, or ply most trades. Many of

them became moneylenders by default, encouraged by a society that needed credit desperately but was forbidden to charge interest. But it wasn't long before the English began to resent the affluence money lending brought the Jews. In addition to financial envy, there was hostility toward their non-Christian religious practices.

Sometimes hostility swelled into violence, as Jewish homes were plundered and Jewish families massacred—despite the nominal protection of the English Crown. By the late 1200s, the Jews' financial reserves were exhausted by heavy and unjust taxes and their emotional reserves were drained by chronic harassment. No longer useful to English society, they were banished in 1290—sixteen thousand people forced to leave England almost immediately.

Reflecting on this history, our young Spanish or Portuguese Jew might decide instead to sail for the safety of the well-established Jewish community in Antwerp, Belgium, making a stopover at Dover, England, along the way. But once in England, he might hear about a small Jewish community in London and choose to join their number—probably less than a hundred. After his awful double existence in Spain, where his family had lived secretly as Jews and publicly as "New Christians," or Marranos, he might be overjoyed to find even a few Jews, especially since they, too, were exiles from Spain and Portugal.

The small community of Jews in Elizabethan London had worked out a relatively comfortable coexistence with Protestant England. Many of them were doctors, merchants, traders, and prominent citizens in the city. Outwardly, of course, they conformed, as everyone had to by the law of the land. They faithfully attended Sunday services at the Protestant Church of Saint Olave's down the street and even held their marriages and funerals there. But once a week, they trod the cobbled streets of the section of London known as Aldgate and, behind the closed doors of the home of a Portuguese Jew, quietly held Sabbath prayers. As a Spanish subject imprisoned in London eventually reported to his government, "It is notorious that in their own homes they live as such observing their Jewish rites; but publicly they attend Lutheran [Protestant] churches, and listen to the sermons."

They knew that to keep their Jewish identity they had to keep it quiet, that being Jew-ish in the eyes of the authorities was better than being outright Jews. Still, a nagging sense of insecurity remained. In the first place, they didn't really have any legal ground to stand on—the decree of banishment handed down in 1290 wasn't officially repealed until 1650, and the government could have kicked them out at any time. In the second place, the English annals of anti-Semitism were too full and well thumbed for any Jew to think that the prejudice had vanished from the land. In Christian eyes, they were infidels just as Turks and Moors were. If "Turk" meant "cruel" and "treacherous," then "Jew" stood for "villainous" and "untrustworthy." Benedick uses this construction to declare his intentions toward Beatrice in *Much Ado About Nothing:* "If I do not take pity of her, I am a villain; if I do not love her, I am a Jew."

The Jew was automatically assumed by the English to be inferior to the Christian. The servant Launce makes this explicit when he issues an invitation to his fellow servant Speed in *The Two Gentlemen of Verona:* "If thou wilt, go with me to the alehouse; if not, thou art an Hebrew, a Jew, and not worth the name of a Christian."

Elizabethan institutions everywhere seemed to support and encourage these derogatory notions about Jews. The Church teachings held that the Jewish people were not only shifty infidels but also the treacherous murderers of Christ, a belief officially repudiated by the Pope in the 1960s. The writers of the time adopted the old medieval stereotypes of wicked Jews; Thomas Nashe's *The Unfortunate Traveller* presented Zachary and Zadoch, two diabolical medieval Jews who gleefully threaten to poison wells and murder Christian children—supposedly favorite Jewish pastimes and the cause of many an anti-Jewish riot in the Middle Ages.

Most playwrights, too, chose one of two caricatures when they came to depict Jews onstage: either a comically ugly figure with a red wig, big nose, and devil-like features, or a horrendously bloodthirsty and scheming villain, such as Christopher Marlowe's Barabas, the *Jew of Malta.* Shakespeare's Shylock in *The Merchant of Venice* is a possible exception.

Although generally no one bothered the Jews, there

were a few incidents with unpleasant implications. The affair of Dr. Lopez was notorious and reverberated long after its conclusion. Roderigo Lopez, a well-known member of the Jewish community, had been Queen Elizabeth's trusted physician for years when the trouble started; as a Portuguese Jewish immigrant, he had also been invaluable to the government in foreign policy matters relating to Portugal. After years of faithful and honorable service to Elizabeth, during which she granted him a manor house twelve miles from Shakespeare's Stratford, Lopez was accused of plotting to poison her.

He swore he was innocent, but he was a convenient scapegoat in the power struggle between the queen's favorites. Done in by the combination of backstabbing Elizabethan politics and anti-Semitism (the State Papers referred to him throughout as "the vile Jew"), Lopez was convicted—on trumped-up charges—and executed in May of 1594. The execution was a major public event and set off ripples of anti-Jewish feeling around the nation that took some time to fade.

There were a few other incidents, although none as big as the Lopez travesty. A German miner who openly professed Judaism lived in England with no problem until he got into a theological argument with a clergyman; after fifteen years of keeping his mouth shut, he was expelled from the country.

But in some respects Elizabethans seemed glad that the Jews were around—especially English merchants and traders. Jews made excellent shipping agents and middle men in English trading activities with Portugal and Spain. Confronted with the desire and need to trade with Spain, England's number-one enemy, these resourceful Englishmen kept their hands clean by employing Jews as "secret" agents. When Spanish goods left Spain as exports for England, they would technically "belong" to the Jewish shippers, who were originally from Portugal or Spain; but by the time they arrived in England as imports, they would have become the property of the English merchants who had financed the voyage in the first place.

Elizabeth's government also benefitted from the presence of Jews, for they brought to foreign policy matters the invaluable combination of knowledge and passion. As ex-citizens of Spain and Portugal who still kept up with

with their old communities there, many Jews in London were experts on Spanish and Portuguese affairs and indispensable sources of intelligence information. Because they had been brutally expelled from Spain in 1492 (and the hidden ones who remained hunted down by the Inquisition ever since then), many of them were zealously anti-Spanish—which fit right in with English foreign policy.

Although the life of the Jews in Elizabethan England was legally unstable and vulnerable to waves of anti-Semitism, by Shakespeare's time things weren't so bad. As long as they made their Jewishness a private matter, publicly fulfilling the minimum daily requirements of citizenship in a Protestant land, the Jews were for the most part tolerated, although they remained outsiders.

ARMADAS AND ARMADOS

IF SPANISH JEWS were guided by signs instructing them to Proceed With Caution and Yield to Oncoming Traffic, Spanish Catholics coming to England would have been greeted by billboards screaming Keep Out! It had been that way for a long time. Even when the Spanish King Philip married the English Queen Mary, during a decade when both the ruler and the Church of England were Catholic, Spanish visitors had been given a cold reception.

After Elizabeth and the Protestant Church were enthroned in 1558-1559, that chill became a downright frost. In Elizabethan London, in fact, a Spanish face was a rare sight; unless he were the Spanish ambassador to the Court, or a sailor on a merchant ship, or, in 1588, a would-be invader aboard one of the ships in the Spanish Armada, it would be extremely unlikely that a Spaniard would venture into English waters.

Religious differences may have been at the heart of what was really a mutual dislike: Protestantism and Catholicism were to these two world powers what Democracy and Communism are to twentieth-century superpowers. But it was not religion alone; in that era, religion and politics were inseparable. The English might not have thought twice about Spanish Catholicism if Spain hadn't also happened to be the greatest political and military power in the world.

It was probably as much envy as fear that caused Elizabethans to believe that Spain was an evil empire that intended to take over the whole globe—beginning, of course, with England. Every move the Spaniards made on the chessboard of international relations was seized on as evidence of their diabolical intentions. For example, the English saw right through the Spanish invasion of Spain's rebelling colonies in the Netherlands; what Spain was *really* trying to do was to build up its military power across the Channel.

To English minds, Spain was an evil second only to the Devil, and they never passed up a chance to vilify their hated rival. Accordingly, Spaniards were described as a bloodthirsty, greedy, cruel, and bigoted lot who would let no one prevent them from attaining their evil ends. They fed Indian babies to their equally bloodthirsty dogs while out conquering the New World and held contests to see who could disembowel a man fastest. They took extraspecial delight in torturing Protestants—although they might be hard put to outdo the diabolical English torturer of Catholics, Richard Topcliffe.

When the Elizabethans weren't busily engaged in Spanish character assassination, they concentrated on mocking and ridiculing the hapless Spaniards. They might have simply been following the example of their queen: rumor had it that Elizabeth considered the Spanish ambassador a pompous fool and made fun of him whenever the opportunity presented itself. Perhaps he wasn't so different from the Shakespearean Spaniard in *Love's Labor's Lost*—Don Adriano de Armado, "a refinèd traveler of Spain, A man in all the world's new fashion planted, That hath a mint of phrases in his brain," and preposterous bombast on his lips: "Arts-man, preambulate," he trumpets, "we will be singuled from the barbarous."

Both Don Armado, in his own swaggering way, and the more serious matter of the Invincible Armada provided the Elizabethans with entertainment that was hard to beat; neither Armado nor Armada did very much to improve the English opinion of Spain. After the highly-publicized fear-inspiring Spanish fleet met its end on the Irish rocks, it was hard for Spaniards to hold their heads up in the international set; and England went mad with the sweet taste of victory. Gloating ballads and pamphlets streamed from English presses, proclaiming the victory as final proof that God really was an Englishman after all—and a Protestant at that. Relations between the two countries continued to worsen. The raids of English pirates on Spanish cargo ships were frequent occurrences for years afterward.

And the legends of Spanish cruelty and bloodthirstiness continued to enjoy quite a following. Anti-Spanish pamphlets made the rounds in London; one, entitled *A Fig for the Spaniard*, described Spain as the natural habitat of those "that like bloody butchers continually thirst after blood." It would take a long time for tensions to ease. Until then, Spaniards preferred to stay put at home, safe from English swords—and English pens!

DUTCH TREAT, PETTY FRANCE

THE PROTESTANT RELIGIOUS refugees who made their way into England might have expected to be welcomed with open arms. After all, they weren't Turks or Africans, Jews or Catholics, but good old Protestants. The King of Spain was flexing his Catholic muscles in the Netherlands, and France was thrown into a religious uproar on the death of its king in the 1570s; European Protestants were in trouble and called on their fellow Protestants in England for help.

But if religious differences ebbed with this particular tide of immigrants, economic jealousies flowed right in to take their place. These Dutch and French Protestants couldn't have picked a worse time to descend upon their Protestant neighbors than the last quarter of the sixteenth century. England had been periodically racked with famine, unemployment, and trade slumps, and the Elizabethans were in no mood to receive groups of destitute foreigners who arrived on their shores exhausted, frightened, and penniless—and also, it soon emerged, skilled.

Evidently the queen—always anxious to swell the Protestant ranks—was happy to see these refugees flooding

English shores and English churches. Perhaps she realized that they could bring desperately-needed skills to her battered economy. And so, glossing over the diplomatic sensitivity of England's welcoming political/religious exiles from allied or rival nations, she declared, "They are all welcome; I at least will never fail them." Many of her top advisors felt the same way, extending warm greetings, well aware of the potential economic improvements to England's backwardness in manufacture and industry.

Unfortunately, the Dutch and French immigrants couldn't live their daily lives among their high-level sponsors. Life among the ordinary Elizabethans—farmers, shopkeepers, artisans, weavers, merchants, and apprentices—wasn't always a cozy affair. Many of them resented the refugees simply because they were strangers, others envied their skills and workmanship, and no one was particularly shy about making his feelings known.

As a result, depending on the city or village, the Dutch and the French refugees found themselves stung by lots of little irritations and petty restrictions. Unscrupulous landlords might jack up the rent for a family of strangers, sometimes charging them seven times as much as a native English tenant. Some villages enforced an eight o'clock evening curfew for immigrants; in others, foreign-born bakers could bake and sell only the inferior wheat bread, while the English bakers enjoyed the monopoly on the more popular white bread. And elsewhere, alien weavers had to swallow their anger and pay "loom money" for permission to weave—on top of taxes that might already be twice as much as the Elizabethans paid.

Foreign craftsmen could hire only English apprentices—a requirement of the law—but the English certainly didn't have to respond in kind by hiring Dutch or French apprentices. Craftsmen from abroad also had to submit to regular monitoring by a supervisory committee of Englishmen—yet another Elizabethan maneuver to extract as many secrets as they could from the foreigners and thus prevent them from gaining a monopoly.

Indeed, the main source of Elizabethan antagonism toward Protestant refugees was fear of foreigners' money-making potential. For as one foreigner noted, the English suspected that most foreigners "never come into their island but to make themselves masters of it, and to usurp their goods"; and when foreigners were as competent and knowledgeable as these Europeans, suspicions were even greater. The immigrants were resented for surpassing their Elizabethan hosts "in dexterity, industry, and frugality," as one fair-minded Englishman said.

And so, instead of tolerating these skilled strangers, many Elizabethans demonstrated their own industry—in making scapegoats of vulnerable groups. The unfortunate Dutch and French workers were blamed for food shortages, price rises, housing shortages, rent increases, and anything else that went wrong.

Sometimes, when Elizabethans could no longer bear the burden of their inferiority, resentment shortened their tempers, turning to riot. English apprentices were usually the engineers of these free-for-alls, leading the way as they smashed market stalls, plundered strangers' goods, and turned their beefy fists on anyone who looked foreign. After three terrible riots in ten years, the government finally cracked down on the apprentices and sentenced five of them to hang. Things quieted down after that.

Actually these Protestant refugees, who gave up everything for their religious principles, had a good measure of religious freedom in England. They lived in their own communities—London had an area that was called "Petty France" because of all the Frenchmen living there—and kept their lives separate but parallel to the English. They attended their own worship services apart from the English. They maintained their own baptismal and marriage records, took care of their own poor, and were even excused from the law requiring weekly attendance at Church of England services.

And so, within the shelter of their communities, they went quietly about their business, despite occasional resistance from the ungrateful English. Gradually, grudgingly, the Elizabethans began to learn from these thrifty, talented craftsmen. The refugees showed their English pupils how to weave silk, make ribbon, and engrave glass; they taught them how to make canvas, parchment, soap, combs, and buttons. The immigrants demonstrated efficient techniques of copper-mining, knife-making, harbor-dredging, and marsh-draining. And one of them revolutionized English fashion when she introduced the practice of starching linen. After that, the upper classes never again had to worry about floppy ruffs, and Mrs. Dingham van der Plasse never again had to worry about money—she grew rich practically overnight.

Local Habitations

Elizabethans were so sensitive to anything foreign or strange that they reacted even to people who came from no farther away than the remote parts of their own islands. Although a Scotsman or an Irishman or a Welshman might not stand out at first—for he *looked* English—the minute he opened his mouth he gave the game away. Regional accents were very strong and immediately recognizable, especially to Londoners who spoke the standard southern dialect that was considered "correct." Whether or not the English reacted with their customary hostility to foreigners when they heard such a "foreign" accent on the street, they certainly found these country yokels uproariously funny on the stage.

A Welsh citizen might be laughed at for the way he stumbled over his *p*'s and *b*'s, his *d*'s and *v*'s; Sir Hugh Evans in *The Merry Wives of Windsor* calls to the fairies, "Trib, trib, fairies. Come . . . Be pold, I pray you." Or he might have reported to his military captain with the classic pronunciation of a Fluellen, in *Henry V*: "there is gallant and most prave passages. Marry, th' athversary was have possession of the pridge."

An Irishman's distinctive accent never deserted him, nor did it ever fail to raise a laugh. Shakespeare has a lot of fun with MacMorris, an Irish comrade-in-arms of Fluellen: "I would have blowed up the town, so Chrish save me, la, in an hour. O, tish ill done, tish ill done; by my hand, tish ill done!" Nor did Scots get off scot-free; their broad vowels struck their southern neighbors in London as hilarious. The Scottish captain Jamy assures Fluellen and MacMorris that "It sall be vary gud, gud feith, gud captens bath." The conversations that occur between these three officers in the army of Henry V are a comical smorgasbord of incomprehensible vowels, idiosyncratic speech mannerisms, and oddly-pronounced words.

*   *   *

In the end, no matter what flag of race, creed, or nationality the immigrants waved, life couldn't have been easy for strangers in a country that considered even its own fellow islanders foreigners. The fabric of English society was woven so tightly that it seemed to exclude anyone who wasn't white, Anglo Saxon, Protestant—and male. For although Elizabeth sat on the throne, everywhere else in England a woman was just as much a second-class citizen as any stranger.

CHAPTER 5

LIKE A VIRGIN: QUEEN ELIZABETH AND THE STATUS OF WOMEN

THE BIGGEST RIDDLE of all, in a society that was riddled with riddles, was how a woman could rule the nation while all other women held such a low status. A woman in sixteenth-century England had no vote, few legal rights, and an extremely limited chance of ever getting an education, much less a job. There was no room for the independent single woman—except, of course, in the throne room.

WOMEN'S STUDIES

AN ABUNDANCE OF forces conspired to keep women in their place. For one thing, most women were denied the chance to be schooled beyond the basics. True, many new grammar schools were being founded as Elizabethans embraced Renaissance learning. But most of them had Male Only signs on the door; the few that did accept girls usually gave them a softer, easier course of study. What was unusual for the grammar schools was unthinkable for the universities of Oxford and Cambridge; in fact, these two famous institutions didn't offer degrees to women equivalent to those they gave to men until the twentieth century—Oxford in 1920, Cambridge in 1948!

No, the most an ordinary young Elizabethan woman could hope for was to pick up basic reading and writing skills at the local village school. After that, she waved good-bye to her brothers every morning as they went off to the grammar school, if the family could spare them.

Things were different in the upper classes. Gentry families often hired tutors to come into their homes and teach their daughters. Baptista showed himself a considerate father in *The Taming of the Shrew*, for he "took some care To get her [his daughter Bianca] cunning schoolmasters to instruct her"; Lucentio and Hortensio both take advantage of this upper-class practice, disguising themselves as schoolmasters to get into Baptista's house and woo Bianca! She, of course, proves to be a more assertive pupil than they had bargained for, insisting, "I am no breeching scholar in the schools; I'll not be tied to hours nor 'pointed times, But learn my lessons as I please myself."

A number of wealthy families, rather than keeping their daughters at home, placed them in other wealthy households to be tutored. And Prospero, tutorless on the uninhabited island of *The Tempest*, teaches his daughter himself: "here Have I, thy schoolmaster, made thee more profit Than other princess' can, that have more time For vainer hours and tutors not so careful."

In any case, some rich Elizabethan girls gained access through their tutors to ancient languages and ancient literature—both classical and biblical—just as their brothers did. An Italian Catholic disparaged the motives behind this: "The rich cause their sons and daughters to learn Latin, Greek, and Hebrew, for since this storm of [Protestant] heresy has invaded the land, they hold it useful to read the Scriptures in the original tongue."

Whatever the motives, the richer classes produced some impressive daughters—Lady Jane Grey, who would rather read Plato than go hunting with her parents in the park; Anne Bacon, who at the tender age of twenty-two published translations of twenty-five Latin sermons about the theological doctrine of predestination; and Mary Sidney, the translator of French tragedy and versifier of Hebrew psalms, who cultivated a circle of literary men and scholars at her stately home.

The fairest of them all, of course, and a valuable role model for the upper classes, was Queen Elizabeth, who had studied Greek, Latin, French, Spanish, Italian, Flemish, mathematics, astronomy, and history by the time she was twelve! Her command of languages was legendary; her old schoolteacher said he once saw her reply simultaneously to three different ambassadors in three different languages (Italian to one, French to the next, and Latin to the third), without missing a beat. Everyone knew the story of how she told off the stunned ambassador from Poland in a stream of spur-of-the-moment Latin—and then turned around to the Court and apologized for being slightly rusty!

The headmaster of the exclusive all-male school Eton observed that it was becoming the fashion at Elizabeth's court for women to engage in intellectual pursuits: "It is now no news at all," he declares, "to see the queen and ladies . . . instead of courtly dalliance, to embrace virtuous exercises of reading and writing, and . . . to apply themselves to the acquiring of knowledge in both liberal arts and Scriptures."

And yet—there were limits, even for women from the upper classes. Their education wasn't preparing them to go on to a university, or to become a doctor, priest, or politician; instead, it was outfitting them for life in the domestic sphere. Rather than history, grammar, and logic, most Elizabethan girls were given instruction in piety, chastity, and "home economics." The schoolteacher Richard Mulcaster uttered the prevailing opinion when he said that a woman should learn "to govern and direct her household, to look to her house and family . . . to know the force of her kitchen. . . ." Another cookbook warned, "Let no body loathe the name of the kitchen."

Spinning, cooking, preserving fruits, keeping accounts, doing needlework, weaving, playing musical instruments —anything that made home life more pleasant—were considered indispensable elements of every upper-class girl's education. Helena gives a glimpse of a girl's studies when, in the middle of a fight with her best friend Hermia in *A Midsummer Night's Dream*, she appeals to their "all schooldays' friendship" when the two of them "with our needles created both one flower, Both on one sampler, sitting on one cushion, Both warbling of one song, both in one key." Desdemona was similarly schooled, if we can believe Othello—"So delicate with her needle. An admirable musician! O, she will sing the savageness out of a bear. Of so high and plenteous wit and invention."

Domestic skills were the staples of an Elizabethan girl's education; all the rest was frivolity. Elizabeth's successor, King James, made this startlingly clear: when he was introduced to an accomplished young woman praised for her knowledge of Latin, Greek, and Hebrew, his only comment was, "But can she spin?" A girl's knowledge of ancient languages was widely considered ornamental. After all, women would never have any practical use for Latin or Greek in the political or business world—but the occasional Greek aphorism or Latin tag did set off the womanly graces quite nicely.

There were plenty of doomsayers who worried about the consequences of giving women any learning whatsoever. One writer compared a woman with an education to a madman with a sword: you just couldn't tell what she'd do with it! Others fretted that chaste young women would compromise their virtue by reading the racy tales of Ovid or equally risqué medieval romances. "Let not your girl learn Latin," parents were solemnly warned.

The final insult to women was that the rare few who managed to do something worthwhile with their education (translating the Psalms, for example), were not praised as educated women but were instead welcomed to the company of men! Sir Thomas More's daughter, Meg Roper, was so well-educated "that she may compare with any notable man." Lady Falkland was remembered after her death as "a woman of most masculine understanding." The daughters of Sir Anthony Cooke were brought up "learning both Greek and Latin, above their sex." Even Queen Elizabeth was the recipient of such a back-handed compliment: a sermon preached after her death celebrated "her masculine graces of learning, valor, and wisdom by which she might justly challenge to be the queen of men!" Apparently it never occurred to these writers and preachers that a woman could be intelligent, capable, or wise and still remain female.

WOMEN'S WORK

EDUCATED OR NOT, a woman always ran up against the one immutable fact of Elizabethan life: she would never be able to enter the professions, because she was a woman. She couldn't become a lawyer. She couldn't be a priest—in fact, some clergymen were still debating heatedly whether or not women even had souls. She couldn't be a professional teacher, although she could take care of her own children's early education. And she couldn't be a doctor; if she wanted to work in medicine she could find a job as an overworked nurse in one of the squalid London hospitals, a midwife in a village, or a "searcher" for the cause of disease in dead bodies.

The only career open to all Elizabethan women was marriage; a wife's job was to run the household and help her husband in whatever he did. Her work varied accordng to his. The tasks of a farmer's wife were "to go or ride to the market to sell butter, cheese, milk, eggs, chickens . . . and all manner of corn. And also to buy all manner of necessary things belonging to a household." The shopkeeper's wife helped in the shop, perhaps keeping the account books, and made sure the household ran smoothly. Poor women's work was spinning and weaving.

Upper-class wives, with a houseful of servants to tend to domestic matters, often had much more free time. The most popular activities of such women were writing letters, singing, dancing, strolling in the garden, playing with dainty little pet dogs, and poring over needlework—everything their education had prepared them for. Although some wives subsisted on the pious diet of religious sermons and the Bible, one upper-class woman spent an entire evening in her husband's chamber reading Turkish history and the poetry of Chaucer.

One foreigner thought that the freedom and leisure of these upper-class Elizabethan women qualified England as "the paradise of married women," elaborating: "They spend their free time in walking and riding, in playing at cards or otherwise, in visiting their friends and keeping company, conversing with their equals (whom they term gossips) and making merry with them at childbirths, christenings, churchings, and funerals; and all this with the permission and knowledge of their husbands."

SECOND-CLASS

BUT THAT LAST phrase about "the permission of their husbands" was the sticky bit for many an Elizabethan woman: whatever freedom she had was granted—and taken away —by her husband. All the current notions about the "ideal" marriage gave him this authority. He was the prince with power—and his wife was his loyal, loving subject. Kate makes this perfectly clear at the end of *The Taming of the Shrew* as she lectures the other women on wifely duties: "Thy husband is thy lord, thy life, thy keeper, Thy head, thy sovereign; . . . And craves no other tribute at thy hands But love, fair looks, and true obedience." In this scheme, the bad wife was a disobedient subject; Kate goes on: "Such duty as the subject owes the prince, Even such a woman oweth to her husband; And when she is froward, peevish, sullen, sour, And not obedient to his honest will, What is she but a foul contending rebel And graceless traitor to her loving lord?"

Both Church and State supported this premise. The Church argued that Eve had played the principal role in the fall of man. Saint Paul had a few words to say in the New Testament about the duty of women in marriage. "Let the woman learn in silence with all subjection," he advised, "But I suffer not a woman to teach, nor to usurp authority over the man, but to be in silence." Elsewhere he urged obedience: "Wives, submit yourselves unto your own husbands." Young wives who followed Paul's writings were "discreet, chaste, keepers at home, good, obedient to their own husbands."

Elizabeth's successor King James enshrined the husband's authority in a book of advice he wrote for his son. In marriage, he said, "Ye are the head, she is your body: it is your office to command, and hers to obey; but yet with such a sweet harmony, as she should be as ready to obey, as ye to command."

Wifely inferiority got a further endorsement from the

law. One foreign observer commented that "wives in England are entirely in the power of their husbands, their lives only excepted." When a woman got married, she traditionally lost all control over her property, even including clothes and jewelry; her husband could sell them, throw them out, or give them away as he pleased. Portia surrenders her wealth to her beloved Bassanio without a peep in *The Merchant of Venice:* "Myself and what is mine to you and yours Is now converted."

In giving up her property, the wife often became her husband's property; Petruchio claims his Kate in *The Taming of the Shrew* with these proprietary words: "She is my goods, my chattels; she is my house, My household stuff, my field, my barn, My horse, my ox, my ass, my any thing." When a wife died, her husband inherited all her lands; if he was the first to go, however, she got only one third of his. She had to take her husband's surname; a contemporary writer reflected playfully, "She that in the morning was Fairweather, is at night, perhaps Rainbow or Goodwife [Mrs.] Foule." She also had to assume his rank in society, even if it was lower than hers; if she married one of her servants, for example, he became a free man and her master in one sweeping motion—"where before he was her footstool, he is now her head and seignior [master]." The legal cards were so stacked against women that one observer was provoked to say, "Methinks here wanteth equality in law." Unfortunately, there wasn't much to be done about it; the Act of Parliament necessary to confer legal equality would be a long time in coming.

Any legal loopholes that might have left some doubt as to women's inferior status were amply filled in by the teachings of biology. The theory of the four humors—or liquids—stated that women's bodies had a greater proportion of the cold and moist humors (while men's bodies consisted primarily of the hot and dry humors). This meant that women were passive, timid, and hesitating—fit to be dominated by men. In *Henry VI Part 3*, the Duke of York denies that his cruel captor Margaret can really be a woman, for "Women are soft, mild, pitiful, and flexible; Thou stern, obdurate, flinty, rough, remorseless."

The supposed yielding softness and frailty of women's bodies was all the proof anyone needed of women's all-around weakness, for most Elizabethans firmly believed that "the disposition of the mind is answerable to the temper of the body." In other words, outer appearance was merely a reflection of inner condition. One Elizabethan spelled it out: "A woman in the temperature of her body is tender, soft, and beautiful, so doth her disposition in mind correspond accordingly; she is mild, yielding, and virtuous." Or, as Isabella cries to Angelo in *Measure for Measure*, "Nay, call us ten times frail, For we are soft as our complexions are, And credulous to false prints."

Indeed, the softer the body, the greater the beauty. Ivory skin, rosy cheeks, a round face, rounder hips, and yielding flesh were all requirements for the beautiful woman. Modern standards of womanly beauty—tanned, thin, and bony—would have struck an Elizabethan fashion plate as very odd indeed.

Of course, complexions aren't perfect in any age; and when Nature refused to deliver, women resorted to various chemicals to conjure up the necessary paleness of skin and rosiness of cheek. They began with a base—not the beige, skin-colored foundation some women use today, but a greasy chemical made of white lead or sulphur, which often had a withering effect on the skin. They smeared this base lavishly over their faces, necks, and upper chests. On top of the white went various dyes to redden the cheeks; these, too, were caked on heavily. Beauty spots were drawn on the cheeks in strategic locations, eyebrows plucked to a dainty thinness, and lips thickly lipsticked. After her hair was powdered, pinned, and perfumed, and the perfumed gloves put on, the Elizabethan lady was ready to face society. Shakespeare plays on both meanings of "face-painting" in the final scene of *The Winter's Tale:* "The ruddiness upon her lip is wet," Paulina warns Leontes as he gazes at the "statue" of his wife Hermione, "You'll mar it if you kiss it, stain your own With oily painting."

Not everyone thought that this face-painting was such a great idea. Puritans thought it was an abomination to try to improve one's God-given appearance: Elizabethan women, one writer fumed, "color their faces with certain oils, liquors, unguents [ointments] and waters whereby they think their beauty is greatly decored [decorated]." And Hamlet speaks for many an opponent of makeup when he says scornfully to Ophelia, "I have heard of your paintings too, well enough. God hath given you one face, and you make yourselves another."

The standards of inner beauty for women were no more accommodating to variety than those of outer beauty. The recipe for a good woman included ingredients of obedience, patience, chastity, modesty, and virtue. Miranda, in *The Tempest*, calls her modesty the most important quality she has, "the jewel in my dower." Talkative women were not considered witty and learned but unpleasant, impudent, and shrewish. Launce intones in *Two Gentlemen of Verona*, "To be slow in words is a woman's only virtue." Indeed, women who spoke their minds too assertively ran the risk of making themselves unattractive to men: Kate warns her fellow wives in *The Taming of the Shrew*, "A woman moved is like a fountain troubled, Muddy, ill-seeming, thick, bereft of beauty; And while it is so, none so dry or thirsty Will deign to sip or touch one drop of it."

Usually, an Elizabethan female who didn't live up to these specifications of submissiveness and silence was labeled as a "bad woman," one of several types. She might have been the shrew who nagged, scolded, and ordered her henpecked husband around. In *The Comedy of Errors*, Antipholus of Ephesus apologizes to his friends for having to run out on them but excuses himself on the grounds that "My wife is shrewish when I keep not hours." As Kate learns, shrews had to be tamed, for they created household havoc and, worse, represented a reversal of the natural order. Lady Macbeth is a formidable and decidedly unfunny version of a woman who dominates her weak-willed husband.

Those who didn't fit into the shrew category might be considered lustful seductresses who welcomed any chance to cheat on their husbands. The ageless fear of wearing the horns of the "cuckold" (the man whose wife had committed adultery) was probably the single biggest anxiety of Elizabethan married men. Certainly Shakespeare's men worry about it. Master Ford, in *The Merry Wives of Windsor*, suffering under the delusion that his wife is committing adultery with Falstaff, cries in anger, "See the hell of having a false woman!" Master Ford is not alone in judging his wife to be the unfaithful seductress: Leontes doubts Hermione's integrity in *The Winter's Tale*, Claudio jilts Hero in *Much Ado About Nothing* on the grounds that she's been carrying on with someone else, and Othello's jealousy and suspicion of his wife Desdemona end in murder.

If ever a woman dared to threaten male authority by talking back, showing independence of mind, or even wearing men's fashions, men usually had a strong reaction. Toward the end of the century it took the popular form of pamphlets against women. No doubt the Elizabethan women who could read them didn't know whether to laugh or cry at all the stereotypes, simplifications, and gross exaggerations contained in these booklets.

There was the old chestnut about women having only two faults: everything they say and everything they do. There was the traditional picture of the hysterical angry female: "A froward woman in her frantic mood will pull, haul, swerve, scratch, and tear all that stands in her way." There were the exaggerated comparisons: "The lion being bitten with hunger, the Bear being robbed of her young ones, the Viper being trod on, all these are nothing so terrible as the fury of a woman."

Of course every war has two sides, and this pamphlet war was no exception. Women volleyed back with pamphlets wondering about men who didn't have anything better to do than "write some bitter satire, pamphlet, or rhyme against women." They also took a few shots at the double standard that indulged drunken men as boys just having a good time but judged drunken women to be of loose morals. The double standard was everywhere: "If a man abuse a maid and get her with child, no matter is made of it but as a trick of youth, but it is made so heinous an offense in the maid that she is disparaged and utterly undone by it."

Furthermore, these pamphlets argued, if women were bad, they had men to thank for it. If wives were deceptive, it was because they learned how to lie to protect their husband's reputation; if they were vain, it was because men flattered them. In *Othello*, Emilia even goes so far as to blame men for women's adulterous actions, telling Desdemona that it's men's fault for setting a bad example: "But I do think it is their husbands' faults If wives do fall . . . have not we affections, Desires for sport, and frailty, as men have? Then let them use us well; else let them know, The ills we do, their ills instruct us so."

Whether women were being attacked or defended, one thing was clear—as ever, they were a hot topic of the times. But in the end, the word battles didn't accomplish much besides generating a lot of paper. The intellectual debate about the nature and position of women did little to improve their situation. As long as the law denied women equality, as long as the fruits of education remained beyond the reach of most, as long as church teachings, biological theories, and long-practiced social conventions upheld women's inferiority, Elizabethan women had no choice but to accept the fact that they lived in a man's world.

MEANWHILE,
BACK ON THE THRONE. . .

WHILE STALWART ELIZABETHAN women were battling it out on the front lines of the household, Queen Elizabeth was proving that a woman was more than capable of mastering a kingdom—and showing herself to be an almighty exception to the rules that governed women's lives.

In the first place, she never got married—despite the universal expectation that women must. For a time after she came to the throne, everyone had simply assumed that she'd be getting married, just as her older sister, Queen Mary, had before her; and there was a great deal of talk about who the lucky man would be. After all, who else but a husband could relieve her of the labors which are better borne by men? as King Philip of Spain suggested.

Members of Parliament—concerned about who her successor would be—tried over and over again to make their wayward queen see the necessity and urgency of marriage. At one point they even threatened to hold back money she desperately needed for the government until she promised to get married. Elizabeth dug in her heels and refused to be blackmailed, declaring instead that she would pray to God "to continue me in this mind to live out of the state of marriage."

In fact, being a single woman served the queen well in

matters of foreign policy. She wasn't above making and breaking diplomatic alliances by dangling the prospect of marriage in the faces of various Spanish, French, and Scandinavian nobles and princes. She would call off the match at the last moment, either because the would-be husband-king was Catholic and therefore unacceptable, or because he refused to come to England and submit himself to a degrading onceover by the queen. If foreigners were unsuitable, an English husband was even more out of the question; to make a king out of a subject, even if he was a nobleman, would be seen as dangerously destabilizing to the country.

Perhaps what it really came down to was that Elizabeth realized early on that marriage meant loss of power. She couldn't be a queen and a wife at the same time. Some Protestant writers thought she could have it both ways—"Why may not the woman be the husband's inferior in matters of wedlock, and his head in the guiding of the commonwealth?"

But Elizabeth knew better, and once the scepter was in her hand, she was determined not to give it up to anyone. "In the end," she declared with satisfaction, knowing that she had won her case, "this shall be for me sufficient, that a marble stone shall declare that a queen, having reigned such a time, lived and died a virgin."

This careful, calculating queen had learned about power and prudence early in life. The storms and tumults she survived as a child taught her a lot about self-preservation. After Elizabeth's mother Anne Boleyn was beheaded by her father King Henry VIII, the young princess was declared illegitimate by an act of Parliament. She then had to get used to four different stepmothers in a row, as Henry went through one wife after another in his quest for a male heir. Her last stepmother remarried after King Henry died, taking Elizabeth to live with her and her new husband—a situation that taught the princess yet another political lesson. Before long, nasty rumors began to circulate about scandalous goings-on between Elizabeth and her new stepfather, who, it was said, visited her bedroom every morning—often before she was fully dressed. Even in a time before inquisitive newspaper reporters were sniffing out improper behavior in political figures, the future queen learned how easily public scandal could erupt as a result of private actions.

The oppressive five-year reign of Elizabeth's Catholic half sister Mary made life for the princess even more difficult. Although born a Protestant, she was forced (along with the rest of the nation) to convert to Catholicism—which she did, at least outwardly. But Mary was still very suspicious of her sister, especially because Elizabeth was so immensely popular with the English people—who knew that she was the rising star. At one dreadful point, she was even accused of treason and sent to the damp, gloomy Tower of London—protesting her innocence all the way.

In order to survive all these perils Elizabeth had had to cultivate wariness, watchfulness, calculation, and patience. She became a born actress, endlessly resourceful at playing whatever role circumstances required. This ability proved to be no less useful when she came to the throne.

Certainly Elizabeth began grandly. The new queen's coronation procession through London was an extravaganza. Even in the middle of the cold winter, exuberant subjects lined up behind the wooden rails on the frozen narrow streets for miles to see the glittering procession: fathers lifted up babies; women held out little nosegays; and everyone cheered and waved as their beloved Elizabeth passed by, resplendent in her golden glitter on the way to Westminster. But the reception the new queen received in international political circles was far more reserved. At first, of course, rulers and governments were holding their breath to see who Elizabeth would marry; when that issue remained unresolved, foreign leaders grew hostile to the very idea of a woman ruler.

The general opinion at the time was that governing was an art accessible only to men; a female head of state was an offense against nature. One Protestant writer published a book called *The First Blast of the Trumpet Against the Monstrous Regiment of Women*, in which he declared that "it is more than a monster in nature that a woman should reign and bear empire above men." This criticism was actually aimed at Elizabeth's predecessor, the Catholic Mary—but unfortunately for the author, the book came out just as the Protestant Elizabeth ascended the throne. Needless to say, there were no more blasts from *that* particular trumpet.

This writer wasn't alone in his sentiments, however; even Elizabeth's closest advisors were convinced that she suffered from womanly weakness of the mind. Two years into her reign, one of her ministers scolded a diplomat for mentioning to the queen "a matter of such weight, being too much for a woman's knowledge." This didn't stop her from establishing herself; the Pope later expressed surprise at Elizabeth's formidable authority: "She is only a woman . . . and yet she makes herself feared by Spain, by France . . . by all."

A FEMININE MYSTIQUE

ELIZABETH DIDN'T WASTE much time worrying about what would in later ages be called feminist principles and sexist attitudes. Her concerns were practical and immediate: how to get on with the business of ruling. Her Court was a large and unruly community whose members, mostly male, were constantly competing with each other for favor, power, and position. It was a chaotic, corrupt place, as hectic as the stock exchange, filled with ambitious young men who had come from all over to rub elbows with the great and mighty. In *The Two Gentlemen of Verona,* Proteus is sent to the Court to "practice tilts and tournaments, Hear sweet discourse, converse with noblemen, And be in eye of every exercise Worthy his youth and nobleness of birth."

The main task Elizabeth faced, even after replacing some of the gentlemen attendants with her own ladies-in-waiting, was figuring out how to maintain control of this male preserve and yet retain her courtiers' loyalty at the same time.

If the Court presented a challenge, it also provided a perfect setting. For the Court was the center of the nation's political, cultural, and social life. All the ins and outs of governing wound their way around the Court; many of the interesting new trends in poetry, drama, and literature flourished there. It was the place for all the fun that high society knew how to have—tournaments, balls, witty conversations, lavish parties. With its rich velvets and shimmering silks, its sparkling conversation, its self-assured air, the glittering spectacle of the Court was the ideal back-drop for Elizabeth's command performance. To overcome the disadvantages of being a woman ruler in the over-whelmingly male world of the Court, she had to play a double role, alternating between the earthly woman and the divine majesty.

Her strategy worked superbly, for if her gender was the problem, it was also the solution. Elizabeth gained control of the Court by capitalizing on the fact that she was a woman—initially a young and attractive one. She shamelessly flirted with her courtiers and mercilessly toyed with their emotions. She played rival factions off against each other rather than letting them destroy her. She gave out her favor and snatched it back without warning, so that no courtier could ever be sure of his standing with her. She was as imperious and moody as Shakespeare's Cleopatra, changing her mind and temper as rapidly as the English clouds covered and uncovered the sun.

Careful as always, Elizabeth never let the game of flir-tation get out of hand. She never allowed a courtier to become her one and only but let several dangle at once. And whenever a courtier went too far, thinking that he could expect her favors, she quickly cut him down to size with her acerbic wit and sharp one-liners. When an angry courtier dared reproach her for refusing to give him money, she replied that anger made dull men witty but kept them poor.

Although Elizabeth won the Court over with her "fem-inine wiles" and flirtatiousness, she also rose far above or-dinary definitions of the feminine. As a divinely ordained ruler, she became the personification of virtue—Modesty, Prudence, Wisdom. By virtue of her unmarried state, the "Virgin Queen" was also the symbol of that supreme fe-male virtue—Chastity. A cult grew up around this queen who was so much more than a queen—a cult that she her-self encouraged. She was acclaimed in poetry, song, bal-lad, and pamphlet as Astraea, Diana (the mythological Roman moon goddess), and the pure chaste shepherdess-nymph of many a pastoral poem. The courtier poet Ed-mund Spenser celebrated her as Gloriana, the Fairy Queen, whose knights rode out to do battle and deeds of honor in her name. Like Shakespeare's Coriolanus, she was hailed as "a thing Made by some other deity than Nature, That shapes man better;" a Swiss tourist remarked with interest that the English worshipped her "not only as their queen but as their god."

No matter if in later years her teeth were black, her white skin shriveled with age, her head weighed down with a huge red wig, her temperament grouchier and more difficult by the day. Elizabeth the woman, subject to the physical weaknesses that affect all human beings and the added "natural frailties" that afflicted all women, was conveniently lost beneath the pomp and paraphernalia of Elizabeth the symbol.

Much of the lavish praise that gushed over the queen in her lifetime exalted her "masculine" virtues of courage and intellect. At times Elizabeth almost had to become a man in order to get anything done, just as many of Shakespeare's heroines—Viola in *Twelfth Night*, Portia in *The Merchant of Venice*, Julia in *The Two Gentlemen of Verona*, and Rosalind in *As You Like It*—had to put on male clothes and boyish behavior in order to enjoy male privileges of freedom and self-determination. Rosalind certainly understands how the game is played—"in my heart Lie there what hidden woman's fear there will—We'll have a swashing [swaggering] and a martial outside."

Elizabeth knew as well as Rosalind that she simply had to maintain that swashing and martial outside, and she didn't let down her guard for a minute. To call attention to womanliness in the wrong way would have been to commit political suicide. On the rare occasion when Elizabeth referred to her gender at all, she drew attention to it as a shortcoming—"my sexly weakness." By emphasizing the weakness of womanhood, Elizabeth was cleverly drawing attention to herself as the overwhelming exception. In her speech to the English troops at Tilbury just before the invasion of the Spanish Armada, she said she hoped no one would hold her sex against her: "I know I have the body of a weak and feeble woman; but I have the heart and stomach of a king, and of a king of England, too."

Elizabeth was too well-versed in the way of the males world to think she could get away with putting any other women in positions of power—even if she had wanted to. Not only were all her councillors male, but apparently she forbade her ladies-in-waiting to mention affairs of state at all!

Like her woman subjects, Elizabeth dwelled in a male world, facing the same traditional barriers of inferiority that Elizabethan women faced, but crossing others, such as education, with upper-class ease. But even though she showed herself to be a powerful, popular, and wise ruler, she couldn't make a difference in the lives of her female subjects, because she succeeded only by repudiating her identity as a woman. The male world accepted her because she was the exception among females. In the end, this great queen succeeded in the Elizabethan world not because she was a woman but in spite of it.

CHAPTER 6

THE TIES THAT
BIND: FAMILY LIFE

IF YOU WOKE up one morning and suddenly found yourself
in a sixteenth-century family, you might be surprised at
how familiar everything seemed. Although you would be
getting off of a lumpy straw mattress and planting your
feet on a floor covered with rushes instead of rugs, when
you went downstairs you would find a very modern-
looking nuclear family—mother, father, and a few sisters
and brothers—sitting on stools around the breakfast table,
drinking their morning beer (*that* might be different!) and
eating their bread and butter before getting on with the
day's work.

A few generations earlier, however, it would have been
quite a different story. In the Middle Ages the "family"
was a much bigger crowd, essentially a clan whose loyalties extended even to distant relatives; "kinship" was an
all-purpose word.

But by the sixteenth century "kin" had become a much
more exclusive club—parents, grandparents, siblings, aunts,
and uncles. Everyone else was left out in the cold as a
distant relative, vaguely hailed as "cousin" or just "friend."
This newly-defined family played a leading role on the
broader stage of society, supplying its economic, repro-
ductive, social, and emotional recommended daily requirements.

The family was the firmest and most entrenched foundation of Elizabethan society; it didn't occur to many peo-

ple that there was life outside it. Indeed, Elizabethan life sometimes seemed to be one long dance—be it a courtier's minuet or a villager's folk dance—from one family to the next: from the original family Elizabethans grew up in to the "surrogate" family they were sent to as servants, college students, or apprentices, to the families they would one day create with their spouses. At any stage of life, the family was more or less a given—an immensely comforting fact. Bewildered and buffeted by fast-paced changes in society, Elizabethans needed something to lean on— and most found it within the family.

They also earned their living in a family setting, whether in a stately manor in the rolling green dales of northern England or in a cramped and tiny cloth shop on one of the filthy and noisy streets of London. And of course the family literally kept society alive by providing it with children. Procreation was one of the principal and sacred purposes of marriage. At the end of *As You Like It*, the god of marriage is applauded for maintaining the population: "'Tis Hymen peoples every town; High wedlock then be honorèd."

DEATH COMES A'KNOCKING

BUT IF HYMEN peopled every town, Death *un*peopled it almost as quickly. For death was the center of Elizabethan life—the other member of the nuclear family that no one liked to think about but everyone sensed lurking in corners.

Death—not divorce—was the great Elizabethan homebreaker. Its preferred victims were infants and children; babies were lucky to survive the perils of birth, much less their first year of life when they were most vulnerable to infectious diseases (the plague or smallpox), malnutrition, and a host of other terrors. Some infants were accidentally suffocated when mothers lay too close to them in bed; others succumbed to birth defects.

The child's environment was no more friendly; it was filled with natural and artificial hazards—stairs to fall down, open fireplaces to walk into, horse's hooves to be trampled beneath, village wells to topple into, and ditches to drown in. No wonder one out of every five Elizabethan children didn't live beyond the age of ten. Shakespeare's son Hamnet died after his eleventh birthday, and too many Elizabethan parents could identify with Capulet when he tells Paris that Juliet is his only surviving child: "earth has swallowed all my hopes but she." Viola's confession to Orsino in *Twelfth Night*, although a fib, certainly has the ring of truth: "I am all the daughters of my father's house, And all the brothers too."

Death left its calling card with adults, too; most Elizabethans had lost at least one parent by their twenty-fifth birthday. Helena, the young heroine of *All's Well That Ends Well*, mourns her dead father—or so the Countess thinks when she observes, "The remembrance of her father never approaches her heart but the tyranny of her sorrows takes all livelihood from her cheek." Ironically, women often died in the process of giving life, for in the hands of untrained midwives without any surgical know-how or anesthesia childbirth was not only "natural" but downright primitive—and extremely dangerous. As for men, many fell on the battlefields of England's constant foreign wars in Europe. Also, famine, poverty, the bubonic plague, and other diseases claimed lives daily.

IN THE NURSE'S ARMS

DESPITE THE MANIFOLD dangers of pregnancy and childbirth, parents welcomed a child as a blessing from God. As the Clown in *All's Well That Ends Well* exclaims, "I think I shall never have the blessing of God till I have issue o' my body; for they say bairns [children] are blessings." With the fear of death uppermost in their minds, parents took care to baptize this new blessing right away, so that the baby's soul would be saved if death staked its claim in the first few months of life. Once that was taken care of, the baby was greatly fussed over in its early years— rocked, sung to, and kept out of the light to protect its tender eyes. Its tiny arms and legs were wrapped with strips of "swaddling cloth" for protection; Hamlet conjures up a ridiculous image of the pompous elderly statesman Polonius when he tells the Players, "That great baby you see there is not yet out of his swaddling clouts."

The mother usually took care of breast-feeding her infant. But many upper-class women, worried that breast-feeding would spoil their figures or their social lives, shipped their babies off to a wet nurse, paying *her* to do it. Not only was this costly, it was risky: because there weren't any surrogate wet nurse agencies, a mother couldn't always be sure what kind of situation she was sending her infant into. One upper-class woman worried about a potential wet nurse: "She looks like a slattern but she sayeth that if she takes the child she will have a mighty care of it, and truly she hath two as fine children of her own as ever I saw." Many nurses were overworked or indifferent—burdened with too many children or not enough food—and were the cause of more than one baby's death. Indeed, Juliet's faithful and affectionate Nurse is unusual in her maternal devotion to her charge: "Thou wast the prettiest babe that e'er I nursed," she tells Juliet, "An I might live to see thee married once, I have my wish."

A FIRM BUT LOVING HAND

THE FACT THAT death might swoop down any day didn't cause a lack of parental affection. In the sixteenth century, unlike preceeding ages, parents were just beginning to bring up their children with tender loving care, worrying about each scratch, sore, or fever—knowing that it might be fatal—and providing the best food, clothing, and shelter they could.

For poor families, raising children often meant a terrific struggle against the enemies of inadequate food, nonexistent heating, dangerously overcrowded one-room cottages, and pitifully thin clothes. Farm laborers in one part of the countryside were "so extreme poor that they are scarcely able to put bread in their children's bellies." But parents often went to extraordinary, even heartbreaking lengths to get food for their children, spinning wool

The aged servant Adam was luckier than many homeless old people who wandered the countryside in lonely poverty, for he had his young master Orlando to keep him company. (Lou Gilbert as Adam in *As You Like It* in 1973.)

PHOTO: GEORGE E. JOSEPH

All photographs from New York Shakespeare Festival Productions, Joseph Papp, Producer.

The alehouse was the place for ordinary Elizabethans to have a beer, take a date, find a job or just hang out, as Falstaff and his cronies know. (Stacy Keach, second from right, as Falstaff in *The First Part of King Henry IV* in 1968.) PHOTO: GEORGE E. JOSEPH

Sir Hugh Evans tests his pupil William on his knowledge of Latin grammar, a subject every Elizabethan schoolboy studied. (Left to right: George Pentecost, Marilyn Sokol, Marcia Rodd and Stephen Austin in *The Merry Wives of Windsor* in 1974.) PHOTO: GEORGE E. JOSEPH

Valentine, (left) a gentleman of Verona, hopes to distinguish himself as a worthy courtier and Renaissance man. (A scene from *Two Gentlemen of Verona* in 1987.) PHOTO: MARTHA SWOPE

This "deposition" scene, where the divinely ordained monarch Richard II (left) is deprived of his rightful crown, was considered too subversive to be allowed onstage in Shakespeare's day. (Peter Macnicol, left, as Richard and John Bedford Lloyd as Bolingbroke in *King Richard II* in 1987.)
PHOTO: MARTHA SWOPE

The charming wood creatures and fairies of *A Midsummer Night's Dream*—a far cry from the traditional Elizabethan conception of fairies—gather in the wood. (William Hurt, third from left, as Oberon and Michele Shay, second from right, as Titania with the fairies in *A Midsummer Night's Dream* in 1982.)

PHOTO: MARTHA SWOPE

These witches are sinister stage versions of the real-life old hags
many Elizabethans suspected of practicing witchcraft. (Joan
DeWeese, Barbara Lester and Nancy Watts in *Macbeth* in 1962.)
PHOTO: GEORGE E. JOSEPH

Shakespeare's portrayal of the pompous Don Armado, a "refined traveller of Spain," is far less derogatory than the anti-Spanish pamphlets circulating around London at that time. (Paul Stevens in *Love's Labor's Lost* in 1965.)

PHOTO: GEORGE E. JOSEPH

Though Shylock is a Jew of Venice, he had a few counterparts in Shakespeare's London, where there was a small community of Jews. (George C. Scott as Shylock in *The Merchant of Venice* in 1962.) PHOTO: GEORGE E. JOSEPH

The exotic, dark-skinned Prince of Morocco wooing Portia chooses the wrong casket, much to her relief: "Let all of his complexion choose me so." Such prejudice was rampant in Shakespeare's England. (James Earl Jones, center, in *The Merchant of Venice* in 1962.) PHOTO: GEORGE E. JOSEPH

The marriage of the Moor Othello and the white Venetian Desdemona violates the Elizabethan principle that like should marry like. (Julienne Marie and James Earl Jones in *Othello* in 1964.) PHOTO: GEORGE E. JOSEPH

The aspiring Lucentio, taking advantage of the upper-class practice of educating girls at home, disguises himself as a tutor in order to woo Bianca. (Deborah Rush and James Lally as Bianca and Lucentio in *The Taming of the Shrew* in 1978.)

PHOTO: GEORGE E. JOSEPH

Blonde, soft-skinned, and rosy-cheeked, Katharina fits the
Elizabethan standards of feminine beauty perfectly.
(Meryl Streep as Katharina in *The Taming of the Shrew* in 1978.)
PHOTO: GEORGE E. JOSEPH

Many Elizabethans fought—and many died—on foreign battlefields similar to this one at Agincourt, where Henry V leads his troops to glorious victory. (Kevin Kline, center, as Henry in *King Henry V* in 1984.) PHOTO: MARTHA SWOPE

The gravediggers are a reminder of the constant presence of death in Elizabethan life. (Peter Van Norden and William Duell as the gravediggers in *Hamlet* in 1986.) PHOTO: MARTHA SWOPE

The pregnant Julietta is an unfortunate victim of the
Elizabethan betrothal system, which considered the mere
promise of marriage as valid as an actual marriage ceremony.
(Amy Taubin as Julietta in *Measure For Measure* in 1966.)
PHOTO: GEORGE E. JOSEPH

Coriolanus, a grown man and a national hero, still shows respect for his mother by kneeling in her presence. (Morgan Freeman as Coriolanus and Gloria Foster as Volumnia in *Coriolanus* in 1979.) PHOTO: GEORGE E. JOSEPH

Hamlet, in a private talk with his mother, accuses her of being seductive and lustful—a common Elizabethan stereotype of women's behavior. (Stacy Keach and Colleen Dewhurst as Hamlet and Gertrude in *Hamlet* in 1972.)

PHOTO: GEORGE E. JOSEPH

The authorities of the city of London lived in fear that stage plays would lead to a riotous gathering like Jack Cade's rebellion that Shakespeare portrays in *The Wars of the Roses*. (A scene from *The Second Part of King Henry VI* in 1970.)

PHOTO: GEORGE E. JOSEPH

through the night or walking all over the countryside to get even the most basic provisions for their brood.

Since there weren't many professionally-written child-rearing manuals, most parents followed the example of *their* parents. The mother's love was generally considered stronger; as one upper-class woman wrote to her son, "There is no love so forcible as the love of an affectionate mother to her natural child."

But a right upbringing involved more than "forcible" love, in most people's eyes; it also required forcible discipline. Although discipline was always strict, whipping was usually a last resort. Some of the few child-rearing books in circulation advocated regular flogging; others (written by women) recommended a lighter touch: "for what disposition so ever they be of, gentleness will soonest bring them to virtue."

The main thing parents asked in return for all the time and energy they spent was obedience—and perhaps a little gratitude (parents were, after all, human). Elizabethan children were expected to honor their parents by obeying them in all matters; children didn't speak without first being spoken to—nor was talking back to parents a frequent occurrence. Middle- and upper-class children were used to kneeling every day to ask their parents' blessing. Shakespeare's valiant Roman general Coriolanus honors his mother this way even after he is a grown man and a famous warrior: "You gods!" he checks himself, "I prate, And the most noble mother of the world Leave unsaluted. Sink, my knees, i' th' earth; Of thy deep duty more impression show than That of common sons." His mother replies, "O, stand up blest!" Most children's greeting to their parents was less dramatic than this, of course—"good morning, father and mother; please, may I have your blessing?"

In poor families, however, children had to do more than just honor and obey; they were also expected to labor and earn. A family that was just scraping by often counted on even its young children for income. Simple chores such as gathering wood, scaring birds away, picking up stones, tending the sheep, or keeping an eye on the newest baby were the normal responsibilities of children in less well-off families.

Few parents, rich or poor, viewed their children as

"social security": elderly parents rarely expected to be taken in and taken care of by their offspring. In the first place, given that the average life expectancy for Elizabethans was somewhere around forty years, not many parents ever qualified for such social security. Many of those who did would probably have to work right up until the day they died anyway, unable to afford retirement.

In any case, the older generation generally thought it stupid or ill-advised to go live with grown children as "sojourners." How could parents give up everything and still expect to retain their children's respect and obedience? King Lear discovers the sad truth of this conventional wisdom too late, of course; after dividing up his kingdom between two of his three daughters, he is relieved—or deprived—of one privilege after another until he cries out in futile rage, "Ingratitude, thou marble-hearted fiend, More hideous when thou show'st thee in a child Than the sea monster!"

HALFWAY HOUSE

WITH THE MAJOR exception of children of poor laborers, Elizabethan teenagers generally left home to go live with another family. Sending children away to spend their adolescence with other people was an almost universal custom for the middle and upper classes. And so Panthino finds it odd that Antonio keeps his son Proteus at home in *The Two Gentlemen of Verona*, "while other men, of slender reputation, Put forth their sons to seek preferment out: Some to the wars, to try their fortune there, Some to discover islands far away, Some to the studious universities."

Although sending their teenagers away might have saved beleaguered Elizabethan parents many headaches, they didn't stop worrying about them. Launce's departure from his family practically undoes them, if we can believe his description: "My mother weeping, my father wailing, my sister crying, our maid howling, our cat wringing her hands, and all our house in a great perplexity." Even the young fellow safely ensconced within the protective high walls of Oxford or Cambridge, looked after by a tutor determined to keep him on the straight and narrow, could regularly expect long letters from his parents asking how his grades were and whether he was getting enough to eat. Not only does *Hamlet*'s Polonius give his son Laertes a stern lecture before he goes back to the university at Paris ("these few precepts in thy memory Look thou character") but he then dispatches Reynaldo (in secret) to "make inquire Of his behavior"—that is, to make sure Laertes is behaving himself.

The wealthiest families usually sent their adolescents either to university or to the Inns of Court. But most teenagers went to work as manservants to wealthy farmers or maidservants to upper-class women; others were apprenticed to craftsmen and tradesmen in the cities. Indeed, thousands of ambitious adolescents from all over England made their way to London to work as apprentices to grocers, candlemakers, spice merchants, barbers, and cobblers, who were often acquaintances of the family.

The master usually took on the role of the boy's surrogate father—on a contractual basis, of course. He would agree to feed, clothe, and shelter his new charge, as well as to teach him the trade; in turn, the boy signed the usual seven-year contract, promising—no doubt with fingers crossed—not to run away, not to fool around with girls, and not to get married. Cockfights, bowling grounds, and tennis courts were off-limits, and hair had to be kept short. Girl servants were governed by a similar set of rules applying to them.

And so the apprentice began his life in a brand new family. It wasn't so different from the old days with his real parents, except that his master didn't always feel obligated to provide the same kind of concern. Horror stories about cruel masters were a dime a dozen: one girl servant was stripped, hung by her thumbs, and given twenty-one lashes with a whip; a male apprentice was hit with an axe. One hapless fellow barricaded himself in an alehouse rather than return to the master he loathed.

Male apprentices were one of the most distinct and noticeable groups in the city. With the "fury of ungoverned youth" (as Shakespeare called it) racing in their blood, they roamed the streets of London in a rowdy, rambunctious fraternity—much like the crowd of loyal prentices in *Henry VI Part 2*, who arrive en masse to cheer on their fellow Peter in single combat against his master—"Be merry, Peter, and fear not thy master. Fight for credit of the prentices," they advise him. Whether they were drinking each other's health in their favorite alehouse, jostling each other in the pit of the Globe Theatre as they stood and watched one of Shakespeare's plays, or competing with each other to chat up pretty servant girls, apprentices did their best to stir up trouble. No doubt most people who encountered them went away muttering something similar to the shepherd in *The Winter's Tale*, who wishes that "there were no age between ten and three-and-twenty, or that youth would sleep out the rest, for there is nothing in the between but getting wenches with child, wronging the ancientry [the elderly], stealing, fighting. . . ."

Apprenticeship—or servitude, or wage labor, or university—was where Elizabethan teenagers spent those strange years sandwiched between childhood and adulthood. They were in the awkward position of being old enough to leave their parents' homes but not old enough to set up their own households, and so society provided a kind of halfway house where they were supervised by people who weren't their parents but were supposed to be *like* their parents. However parentlike they might have been, these caretakers actually gave teenagers a lot of leeway.

OUT FROM UNDER

ALTHOUGH IT WOULD be a while before Elizabethan teenagers would actually tie the knot in marriage, they weren't averse to casting out a few lines here and there. For at their age, as one writer said, "Cupid and Venus [the gods of love] were and would be very busy to trouble the quiet minds of young folk." Teenagers might have several liaisons before settling down for a long-term one, and, of course, the fact that they were away from home gave them the freedom to experiment.

The opportunities for socializing must have seemed endless, particularly for enterprising young teenagers. They might dance cheek to cheek at a village celebration, trade sweet nothings in the dark back booth of an alehouse, take in the sights and stalls at country fairs and markets, stroll along back lanes, or do goodness-knows-what behind the back stairs of the master's house. Perdita and Florizel declared their love at a village sheep-shearing festival in *The Winter's Tale*. Of course, a girl had to be careful—if she walked out with more than one man within a short period of time, she might find herself the target of unpleasant gossip. But on the whole these young folk were left to their own devices, unchaperoned and unhindered.

Even children of upper-class families who didn't enjoy the freedom from parents' watchful gazes could find some ways to spend time alone with one another—although daughters were more sheltered. They might go sight-seeing around the countryside in a coach, dance close together at balls, or talk to each other at lavish upper-class parties during the London season. Flattering letters declaring undying love were another good gambit; in *The Two Gentlemen of Verona*, Proteus glibly advises Thurio on the art of letter-writing: "Say that upon the altar of her beauty You sacrifice your tears, your sighs, your heart." And upper-class swains often sent trinkets and gifts as tokens of their affection; Proteus' plan to win Silvia by presenting her with his pedigree lapdog backfires when his servant Launce substitutes his own mangy cur instead.

THE PARTY'S OVER

THINGS CHANGED, HOWEVER, as teenagers approached marrying age; freedoms were curbed. Upper-class children in particular found their parents suddenly taking a lot more interest in their romantic affairs. Even though it was no longer fashionable for parents to arrange and force a marriage against a child's will, as Juliet's father tries to do, the child still wasn't entirely in control of his or her marital fate.

As parents explained over and over, the property gains and family alliances that a good marriage could bring were just too important to be left in the hands of children. The

Margaret Dakins story showed the lengths parents could go to in their quest for a good match: because she was the only child of a wealthy couple, the future status of the family depended on her marriage, and her parents looked long and hard to find just the right combination of property and prestige. But evidently they were better judges of wealth than health, for both of her first two husbands died within a few years of marriage, and by the age of twenty-five, she was on her third husband!

For many a matchmaking parent, wealth and property were the only considerations. Valentine, one of the two gentlemen of Verona, disparages Thurio as "My foolish rival, that her [Silvia's] father likes Only for his possessions are so huge." And in *The Merry Wives of Windsor*, Sir Hugh Evans observes, with his inimitable Welsh flair, that Anne Page is well endowed where it counts: "Seven hundred pounds and possibilities," he says, "is goot gifts." Anne herself rejects these criteria for choosing a mate— "O, what a world of vile ill-favored faults Looks handsome in three hundred pounds a year!" she says of her suitor, Slender.

Equality of status, religion, and age were important too. Couples of different ages, races, religions, or social standing were certainly not encouraged, and even highly disapproved of in some quarters. Desdemona's marriage to the Moor Othello shocks and angers her father. Polonius, as he tells Claudius and Gertrude in *Hamlet*, has warned Ophelia that "Lord Hamlet is a prince out of thy star; This must not be." And in *The Winter's Tale*, King Polixenes is outraged that his princely son consorts with a lowly shepherdess: "Thou art too base To be acknowledged. Thou a scepter's heir, That thus affects a sheephook!"

If parents presented a child—a daughter—with a match that met their criteria, one of two things could happen. She could resign herself to the inevitable (as Margaret Dakins did) and go through with it; or she could put up a fight—at the risk of incurring her parents' anger. Juliet's father cannot believe his ears when she refuses his generous offer of the Count Paris; after all he's done for her, "to have a wretched puling fool, A whining mammet, in her fortune's tender, To answer, 'I'll not wed, I cannot love, I am too young; I pray you, pardon me'." But if a rebellious

daughter or son resisted a match with enough energy—
Anne Page, in *The Merry Wives of Windsor*, vows that she
would "rather be set quick [alive] i' th' earth And bowled
to death with turnips" than marry Doctor Caius—the marriage might be called off.

Upper-class parents didn't always try to choose for their
offspring; often children were free to select their own
spouses. Whoever made the choice, the important thing
was to get the consent of everyone involved. Tranio recognizes that winning Bianca's heart is only the first step
for Lucentio in *The Taming of the Shrew*: "But, sir, love
concerneth us to add Her father's liking." Ferdinand (*The
Tempest*) apologizes to his father for wooing Miranda
without consulting him: "I chose her when I could not ask
my father For his advice." Master Page refuses to allow
Anne to marry until he bestows his approval in *The Merry
Wives of Windsor*: "The wealth I have waits on my consent,
and my consent goes not that way," he says of her beloved
Fenton.

But in the end—like many a hapless Elizabethan
parent—Mr. Page accepts his daughter's choice: "Fenton,
heaven give thee joy! What cannot be eschewed must be
embraced." Another upper-class woman writes despair-
ingly to her husband about their wilful daughter: "She is
so great with Mr. Candish's son that she is fully minded
to have him . . . Whether you like it or not it must go
forwards and be a match."

Things were much less difficult and constrained on the
lower rungs of the social ladder. Less well-to-do young
people were not only freer to shop around, but also to
marry whomever they wanted. Since grand property deals
and shrewd marital investments weren't being made, parental consent wasn't usually a problem.

But this didn't mean that money didn't matter. Although a servant or apprentice might have had fewer possessions, he still had economic interests to think about.
Survival in the rough waters of the Elizabethan economy
was impossible without a good helpmate through life, and
it was crucial to look before leaping. A potential diver into
the marriage market would probably give a lot of thought
to how good a provider or housekeeper a prospective part-
ner was likely to be. In *The Two Gentlemen of Verona*,

Launce lists the virtues of the milkmaid he plans to marry: "Here is the catalog of her condition," he pronounces: she can fetch and carry, milk, brew good ale, sew, knit, wash, scour, and spin. In fact, this woman was a real find, for such skills were crucial to running an efficient and thrifty household, and not everyone had them in equal measure; as Rosalind reminds the haughty Phebe in *As You Like It*, "Sell when you can, you are not for all markets."

Marriage wasn't always a cut-and-dried financial transaction; the Duke of Suffolk, encouraging King Henry VI to marry for love instead of politics in Shakespeare's play, insists that "Marriage is a matter of more worth Than to be dealt in by attorneyship." Among the poorer classes especially, love mattered. Many was the young man who swore passionately that he could not survive without the lifelong presence of his beloved, and many the young woman who vowed to love her chosen one till not a breath was left in her belly.

TYING THE KNOT

THESE WERE THE sorts of heartthrobs and undying loves and marital fantasies that occupied the minds and hearts (and hormones) of most Elizabethan teenagers throughout the "age of adolescency." They wouldn't actually do anything about them for several years, for the marriage age was surprisingly late—for girls, twenty-five or twenty-six and for boys, twenty-eight or twenty-nine. Baby brides like Juliet, who "hath not seen the change of fourteen years," or fifteen-year-old Miranda of *The Tempest*, were the exceptions, even for the upper classes.

There were very practical reasons for putting off marriage. Later marriages meant smaller families—and in a society that was already bursting at the seams with people, big families meant big problems. Delayed marriage was the insurance policy Elizabethan society took out to guarantee that married couples would be financially able to support a family. The law that required apprenticeships to last seven years was passed specifically to "curb over hasty marriages and over soon setting up of households by youth." In other words, people weren't allowed to marry until they were economically independent. And they weren't economically independent until they had reached an age where they had either saved money from their period of apprenticeship or inherited it from their parents.

This reasoning was well founded. Babies often followed close on the heels of marriage and were quite possibly the major cause of it; probably one out of every three blushing Elizabethan brides was pregnant on her wedding day. This happened to the newlywed Shakespeare, whose first child was born a few months after his marriage to Anne Hathaway; and it happened to another Elizabethan couple, who had themselves married and their baby baptized on the same day!

It wasn't always that these couples were playing fast and loose with each other; it had more to do with how people usually went about getting engaged and married. The way the system worked, a promise to marry someone was considered just as valid and binding an agreement as the actual ceremony. Once intentions had been declared (honorable or not), the couple was free to act as if they were married.

This was widely accepted but not universally embraced. Although he celebrates the betrothal of his daughter Miranda, Prospero feels called on to warn Ferdinand of dire consequences "If thou dost break her virgin-knot before All sanctimonious ceremonies may With full and holy rite be ministered." Often these betrothal arrangements spelled trouble, especially for young women. When Claudio and Julietta make just such an agreement in *Measure for Measure*—"upon a true contract I got possession of Julietta's bed," Claudio vows, "You know the lady; she is fast my wife, Save that we do the denunciation lack Of outward order"—Julietta becomes pregnant.

These pregnancies before-the-fact were generally tolerated—as long as the pregnant *maid* became a pregnant *bride*. But sometimes, for one reason or another, the marriage ceremony didn't happen. The young girl's fiancé may have been forced into military service by a press-gang. Or perhaps the groom-to-be called things off when the bride's dowry didn't meet expectations, as Angelo is said to have done in *Measure for Measure;* when Mariana's brother was shipwrecked and her dowry lost just before the marriage, the treacherous Angelo "swallowed his vows whole, pretending in her discoveries of dishonor." Or perhaps the betrothed was one who "never means to wed where he hath wooed," as Katherina says in *The Taming of the Shrew*.

When someone who, under better circumstances, would have been a pregnant bride became an unwed mother instead, the consequences were dire. She might be fired from her job and kicked out of the parish; and even as she was in the throes of giving birth to this bastard infant, the midwife would refuse to lift a finger until she gasped out the name of the father.

In a society where resources were already drained, women who brought bastards into the world—unless they could manage to find a man to support them—paid dearly. Small wonder that some women resorted to the horrifying alternatives of herb-induced abortion and infanticide by poison or suffocation.

Once a happy young Elizabethan couple had fulfilled all the requirements—financial independence and parental approval—they could crown their courtship with an actual church wedding. This was a great occasion, full of fun and festivity: as Petruchio declares in *The Taming of the Shrew*, "We will have rings and things, and fine array; And kiss me, Kate, we will be married o' Sunday." The church ceremony was the standard Church of England formula, complete with promises to love, honor, and obey.

But the real fun started with the reception or wedding feast—what Elizabethans called the bride-ale and what Puritans referred to as "public incendiaries of all filthy lusts." This was usually quite a party, replete with food and drink, jigs and dances, bawdy songs, and gifts for the guests. Poor couples' celebrations were fairly modest—a simple dinner, party favors of ribbons and gloves, lots of noisy bell-ringing—but the upper classes generally put on a spectacular show, often drawing people from neighboring villages and parishes to gape and gawk. Such feasting, drinking, and all-around extravagance could go on for several days. The affair finally ended when friends of the newlyweds subjected them to the bawdy ceremony of "bedding" on their first night as man and wife. And so married life began.

THE DYNAMIC DUO

THERE WAS NO shortage of writings and sermons by contemporary critics and preachers advising a new couple on how to have the ideal marriage. The pair who followed their advice might achieve what the Duke of Suffolk (*Henry VI Part 1*) calls "a pattern of celestial peace."

The wife was, of course, enjoined to be meek, patient, quiet, and willing to put up with whatever her husband dished out. The husband had a responsibility to look out for his wife, to provide for her, and to be patient with her womanly frailties and shortcomings. He was to be careful not to abuse his power over her but to treat her with kindness. After all, Eve was created not from man's head or foot, but from his side, and so his wife should be, to some extent, his companion.

In fact, marriage probably turned out to be much more of a partnership than these writings implied. In a sense it had to be—the game of survival was too strenuous for half of the team to sit idly on the bench. For the class of poor landless laborers who depended exclusively on wages for a living, it was particularly crucial for both spouses to work. The wife might spin wool to sell to her weaver-husband's employer, help with the weeding, the haymaking, and the harvesting, work in the village alehouse, take in washing, and do any other odd job that might bring in a little more income.

At the other end of the economic spectrum, upper-class women often seemed more ornamental than essential to the operations of the household. But, in fact, many of them had a large hand in running the estate, particularly the wives of husbands who traveled on business. The wife would oversee the estate manager who collected the rents from tenants, handle a large staff of servants, and supervise the various other operations that went with running a household and the accompanying acres of land. She might also be called on for her knowledge of delivering babies, mixing herbal remedies, or making repairs.

The spouses who worked together played together, too, and spent their free time engaging in any number of activities. Young gentry couples held dinners or went to Lon-

don for parties; the less well-off sampled the newest batch
of beer in the local alehouse or danced a measure at the
village harvest celebration. Many couples spent whole eve-
nings just talking to each other, or reading together, and
there is every reason to believe that most felt a deep and
abiding affection for each other. After all Margaret Dakins
had been through, she seemed to have found happiness
at last; her third (and final) husband spoke in his will of
"the extraordinary affection that was between her and myself in our life-time," and wore a bracelet with her picture
inside it until the day he died. Another affectionate old
man wrote to his wife, "Of all the joys I have under God
the greatest is yourself. To think that I possess one so
faithful, and one that I know loves me so dear, is . . . the
greatest comfort this earth can give."

But where there was room for happiness, there was
also room for discontent. Some couples quarreled frequently. Perhaps the wife proved unexpectedly insensitive,
or the husband felt that he was locked into an arranged
or forced marriage he had never wanted in the first place.
As the Duke of Suffolk asks (with his own ulterior motives)
in *Henry VI Part 1*, "For what is wedlock forcèd but a hell,
An age of discord and continual strife?" When Helena
confides in Diana that her husband Bertram hates her, in
All's Well That Ends Well, Diana sympathizes: "Alas, poor
lady! 'Tis a hard bondage to become the wife Of a detesting
lord."

And bondage it often was. Marriage was indeed a "world-
without-end bargain," as the Princess reminds the King
in *Love's Labor's Lost*. If the quarrels didn't resolve themselves, or if one person realized that the marriage should
never have taken place, there simply wasn't much that
could be done about it. Divorce was unthinkable: only a
private act of Parliament could procure one, and that,
obviously, was a rarity. Church courts could annul (or
cancel) the marriage but first required proof that the spouse
was already married to someone else, or that the marriage
was unconsummated. The same court could also order a
physical separation on the grounds of adultery or physical
abuse (battered wives, for example), but this, too, was
unusual.

.   Once again, the poor were freer; they actually had a
couple of escape hatches. The couple could simply sepa-

rate unofficially, and no one would take much notice. Men could exercise another option—walking out. Given the primitive communications and the terrible roads, a deserting husband could be pretty sure he'd never be tracked down by a vengeful wife. He might even marry again and start a new life elsewhere. More often, though, these runaway husbands became homeless vagrants or criminals.

That was all well and good for the poor. But for those who had serious wealth or property to think about, desertion was out of the question. Short of following Othello's example and killing the hated spouse, unhappy husbands or wives just had to put up with their predicament until death relieved them of the burden. Given the low life expectancy, however, an unhappy couple might not have too long to wait; "till death do us part" could be a matter of years, not decades. Rare was the Elizabethan couple who celebrated a golden anniversary; the average marriage lasted around twenty years.

When death brought an end to a happy marriage, as it so frequently did, the surviving spouse was often devastated. Many Elizabethans were cast into deep depression by the death of their mate; a few even committed suicide. One upper-class woman refused to leave her room for a full year after her husband's death. In *The Two Gentlemen of Verona*, Silvia appeals to her friend Eglamour's memory of his beloved: "Thyself hast loved, and I have heard thee say No grief did ever come so near thy heart As when thy lady and thy true love died, Upon whose grave thou vowedst pure chastity." Aegeon's wife in *The Comedy of Errors* follows a similarly chaste existence after she is separated from her husband in a shipwreck: she enters a convent.

More often than not, bereaved husbands and wives chose neither death nor chastity but remarriage. A young Elizabethan man or woman who had had an unhappy first marriage might be eager to make it work the second time around. Even many of those who grieved eventually resigned themselves to remarrying—it was virtually a necessity. A middle-aged merchant simply couldn't cope with the children on his own; a young widow needed help with the farm she'd inherited—and indeed, such a propertied woman would have plenty of suitors, for many an aspiring

Elizabethan male hoped to build a fortune and a career by marrying a widow.

Remarriage was pretty much taken for granted during Elizabethan times. In *The Merry Wives of Windsor*, Master Ford, commenting on his wife's close friendship with Mistress Page, speculates, "I think, if your husbands were dead you two would marry." Mistress Page's retort—"Be sure of that—two other husbands"—points to the inevitable realities of English life in the sixteenth century. For Mistress Page knew, as many Elizabethans did, that no matter how discouraging the setbacks and how great the obstacles, the show must go on. And marriage, in the end, was the only real show in town.

PART III

SHAKESPEARE ALIVE!

In Shakespeare's London, all the world seemed to be a stage. (The opening scene from the 1983 New York Shakespeare Festival production of *King Richard III*.) Photo: Martha Swope

CHAPTER 7

THE REVOLUTION OF 1576: THE THEATRE IS BORN

SOMETHING HAPPENED in 1576, a history-making event that had a profound impact on the course of world theater. A man named James Burbage, who had worked much of his life as a carpenter before becoming a full-time actor, signed a lease on some land outside London, and constructed a building—the Theatre—exclusively for dramatic representation in the English language.

Without this shrewd and courageous move, actors, playwrights, and English drama itself might never have gained the permanence, independence, and truly professional status they needed to live and flourish. The construction of the first permanent, custom-built playhouse in England was without a doubt an event that altered everything in the theater forever after—especially since it became the first theatrical home for the greatest dramatist in the English language, William Shakespeare.

THE WORLD BEFORE
THE THEATRE

OF COURSE THE fact that there hadn't been any playhouses in England before 1576 didn't mean that there hadn't been any plays or actors. Quite the contrary. In the little villages and hamlets sprinkled across the country, drama was a part of daily life. Throughout the Middle Ages and up until 1576, acting in plays wasn't a separate occupation limited to trained professionals in a permanent theater. It was merry-making, a participatory activity, something everyone could do for fun during holidays, church festivals, and harvest celebrations. Plays and entertainments, colorful pageants, tumbling and juggling, various games, and group dancing were all basic features of such seasonal parties and one-time occasions. There were also, of course, traveling minstrels attached as "servants" to the households of noble patrons. These entertainers crisscrossed the countryside singing and dancing for any audience they could scrape together.

Despite a small degree of organization within this apparent chaos, the theater was still pretty much a slap-dash affair. Throughout the medieval period, drama was for amateurs. In the early days, respectable craftsmen—woodworkers, carpenters, cobblers, and so on—put on Bible-based plays under the auspices of their particular guild organization (a cross between a trade union and a social service club). These plays, financed by a guild and traveling from town to town on colorful pageant wagons, brought to life the biblical stories of Adam and Eve, Noah, or Moses, of Jesus' birth, and of the Devil's attempts to lure mankind into eternal damnation. Such plays were performed entirely for the glory of God and were very definitely not-for-profit affairs—vivacious, fast-paced, brightly-painted and gorgeously-costumed spectacles, crammed full of action and display, and laden, of course, with moral teachings.

In the decades leading up to the great year of 1576, these old traditions were combined and transformed into a kind of itinerant theater. Groups of actors, or strolling players, would travel around England, drumming up audiences and putting on plays whenever and wherever they thought they had a chance of financial success. Unlike their medieval predecessors, these players were semi-professionals; many of them earned the better part of their living from the hat they passed around at the end of their performances. To keep that hat full, they had to keep giving their audiences what they wanted and what they were used to—lots of characters, rich costuming, and such elaborate stage effects as Hell belching smoke, angels descending from on high, frightful earthquakes, loud thunderous storms, and burning altars.

These strolling players had inherited the old pageant traditions of theater, the lively spectacles, the vivid sound and sight effects, and the fast pace of earlier theatrical presentations. At the same time, they had to contend with a problem that the craft guilds had not had to worry about: far fewer resources.

To start with, an average group of strolling players was much smaller than the old-style craft guilds, usually somewhere between five and eight people. Because these actors were always on the road (in a time before big tour buses and trucks were around to carry heavy equipment and costumes) and were limited to one or two packhorses and a small wagon or two at best, they had to keep baggage to a minimum. What's more, because they were earning their living from performing, it was in their interest to hold down the operating costs as much as possible. This meant that they were severely restricted in the props, costumes, and stage machinery they could take along.

The result, of course, was a starkly simple production. The stage was nothing more than a rectangular wooden platform resting on top of several barrels. A cloth-covered booth functioned as a kind of makeshift dressing room, hiding the actors while they changed costume. There weren't many props or much scenery. The limited cast meant that doubling of parts was absolutely essential; an actor could routinely expect to play three or four parts in the course of a two-hour play. The notion of hiring extras to fill in the gaps was laughable, given the already stretched financial resources of the group. The actors just had to do the best they could.

And yet with energy and inventiveness, the strolling players managed to overcome these obstacles and offer to their nationwide audiences a truly popular theater. The play they presented, whether a Biblical story or a morality play, was a great combination of slap-dash and energy, as actors dashed backstage to change tie-on beards from gray to blond or ginger to white, caps from a nobleman's to an apprentice's, and gowns from a Moorish servant's to a woman's—all in time to re-enter two minutes and twenty-five lines later as a completely different character.

Their plays mingled the comic and the tragic without apology, disregarding classical theories of drama going back to Aristotle that drew a firm line between "Comedies, [which] begin in trouble, and end in peace," and "Tragedies, [which] begin in calms, and end in tempest," as an ancient saying had it, and insisted on unity of time, place, or action. As far as the itinerant players were concerned, if the audience liked a play, theories of genre could go by the wayside. It wouldn't be at all unusual to see a new play at this time billed as "*Conflict of Conscience* ... An excellent new comedy ... containing the most lamentable history, of the desperation of Francis Spera"; and Shakespeare pokes fun at the company of players in *A Midsummer Night's Dream* who perform "A tedious brief scene of young Pyramus And his love Thisbye; very tragical mirth."

As these popular actors were strolling their way through the sixteenth century, traversing England in search of a livelihood, London was growing by leaps and bounds. The city was fast becoming the economic, political, and cultural capital of the nation, the center of trade, the home of the royal Court, and the final destination of an increasing flood of migrants from the countryside. London, in short, had it all; it was a city that offered unlimited opportunities to the sharp-witted and profit-minded. It didn't take enterprising actors long to realize that where there was a large population and a lot of commerce, there would also be large audiences. And so without further ado, they packed up their bags, loaded up their packhorses, and moved to the big city.

Once an acting troupe had made its way inside the city gates, it might make arrangements with the owner of a popular London tavern or inn to set up a stage, on a somewhat temporary basis, in the enclosed but roofless yard of his establishment. This arrangement satisfied everyone. The manager of the inn was happy since, in addition to the fee he charged the acting company for using his facilities, he was also selling more beer and alehouse buns to the audiences. The actors were delighted to have a place to perform, a ready-made audience of drinkers and eaters to perform for, and sometimes even a place to store costumes and props inside the tavern. No doubt they felt right at home there at the Boar's Head or the Bel Savage or the Red Lion, performing on a platform stage just like the one they'd used in the traveling days, surrounded by an audience on three sides. Of course, if there was no room at the inn, an acting troupe might be able to set up a temporary stage in one of the outdoor bearbaiting arenas, a rounded building with a two-story gallery and a sandy unpaved yard where the bear fought off attacks from trained dogs.

In general, these two pre-1576 outdoor arrangements served the acting troupes well. But city officials, who considered the bands of players irresponsible vagrants, instigators of unrest, and ringleaders of riotousness, were constantly trying to prohibit the actors from playing in the innyards or bearyards (which were within their jurisdiction), put them out of business, and throw them out of London. At first, because the actors preferred the convenience of performing within the city limits, they were willing to put up with this constant hassle, and they were able to withstand the assaults because of the backing of the noble patrons. But after a while it became too difficult.

You can almost imagine James Burbage sitting down with a quill and parchment one afternoon, after a particularly heated argument with the proprietor of the innyard (who had just had a particularly unpleasant visit from the city authorities), to make a checklist of the ideal conditions under which he and his fellow players could continue acting professionally. Leaving out the patronage and protection of a nobleman, which he already had, he would probably have written down "location"—outside the city's walls and the city's jurisdiction; "structure"—probably an outdoor building, with no more than a couple of entries to ensure that no one got in without paying; "size" —enough capacity to hold a large paying audience; and "reliability"—the actors had to be able to count on having a place that they wouldn't be thrown out of on a moment's notice.

Perhaps it was at just about this time that a plot of land came up for rent in the parish of Saint Leonard's, in the Shoreditch area about a mile north of London. Disgruntled, fed up, but nonetheless determined not to let the city officials close him down, Burbage seized the day, borrowed the capital from his brother-in-law (a prosperous grocer and businessman), and within a short time, signed the lease. Construction started in the spring of 1576; several months later, the building was complete. Burbage named it the Theatre—the first time that word had been used in English to refer to a place for plays.

THE PLOT HEARD ROUND
THE WORLD

THE WONDERFUL STRAIGHTFORWARDNESS of its name—the Theatre—was matched only by its architecture—simple and functional, designed to hold as many people as possible. In building his outdoor or open-air theater, Burbage took his cue from the bear-gardens his acting troupe had previously performed in; like a bearbaiting amphitheater, the Theatre was a round (or rather, many-sided), unroofed, wooden building. But with an eye on bigger profits, Burbage made some improvements on this model. Instead of settling for a dirt yard that could turn all too easily to mire and mud, he paved the "pit," as it was called, with brick or stone. And he added a third floor of gallery (or balcony) seating to the standard two-story theater, thereby increasing the capacity of his playhouse considerably, perhaps to over two thousand people.

The stage, too, underwent revision. Burbage's stage was no temporary slab of wood; rather, it was a permanent rectangular platform, probably twenty-five by forty-five feet. Instead of resting on barrels, it was supported on sturdy posts and extended well out into the yard. At the back of the stage was a wall with a couple of doors, for entrances and exits, and behind this wall was the players' dressing room, or the "tiring-house" (for their attire). The stage cover, called the "heavens," stretched out over the stage platform, from the tiring-house to the pillars at the front of the stage. On top of the heavens was a little hut where the trumpeter proclaimed the start of a performance, stagehands operated the stage machinery, and the company flag fluttered in the breeze.

With this building, a trend was being set in theater architecture that would last for decades. Aside from a few individual variations, all subsequent public theaters of this time, unlike the indoor private theaters that offered more elitist entertainment, followed Burbage's basic plan. The lyrically-named theaters—the Curtain, the Swan, the Rose, the Fortune, and the great Globe itself—were many-sided open-air amphitheaters with a wooden frame, a paved yard, a projecting stage, and the rest.

In building the Theatre, Burbage helped establish actors and drama as permanent and accepted aspects of Elizabethan life. Not only did his theater encourage a regular audience and therefore regular profits, but it could physically accommodate the storage of a larger number of more substantial props and costumes. It provided the money and the resources to support a larger permanent cast, to hire extras, to acquire the best plays, and to improve the facilities. In short, the Theatre gave security and independence to drama, conditions under which it could expand and develop.

Now theater people could flap their wings as much as they wanted—provided, of course, that they did so beyond the city limits and beyond the legal reach of the city authorities, who would have liked nothing better than to pluck their feathers. Because the outdoor theaters attracted such large audiences and supposedly promoted a dangerous, unrestrained atmosphere, acting troupes preferred to remain safely outside the city, in the suburbs to the north and south of London.

There were indoor theaters closer to the city, like the one in Blackfriars. Small and intimate, they had a capacity of only five or six hundred compared to the two or three thousand the Globe or the Swan could hold. They were lit by candlelight, charged six times as much admission as their public counterparts, and had no friendly standing room equivalent to the yard of the outdoor theaters. For a while indoor theaters were used mainly by the companies consisting exclusively of boy actors, who offered a particular kind of play replete with literary devices and rich in clever satire. Early in the seventeenth century the adult companies, led by the King's Men, took over these theaters and began using them for the winter season, inheriting the boy companies' audiences.

Although these private houses would one day become theater headquarters, for the moment the outdoor public theaters held sway, proliferating on both sides of the Thames. For the first few years after 1576, they were located mostly to the north of London in the Shoreditch area. The Theatre was about a mile north of London's east end, across Finsbury Fields. The Curtain went up nearby, shortly after the Theatre was finished, while the Fortune's lot was further toward the city's west end. The Red Bull, an inn converted to a playhouse, stood even further west, completing the northern group.

Gradually, though, there was a general migration south across the Thames to a suburb called Southwark, an area with a fine open meadow and lots to do (taverns, gambling houses, bearbaiting arenas, brothels, and so on). In 1587, a particularly powerful theater entrepreneur named Philip Henslowe opened the Rose Playhouse in the garden of an inn in Southwark. The Swan appeared a few years later, and just before the end of the century, the Globe was built by Shakespeare's company.

In the late 1590s, dramatic activity was flourishing in the public theaters. A different play was performed every day at each of the several public playhouses outside London; the two "theater districts" to the north and south of the Thames were bustling with activity; and the profits were rolling in.

Tourists from abroad often commented admiringly on the quantity and quality of dramatic activity around London. One tourist praised the pleasing physical aspects of the theater: "The playhouses are so constructed that they play on a raised platform so that everyone can see the whole spectacle. The actors are most expensively and beautifully dressed. . . ." And another visitor summed up the London scene: "Without [outside] the city are some theaters where English actors almost every day represent tragedies and comedies to very numerous audiences; these are concluded with excellent music, variety of dances, and the great applause of the audience."

BATTLE LINES DRAWN

UNFORTUNATELY NOT EVERYONE wore the enchanted spectacles of tourists. London in the 1580s and 1590s was also the setting for numerous clashes between enemies and friends of the theater; London city officials, flanked by several special-interest groups, squared- off against the Privy Council (the ruling cabinet, composed of the most powerful nobles in the land), Court aristocrats, and ultimately Queen Elizabeth herself.

The Court aristocracy leapt—gracefully, of course—to the aid of the embattled actors time and time again, and the Privy Council (whose members included the patrons of the two leading London companies, the Lord Chamberlain and the Lord Admiral) did their best to thwart the peevish city authorities, unless it was politically impossible. After all, entertainers and players had been under noble patronage as far back as anyone could remember. Medieval minstrels had delighted aristocratic households with singing, playing of instruments, tumbling, conjuring tricks, sword fights, poetic recitations, and puppet shows; attached to—and protected by—a nobleman, actors provided entertainment for his parties and celebrations. It was an old and proud tradition that the nobles intended to uphold now that companies were establishing themselves permanently in London.

The theater was also an important part of the aristocratic social and cultural life. The actors brought the latest hit plays to Court every winter season, performing in the indoor halls for the queen and her courtiers. For this reason—and the additional fact of the noblemen's own love of the arts—the Court defended theater activities; its support was often what saved the actors from an ignominious end at the hands of the city bureaucrats.

Many Londoners who had to live on location with the theaters and actors were much less enthusiastic than the Court aristocrats. Everyone seemed to have something to say about the theater—outraged Puritans, disgruntled entertainment competitors, and protective London authorities. The growth of drama into large-scale, popular entertainment was raising a lot of questions and fears in

people's minds. No longer were productions just ama-
teurish activities confined to noblemen's households or
seasonal church and agricultural celebrations. Drama was
now a fearful commercial force to be reckoned with.

In general, the Lord Mayor and his council of aldermen
(or henchmen, as they sometimes seemed to be) did everything they could to make life miserable for acting companies. To these officials' way of thinking, the new popular
theater might have unpredictable and alarming consequences. How would it affect peace and order on the city
streets? Would impressionable young people get evil ideas
in their heads from this unrestrained type of visual entertainment? What if neighborhoods where theaters were
being built protested that they didn't want all the noise
and riffraff? And who would control how much the players
should charge, and when they could perform?

The mayor and the city councillors seemed to be most
worried about the consequences of bringing large groups
of Londoners together in a public theater. In the first
place, the dreaded bubonic plague could spread quickly
and uncontrollably in a tightly-packed arena. As one re-
straining order explained, "In time of God's visitation by
the plague such assemblies of the people in throng and
press [crowds] have been very dangerous for spreading
of infection." This rule didn't just apply to theaters; all
public gatherings were prohibited during outbreaks of the
notorious epidemic.

But city officials were also plagued by a fear of the
moral contagion of the theater. Although they weren't familiar with the term "mob psychology," the likelihood of
a large boisterous crowd turning into a riotous mob ter-
rified the officials. If a riot did break out, they had no
means of controlling it—no police force, no National Guard,
no standing army.

The one or two theater-related incidents that did occur
were more than enough to convince the authorities
that they were right. The street rioting that broke out one
morning after a young dandy "prodded" the stomach of a
young apprentice sleeping outside the Theatre—although
it wasn't directly connected with a performance—was
enough to vindicate the authorities in their own eyes. As
far as they were concerned, such an incident *could* have

been performance-related; actors could communicate dangerous ideas by portraying rebellion in a play. To guard against this, the Revels Office insisted that anything considered even slightly provocative be cut out. Shakespeare himself felt the muscle behind this prohibition: the deposition scene in *Richard II*, where the rightful monarch is deprived of his throne and royal powers, was seen only once in his day—and illegally at that. The Revels Office had censored the scene as politically subversive, but the Earl of Essex, planning a rebellion against the queen, persuaded the Lord Chamberlain's Men to give a special performance that included the deposition scene. As a result the actors were hauled into court, although they were subsequently let off.

Sometimes the city authorities carried their anti-theater campaign onto legal battlefields. They tried to regulate exactly how many performances the players could give each week, what time they could start, which days were to be allowed as performance days. Several times they actually tried to shut down the playhouses. But even when the antagonistic authorities were successful in prodding the Privy Council to issue an order closing the theaters, there was no guarantee that it would be obeyed. Late in the 1580s, for example, acting on the orders of the Lord Treasurer of the Privy Council, the Lord Mayor of London (no doubt rubbing his palms with undisguised glee) sent for the two leading companies in London and commanded them to stop playing; one of the companies "very dutifully obeyed," but the other group of actors, fumed the Lord Mayor, "in very contemptuous manner departing from me," went straight to the Cross-Keys, a London innyard, and gave a performance that very same afternoon!

Several years later, responding to international outrage over a seditious play called *The Isle of Dogs*, the Privy Council ordered that plays be stopped and playhouses "plucked down"; but theater people just kept a low profile for a while and the order was never really carried out. Though their voices grew fainter, the city authorities kept protesting without much hope of getting their hearts' desire, namely the permanent closing of the theaters. For that, they would have to wait until almost halfway through the next century.

* * *

Although the creation of new theaters spawned a great variety of jobs—for builders, contractors, architects, draftsmen, surveyors, carpenters, plasterers, painters, property men, carters, printers, lawyers—there were some tradespeople who clamored against this new industry, particularly those who stood to lose financially from the theater's gain. Their basic gripe, or so they said, was that plays were drawing apprentices and servants from their work. But the truth of the matter was that they greatly resented actors as rivals and competitors.

For although players were nominally professional craftsmen, they remained free of confining guild obligations such as dues and rules; they grew rich by selling their "wit," an intangible commodity that couldn't be regulated by commercial restrictions. This freedom infuriated merchants and business people who *did* have to operate under limitations, and they refused to accept that "playing" was working.

The sellers of rival forms of entertainment were also distressed by the possible loss of business that theaters might cause them. For with an admission price of only a penny, playhouses could undersell all other popular diversions except bearbaiting, which also cost a penny. Business at the taverns, the eating places, and the gambling houses might fall off if people began to flock to the theaters. Only the watermen, ferrying audience members back and forth across the Thames, were sure to profit.

Joining the ranks of rival businesses, preachers and Puritan citizens lent their moral soldiery to the attack on the theater. They spoke out vehemently against all aspects of dramatic entertainment, denouncing actors, audiences, playwrights, and everyone who had anything to do with them as wicked and corrupt. The playhouse is "Satan's synagogue," said one minister; another called it "the nest of the Devil and the sink of all sin." One preacher even blamed theater for the plague; with an irrefutable syllogism he reasoned, "The cause of plagues is sin, if you look to it well: and the cause of sin are plays: therefore the cause of plagues are plays."

From the pulpit and in pamphlets, these groups objected to the extravagance and high costs of this temporary pleasure, "the waste of expenses in these spectacles that scarce last, like shoes of brown paper." The playhouses themselves were "a continual monument of London's prodigality and folly."

They condemned what in their eyes was the shockingly lustful behavior of the audience, particularly of the young men who scanned the audience for a likely pickup: "In our assemblies at plays in London, you shall see such heaving, and shoving, such itching and shouldering, to sit by women," one writer ranted. Another raved that the wicked flock to the theaters, where "such laughing and fleering; such kissing and bussing; such clipping and culling, such winking and glancing of wanton eyes, and the like is used."

Playwrights were held to be no better, accused of sacrificing virtue and truth to the power of the almighty pound. And actors were nothing more than double-dealing counterfeiters; the boy players who dressed up in women's clothes came under special attack for provoking men to lust and lechery.

Some Puritans discovered a converse—and adverse—relationship between playgoing and churchgoing. "Are filthy plays," asked one peevishly, "comparable to the word of God?" In fact, part of what so enraged the preachers was that the plays were taking away *their* audiences: "Do they not draw the people from hearing the word of God, from godly lectures, and sermons?" While the church was empty, the yard of the theater was crammed with eager spectators, who were gratifying their desires while damning their souls. A mere two years after the opening of Burbage's rival Theatre, a preacher/schoolteacher expressed his frustration at religion's low ratings: "Will not a filthy play, with the blast of a trumpet, sooner call thither a thousand, then an hour's tolling of a bell bring to the sermon a hundred?" The preachers were in the same competitive position (although they might not have admitted it) as alehouse owners; instead of money, however, the burning issue was people's souls.

Aside from the spleen being vented by the puritanical sect, there *was* a broader sense of uneasiness about the nature of theater. Puritans weren't alone in feeling uncomfortable with the dramatic illusion—that is, the built-in pretense, or lie, of the theater. An actor onstage in costume was pretending to be someone he wasn't; a stage was giving the impression that it was a location it wasn't; a play was a fiction, from start to finish, and yet it was a fiction that masqueraded as the truth. The uncertain boundaries between what was true and what was false made lots of morally-inclined observers of the theater squirm.

Every time these people went to a play they were reminded of the ambiguity of it all, for drama, especially Shakespeare's, is constantly reflecting on its own nature. He delights in creating plays within plays, prodding his audience to think about the nature of the dramatic event they are sharing, as in *Hamlet*'s play-within-a-play.

Shakespeare's characters also ponder their dual existence as the characters within the play and the actors of the play, knowing that they are double agents who are involved as both at once and reminding the audience of it repeatedly. Cassius and Brutus pause after the stabbing of Caesar to consider this. Cassius says, "How many ages hence Shall this our lofty scene be acted over In states unborn and accents yet unknown!"

Shakespeare was constantly exploring and referring to the world of the theater—audience, scene, role-playing, the Globe itself—and exploring the gap between appearance and reality. This didn't do much to calm the palpitations in the breasts of worried moralists. One writer got right to the heart of the matter: "In stage plays for a boy to put on the attire, the gesture, the passions of a woman; for a mean [lower-class] person to take upon him the title of a Prince with counterfeit port [bearing] . . . is by outward figures to show themselves otherwise than they are, and so within the compass of a lie."

The notion that someone could change identity, gender, or social class simply by putting on a costume had social implications that worried many upright Elizabethans. In a society where the clothes someone put on in the morning were a sign of his social class and strictly regulated by law, costuming in the theater packed a real punch.

For a lower-class actor to parade around the stage in the lavish fabrics and rich jewels of his social betters was also a sign of intolerable disorder. Worse still, it might put subversive ideas into the heads of the socially inferior people in the audience.

It wasn't plays on the page but plays on the stage that were considered dangerous. The open and unashamed pretending of stage performance, the shifting and unpredictable dynamics of the relationship between the actors and their audiences, the dishonesty of portraying something untrue as true made live performance seem far more frightening and uncontrollable than docile printed black letters on a sheet of paper. And so while reading plays was acceptable, going to see them was not. For, in the words of one Puritan, "Whatsoever such plays as contain good matter, are set out in print, may be read with profit, but cannot be played, without a manifest breach of God's commandment." To put a play onstage—or to see it enacted —was to be an accomplice in the untruths of acting and the theater; audiences were just as guilty and wicked as the actors.

Luckily, most of this opposition was the work of only a few vocal ministers and writers and didn't reflect popular opinion. Backed by the theater-loving queen and Court, actors suffered very little actual damage, other than perhaps wounded egos.

By the 1590s, London was the theater capital of the world. An Englishman who had traveled in many countries sang the praises of the London theater, declaring that "as there be, in my opinion, more plays in London than in all parts of the world I have seen, so do these players or comedians excel all other in the world." And early in the next century, the man who supervised all the dramatic activity in London, the Master of Revels himself, would exclaim, "That most ancient kind of poetry, the dramatic, is so lively expressed and represented upon the public stages and theaters of this city," that it outdid even the great days of ancient Rome.

Despite the protests, actors and stage-plays were in London to stay. They had made their position clear in 1576 when the rise of Burbage's Theatre made a more eloquent declaration of theatrical independence than any written document ever could. But the opposition didn't give up so easily, and in a few decades the lively and crowded public theaters would become empty and lifeless spaces, boarded up and closed down when the Puritans finally won the day.

These reversals were still in the future. For the time being, in late sixteenth-century England, all the world seemed to be a stage.

CHAPTER 8

IN GOOD COMPANY: THE SIXTEENTH-CENTURY ACTING COMPANIES

IF THE YOUNG Mr. Shakespeare had arrived in London in the mid-1570s and asked the way to the theater district, he probably would have met with blank stares—or, if he were unlucky enough to have stopped a Puritan with his question, he might have gotten a half-hour lecture on the evils of stage-plays!

In Shakespeare's London there was nothing like New York City's Broadway or London's West End. Anything approaching theatrical organization was just beginning to crystallize. At the core of this process were the professional acting companies of men and boys, which were evolving through the years from groups of itinerant players to permanent organizations based in London.

ORIGINS

THE MINSTREL BANDS of the Middle Ages, the wandering forefathers of the sixteenth-century actors, split into two groups over time: the musicians (what we now think of as minstrels), and the professional dramatic players who were still under the protection of a nobleman.

For these strolling players, being on tour was a way of life.

But their touring wasn't a matter of fixed concert dates, enormous stadiums, record-breaking advance sales, or wildly screaming fans. They moved randomly from town to countryside, from aristocratic banqueting halls to humble village greens, sometimes heading to London for the winter Court season and innyard performances—going wherever the business might be. Traveling in small groups of usually no more than three or four men, with a couple of small wagons and a horse or two to carry the heavier baggage, their usual procedure upon arriving in a new town was to meet with the mayor, present their letter of introduction, and get a license from him allowing them to perform in the town square or in the cloisters under the town library.

These strolling troupes of actors lived from hand to mouth, never sure what kind of reception or earnings lay inside a town's walls. They were casually organized, loosely-strung together, and living for the moment. In fact, they were *too* casually organized for some village and town authorities, who considered them annoyances, as much a threat to a community's peace and quiet as any other vagrant and homeless types.

But whenever any authority figure threatened to make real trouble for them, the players scurried to take refuge in their status as servants of a nobleman. They would wave their letters of introduction or recommendation in the face of any petty official who had the nerve to threaten them, daring him to go against the honorable protection of the Earl of Such-and-such or Lord So-and-so. Few local authorities brazened out *that* dare.

The truth of the matter, however, was that many of these noble patrons didn't have the slightest idea of what their alleged "servants" were actually doing. Many times the traveling players were servants in name only, wearing the protective colors or the livery of the household without performing any of a typical servant's duties and without receiving regular wages. They had the best of both worlds: the freedom accorded to vagabonds and the protection accorded to employees of a household.

DOUBLE TROUBLE

BY THE SECOND half of the sixteenth century, the control and supervision of these wandering actors had grown very lax. Small bands were wandering all over the countryside without any regulation, their numbers multiplying. Finally the government took steps to remedy the situation, first by passing an act against illegal retainers or "masterless men," servants who wore the livery but didn't do the work. The crackdown continued with the Act for the Punishment of Vagabonds, which put the traveling actors outside the law:

> All Fencers, Bear-wards, Common Players in Interludes, & Minstrels, not belonging to any Baron of this realm or towards any other honorable Personage of greater Degree, shall be taken, adjudged and deemed Rogues, Vagabonds, and Sturdy Beggars . . .

The law was unequivocal, and the penalties brutal; on the first offense alone, these unfortunates were "to be grievously whipped, and burnt through the gristle of the right ear with a hot iron."

The poor players were in a no-win situation: if they were found wandering around performing *without* the protection of a nobleman, they were vagabonds; if they *did* have a noble's patronage, they had to prove that they were servants in the true sense of the word, and not actors. The effect of the Act of 1572 might have been to squelch English drama for good. But what happened instead was that many of the hangers-on disappeared, while players who really did have aristocratic backing found other ways to continue their playing—namely, as permanent professional companies in London.

The story of the Earl of Leicester's Men is a perfect example of how a company survived the stringent new regulations. When the statute against illegal retainers first came out, these actors panicked, for although they were card-carrying members of the Earl of Leicester's household, they really didn't have much formal standing with him. They wrote a letter immediately, begging him to keep them on as legitimate servants so they could still claim his patronage and protection under the new law.

The earl's reply was far more generous than they could have hoped for: not only did he offer them his protection, but in 1574, word came down from the queen herself (overriding the opposition of the city authorities was one of the privileges of being queen) that the Earl of Leicester's Men were to be allowed to perform their plays in London. The document conferring this privilege royally proclaimed that Leicester's Men could now "use, exercise, and occupy the art and faculty of playing Comedies, Tragedies, Interludes, [and] stage plays . . . as well for the recreation of our loving subjects, as for our solace and pleasure when we shall think good to see them." The group of actors must have been overjoyed—what better protection could there be than that given by Queen Elizabeth herself?

One of Leicester's players was James Burbage, that ex-carpenter turned full-time actor. Combining his two crafts, Burbage used the royal support as the cornerstone for the first custom-made theater building in England.

And so by the late seventies, prospects looked bright for Leicester's men and acting companies in general. The first-ever royal permit had been granted to an acting company to ply its trade in London, and permanent headquarters had been established in the brand-new Theatre. Indeed, in the next two decades the drama business grew rapidly; as new theaters went up, one after another, regular paying audiences began to provide a steady income, and aspiring actors joined the ranks of established companies.

But growth can be an untidy thing. Throughout the 1580s and 1590s, different groups were rising and falling in popularity, forming, disbanding, and re-forming, scooting from one innyard to another, leaving town to tour the provinces, reappearing without notice. If an acting group's legitimacy was ever questioned by suspicious city authorities, the group (echoing the earlier appeals to the protection of noble patrons) usually professed to be "the Queen's Players."

In fact, there *was* a real company called the Queen's Men in the eighties, formed in 1583 by the Master of

Revels. It was a sort of all-star team of actors from the different acting companies around London, and it was definitely the most prestigious group in town. For several years its chief drawing card was Richard Tarlton, the curly-haired, squint-eyed, flat-nosed, drum-beating clown who specialized in dancing jigs and making up verses on the spur of the moment. In 1588, when Tarlton died, the fortunes of the company took a plunge. But one of the tenets of the theater profession is that one group's exit is another's entrance, and there was certainly no shortage of acting groups willing to take over the position of the Queen's Men as the premier company of the day.

The only constants in this easily changing environment were the theaters, which anchored the drifting companies to solid ground. Indeed, a company's first order of business once the performing patent (or permit) had been secured was to find a playhouse. The usual method was to approach the theater owner or manager (called the house-keeper) who had subleased the theater and make a deal with him: in return for half of the gallery profits, the actors would be allowed to occupy the theater building—and call it theirs—for a set period of time.

The situation pleased everyone. The owner or manager had a steady paying tenant, and the actors had the security of a long lease and a place to call their own.

In these wooden, outdoor theaters, the once-itinerant acting troupes found a relatively permanent home. The lease on the theater gave them a new lease on life: those who were previously vagabonds and "unrespectable" rogues could now leave the wandering life, settle down in theaters that belonged to them and get on with the business of playing to eager audiences.

And so, as a contemporary historian tells us, acting went from being a pastime for amateurs to becoming "an occupation; and many there were that followed it for a livelihood." From the 1570s on, acting was considered a trade—but not a completely respectable one.

Establishing themselves as serious professionals was a struggle; in a society that was acutely sensitive to every shade of order and degree, actors were in the awkward position of having *no* position, no obvious status. People weren't quite sure where they belonged or how they would be kept in their place once that place had been decided. This uncertainty sometimes led to dislike and resistance.

Another strike against the actors was the fact that many of them had left their god-given trades to pursue the god-forsaken craft of acting. This was a slap in the faces of those who believed that each person had one and only one proper calling (or vocation) in life, given to him by God. Falstaff defends his thievery on these grounds in *Henry IV Part I:* "Why, Hal, 'tis my vocation, Hal. 'Tis no sin for a man to labor in his vocation."

The actor James Burbage, for example, had once been a carpenter, but "reaping but a small living by the same, gave it over and became a common player in plays." Another member of his company, Robert Armin, had been apprenticed to a goldsmith before the theater lured him away.

Most actors had come from the artisan class, and thus were of humble origin. The fact that many were actually making a profit from acting only made matters worse. As a citywide proclamation announced, "It hath not been used or thought meet [appropriate] heretofore that players should have or should make their living on the art of playing."

A RUNG ON THE LADDER

DESPITE THESE DISAPPROVING words, actors went right on pursuing the art of playing. Because commercial theater was nothing if not a business enterprise, it was not surprising that sixteenth-century acting companies organized themselves along much the same lines as other profit-making institutions, complete with stockholders ("sharers"), managers ("house-keepers"), regular employees ("hired men"), and young interns ("boy apprentices"). Each of these had a specific place in the hierarchy of the company, with specific duties and privileges.

There were usually about ten actors who owned shares in the acting company; Shakespeare's company grew from eight to twelve. As sharers, these men were the core of the company, splitting both the costs and profits of putting on a play. They were the ones who made all the decisions about how to spend the company's money. Will Juliet be able to wear one of Cleopatra's old gowns? Can we afford to hire a third musician for the wedding celebration in *As You Like It*? How can we possibly produce *Macbeth* without buying more daggers and replacing the armor? The new stagehand keeps putting Claudius' throne of state in the wrong place onstage—should we hire another?

But if they shared the problems, they shared the profits, too. More than one actor-sharer in a company—Shakespeare among them—became prosperous middle-class citizens as a result. Because a sharer owned his shares, he was free to do whatever he wanted with them—sell them, buy them, or bequeath them to someone else, just as he pleased. When the famous clown Will Kempe left the Lord Shakespeare's company, he gave his share in the company to Shakespeare and two other actor-sharers to split three ways; Richard Burbage left his percentage to his wife when he died.

The next level in the company's organization was occupied by the hired men, who usually worked on a two-year contract for weekly wages. In addition there were the musicians who provided instrumental music for the songs that were so essential to the play; the tire-men who helped in the tiring-house, or dressing room; and the gatherers, or ticket-takers—often old widows. There were also several stagehands to do the menial labor and plenty of extras around to fill in the stage-crowd for a procession or wedding or parade during the play.

But probably the most important of all these employees was the book-keeper, whose responsibilities were endless. This man attended to all the details relating to the play itself, both the written and the stage versions. He took care of getting the necessary license from the Revels Office, insured that the play was revised and altered as directed by this office, copied out the parts of the play, and delegated his many responsibilities among the various stagehands under his command. Once the play was in performance, he worked as the prompter and also as general stage manager, making sure everything ran smoothly during the show.

None of these theatrical employees, not even the book-

keeper, could expect to make a fortune from his job in the
theater; most survived on several (six to ten) shillings a
week. Although this doesn't sound like much, compared
to what middle-level workers (or journeymen) in other
trades were earning, theater employees were at the top of
the market.

Next in rank to the sharers and the hired men were
the trainees, young boys who received their theatrical education at the hands of the more experienced adult actors
in the company. These boys joined the company between
the ages of ten and thirteen, agreeing to serve apprenticeships of at least seven years. A trainee's curriculum
included speech, movement, music, fencing, dancing, and
singing—everything he needed to prepare him for the ri-
gors of performance in a public theater.

Boys in adult companies such as the Lord Chamberlain's Men played the women's roles, since a government
statute as well as social norms of seemliness and modesty
would keep women off the supposedly lewd and unchaste
English stage until 1660. This is why Cleopatra fears that
her sublime dignity will be degraded and ridiculed in the
theater: "I shall see Some squeaking Cleopatra boy my
greatness I' the posture of a whore." It was a given that
all the women's roles would go to the boys—anything else
was inconceivable. But in other countries it was quite
different. An Englishman traveling in Italy in 1608 recorded his surprise: "Here I observed certain things that
I never saw before. For I saw women act, a thing that
never saw before. . . ."

These young boys had to be spirited and skilled per-
formers, for they were the ones who played Juliet, Viola,
Lady Macbeth, Desdemona, Ophelia—as well as servant
girls, nurses, old crones, and royal women of all ages,
including queens. Those who made the cut were eventually elevated to hired men (perhaps after their voices
changed!) and then possibly to sharer status. As apprentices they were paid even less than the hired men, perhaps
only two or three shillings a week, but it was an excellent
education for those willing to work hard.

The role of the theater manager, or the "house-keeper,"
varied from company to company. Sometimes he was a
part of the company itself, and its best interests coin-
cided with his. Or he might be a separate agent who ruled

the company's affairs with a firm, even dictatorial hand, taking care of their needs—furnishing props, buying costumes, lending money to the actors or playwrights, financing the company's productions, and even building a new theater.

One of the most famous and powerful of these housekeepers was the impresario Philip Henslowe, for many years the manager of the Lord Admiral's Men, chief rivals of Shakespeare's Company, the Lord Chamberlain's Men. Although this shrewd businessman's policies were probably similar to those of other companies, Henslowe seems to have ruled the Admiral's Men with an especially iron hand. He demanded deposits from actors in order to hold them to their agreements to remain with the company. He also fined actors for missing or being drunk during rehearsals and performances.

Even a company with a hard-nosed autocrat such as Henslowe for a manager was by and large a collective enterprise. Decisions about everything from distributing the roles to dividing the profits were made jointly by the shareholders and carried out by them, their employees, and their apprentices, necessitating a good deal of cooperation.

DOUBLE THE FUN

BUT IF ALL had to be harmony *within* a company, things were slightly less peaceful in relationships *between* companies. As theaters grew up north and south of London, and as companies grew more established and well known among the general public, the competition for that public's money grew heated. Given that London's population was that of a small modern city, around 160,000, the rivalries must have been fierce. It was a fairly intimate kind of competition; most of the actors knew each other, for theater circles were relatively small. The competition didn't escape the notice of a German tourist: "Daily, at two in the afternoon, London has two, sometimes three plays running in different places, competing with each other, and those which play best obtain most spectators."

In fact, throughout the late 1590s and into the early 1600s, the London stage was dominated, even controlled, by two major companies, the Lord Chamberlain's Men and the Lord Admiral's Men, because of a decree of the Privy Council in 1598 to limit the chaos of the burgeoning theater scene.

The Lord Admiral's Men had sailed into prominence when the Queen's Men declined in popularity in the 1580s. By the early nineties, with their lineup of actors and their hot-shot manager Henslowe, they were a hard act to follow. Edward Alleyn, the company's principal actor (and Henslowe's son-in-law) would be considered a superstar by later standards, for he was the most famous actor of his day. How could people forget such a deep voice, a striking presence, and a height that was estimated at seven feet!

But however popular Alleyn and the Admiral's plays might have been, by the end of the nineties, everyone who knew anything about the theater knew that the up-and-coming new company was the Lord Chamberlain's Men. These actors, who had spent much of the eighties touring the provinces, now became increasingly popular with the London public. The repertoire of plays the Chamberlain's Men performed was a varied one, ranging from Shakespeare's masterpieces to light comedies, plays that taught a moral lesson (such as *The Miseries of Enforced Marriage*) to experimental new plays, and anything else that struck their fancy. Their successes were crowned and their number-one position confirmed when, after the death of Queen Elizabeth in 1603, the new King James promoted the "Lord Chamberlain's Men" to the "King's Men," while the "Admiral's Men" were elevated only to the level of "Prince Henry's Men."

Within the theater world the reputation of the Chamberlain's Men also rose steadily throughout the 1590s. They had more and better theaters than any other company; their roster boasted the best playwrights; they promoted from within their ranks; they were, in short, the company to be associated with—that is, for anyone lucky enough to find his way in. After all, there were no more than eight or ten leading actors in the company, and only a handful of hired men and boy actors. Openings didn't come up very often: in ten years, the Lord Chamberlain's Men had to replace only two actors—both times because someone had died.

However, life wasn't always as easy as it seemed over at the Theatre, where the Lord Chamberlain's Men were based. The biggest threat to their survival came in the late 1590s, when the lease that Burbage had taken on the Theatre's land was about to expire. The landlord decided to be completely unreasonable about renewing it, insisting on a rent increase and threatening to tear down the Theatre to build "something better" on his land. In the middle of the negotiations, Burbage died and the lease passed to his sons, Richard and Cuthbert.

Exploited by their landlord, blocked in their attempt to move to an indoor theater, and losing ground to their competitors, the Chamberlain's Men had to do some fast footwork. Acting aggressively, if somewhat illegally, they won the day by staging a bold and daring coup.

Just after Christmas in 1598, while the landlord was away at his country house, a handful of actors trudged silently but resolutely across Finsbury Fields sometime around midnight. Reaching the Theatre, they pulled out their tools, rolled up their shirtsleeves, and proceeded to pull it down, timber by timber, under the direction of the carpenter and architect Peter Street. As the landlord later described it in his (unsuccessful) lawsuit against the actors, they were "then and there pulling, breaking, and throwing down the said theater in very outrageous, violent, and riotous sort."

A few days later, the actors transported the contraband wood south across the river to a plot of land on the Bankside, 150 yards south of the Thames. A contract was signed giving half of the lease to the Burbage brothers and the other half to five of the actors in the company. No doubt the sour experience with the landlord of the Theatre had taught these men the value of directing their own fate, and they made sure to maintain control. Instead of leasing the Globe from a separate theater owner/manager, the actors in the Lord Chamberlain's men owned the lease themselves. This was unique in London; no other theater company actually owned the building it performed in.

GLOBAL DIMENSIONS

WITHIN SEVEN OR eight months, the Globe Theatre was finished—a stage for the Chamberlain's Men and for William Shakespeare. The move to the Globe was the beginning of a new era of prosperity for the company. The location of the new theater was ideal—just south of the riverbank, a few hundred feet from the competing Lord Admiral's Men at the Rose, and not far from the bear-baiting arena.

Several of the Globe's actors became nationally famous. Richard Burbage made his name as an actor who portrayed emotion realistically and convincingly. Some of Shakespeare's great tragic characters were probably written for him—including Hamlet, King Lear, and Othello. Will Kempe was the company's knockabout comedian, most famous for his ability to dance jigs. In fact, he had such a love of dancing that when he left the company, he did a morris-dance (an English folk-dance) all the way from London to the city of Norwich, a distance of over one hundred miles—and took only nine days to do it! Kempe's successor was Robert Armin, a more sophisticated, less rough-and-tumble character who probably played Feste in *Twelfth Night* and the Fool in *King Lear*. And, of course, the Lord Chamberlain's Men had the most popular playwright in England—William Shakespeare.

Not everyone in the neighborhood was rapturous over the success of the Lord Chamberlain's Men. The Lord Admiral's Men had been at the Rose for over a decade before their archrivals moved in practically down the street. The Rose's structure was already showing signs of aging, and the damp marshy ground it stood on often got mucky and impassable in the rain. And so it wasn't long before the Admiral's Men moved back across the Thames to the north. They hired the man who had been the Globe's builder/carpenter, Peter Street, to build a new theater, along the lines of the Globe, in Finsbury. They called it, perhaps with hope for the future, the Fortune. And so the rivalry continued.

Although these two companies held the *legal* monopoly on theatrical activity in London, in practice their dual position didn't go unchallenged. Toward the early 1600s, there was a revival of the boy-only companies, which had been popular for a while in the 1570s and 1580s. These groups of little boys had started decades before as choirboys associated with particular chapels (Saint Paul's and the Chapel Royal), under the direction of a choirmaster. Gradually, they began giving dramatic performances for the public and discovered that there was quite a market for the witty and satirical plays which were their specialty. Soon they were as professional as any other company, sometimes managed by greedy adults motivated purely by profit.

Having survived the growing pains of the London theater world, the boy companies enjoyed a revival in the late years of the sixteenth century—much to the dismay of their adult rivals. Audiences were drawn to the combination of the boys' small, elflike appearance and their childish voices speaking the scurrilous lines of plays that were written especially for them. Rosencrantz's description of them in *Hamlet* suggests the general attitude toward the boys among the older professional companies of the time: "there is, sir, an aerie of children, little eyases [young hawks in training], that cry out on the top of question and are most tyrannically clapped for 't. These are now the fashion, and so berattle the common stages—so they call them—that many wearing rapiers are afraid of goose quills and dare scarce come thither."

Meanwhile, various provincial companies were ambling in and out of London. From time to time, the Earl of Derby's Men, the Earl of Hertford's Men, and other companies from England's rural counties arrived, gave a few performances, and went back where they came from. They posed no serious threat to the major companies.

The real trustbusters, who actually did manage to break the double monopoly in the seventeenth century, were the Earl of Worcester's Men. Eventually setting up at the Red Bull, another theater north of London, they carved out a niche for themselves with a repertory of English "domestic" comedies (offering lots of local humor) and swashbuckling adventure plays.

Ultimately, then, all three companies—the Chamberlain's Men at the Globe, the Admiral's Men at the Fortune, and Worcester's Men at the Red Bull—were competing for audiences. In order to stay afloat in this cutthroat environment, the companies had to provide their audiences with something new all the time—which meant an extremely varied and ever-changing schedule of plays. In a typical season—indoor, outdoor, and touring—a company might play six days a week, forty-nine weeks a year, and perform around forty plays, over half of them brand-new.

To make things busier still, the same play was never performed two afternoons in a row! In two weeks a single company might typically put on eleven performances of ten different plays—some new ones, some old ones—without batting an eye. The scheduling of plays was random, so that an actor might arrive at the theater to find that instead of playing Macbeth he had to brush up on the part of Orsino in *Twelfth Night*—a role he hadn't played in six months. The acting company of "rude mechanicals" in *A Midsummer Night's Dream* operates on just such a schedule: their manager, Quince, says, "But, masters, here are your parts. And I am to entreat you, request you, and desire you to con [learn] them by tomorrow night; and meet me in the palace wood, a mile without the town, by moonlight. There will we rehearse."

New plays were introduced frequently, usually about every two weeks. Old plays could be revived on extremely short notice. Most plays ran for seven or eight performances, spread out over the season. A "long run" was defined as any play that was performed more than twenty times over a period of years.

It wasn't as if this hectic pace ever eased up. The companies played practically year-round, with some variation according to the season. There was usually a break during the Church season of Lent; a summer recess (during plague years) usually from July to September or October; and a slowdown in the schedule during the Christmas season.

A company that could maintain this frantic schedule and still produce the season's hits would be invited to perform at Court for the queen (or king, after 1603). The performance at Court, usually sometime over Christmas, was a regular feature of a successful company's season and an honor that all the companies prized. In addition, Court performances were crucial to keeping the public theaters open for the rest of the year. City authorities were frequently reminded that the actors were "rehearsing" for the queen.

In the summertime, when the plague descended upon London and closed the theaters, the companies often took to the road again, recapturing the days of the strolling players. They drummed up audiences just as their wandering predecessors had done, going from Dover to Canterbury, Oxford to Bath, and from York to Norwich.

But now that the actors had tasted the sweets of a permanent establishment, they returned only reluctantly to the subsistence fare of a touring company: half the usual number of actors, pay cuts, fewer props, and playing conditions that (unlike the nice roomy theaters in London) were unpredictable and often not very good. Touring was far less profitable than performing in the public theaters; it was an act of necessity, not choice.

Occasionally some of the actors in a company went farther afield, traveling across the English Channel to Europe. Germany and the Netherlands were the most popular touring grounds for these adventurous actors. They usually carried letters of introduction from their noble patron, asking foreign officials "to show and afford them every favor in your countries and jurisdictions," and not to keep them "from practicing their said profession everywhere." "Said profession" covered more than just acting; it included music and gymnastics as well.

Wherever they went in Europe and however makeshift their performances, the English actors were given a warm reception. Despite the fact that most of the foreigners didn't understand a word of English, they loved watching the actors' gestures and actions. One English traveler reported, "I have seen some straggling broken companies that passed into Netherland and Germany, followed by the people from one town to another, though they understood not their words, only to see their action."

Still, the actors knew that the real core of the theater world in sixteenth-century England was to be found not on the Continent, not in the provinces, but in the city of London. That was where the permanent playhouses were; it was where the investors and financial backers were and where the audiences were. The heart of theatrical activity in London was, of course, the company of professional actors.

GETTING THEIR ACTS TOGETHER: PLAYWRIGHT AND AUDIENCE

THE ACTING COMPANIES weren't the only "players" on the sixteenth-century theater team; two other groups were just as important—the playwright (or the "poet," as he was then known) and the audience.

WIELDING THE PEN

NO MATTER HOW beautiful and spacious the public theaters, and no matter how well-organized and efficiently-run the companies, if the playwright wrote a dud play, the audiences would stay away. Of course a playwright of any era has to think about his audiences. But unlike a modern playwright, a sixteenth-century "poet" often couldn't even call a play his own; many plays in Shakespeare's day were written by several people in collaboration, each individual writing one act. One playwright boasted that he had had a hand in two hundred twenty plays; others tallied up the more modest sums of fifty or sixty-nine plays. Scattered throughout Henslowe's business records are such entries as "Lent unto Thomas Downton the 29 of May 1602 to pay Thomas Dekker, Drayton, Middleton, and Webster and Munday in full payment for their play called Two Shapes, the sum of . . . £3."

Nor was playwriting a very reputable line of work, as it is now. Like a modern Hollywood screenwriter, once a poet sold his play to an acting company, he had almost no control over what happened to the manuscript as it was being prepared for performance; his wishes were rarely taken into account. Because plays weren't often published in printed form, dramatists didn't enjoy the prestige of seeing their works sold as books. And playwrights were almost universally looked down upon by other kinds of writers as cheap, low-grade drudges.

As commercial theater boomed in the 1580s and 1590s, playwrights became more important as suppliers of the goods—wit and entertainment—that were being packaged and sold. Just as television introduces programming changes every season—or mid-season—the theater of the late sixteenth century required a new play every two weeks; there was a constant and enormous demand for fresh drama to satisfy the voracious appetite of companies and audiences.

This quick turnover of plays was part of what gave playwrights their reputation as hacks. A playwright couldn't afford to be painstaking or to spend months carving out a jewel of a play. It was a question of getting the top ratings; the best play was the one that brought in the biggest audiences, not necessarily the one that would earn the praises of later critics as a work of literary genius.

If there was a great demand for hack-writing, there was an even greater supply of hack-writers, many of whom were well-educated graduates of English schools and universities. London was full of young men hoping to make a living off of their wit (a good living wasn't always easy to find in those days, even for college graduates). This surplus of aspiring playwrights meant that it was definitely a buyers' market: the acting companies were the ones with the money and the job opportunities, and the playwrights were generally at their mercy.

There were two ways for a playwright to enter that risky market: as an independent free-lancer or under contract to an acting company. A free-lancer peddled his plays to any and all buyers for a fixed amount of money. If a company accepted his play after hearing a first draft or a plot outline, often in a local bar, he would be paid a series of advances until he finished it. But even after signing for a play and paying sums in advance, the company reserved the right to reject the final version, in which case the luckless playwright had to pay back all the advances. The going rate for a play, about six pounds, was equivalent to more than four months of a laborer's salary; it was also the amount a company might spend on a single costume.

The alternative to free-lancing was to work as an "ordinary poet," a playwright under exclusive contract to an acting company. In this capacity a playwright would sign a contract promising to write two or three plays a year over two or three years for that company only, and no other, in return for a weekly salary (possibly), a fixed fee per play, and the usual benefit performance (box office receipts from one performance of his work). This was the kind of arrangement Shakespeare probably had with the Lord Chamberlain's (later King's) Men at the Globe. Of course, even if the playwright was bound to write for one company only, that company wasn't bound to buy only his plays and no one else's; the actors were constantly on the lookout for new pieces to perform.

But even with contractual work, the playwright couldn't just sit down and churn out plays thoughtlessly. He lived and worked in a theater that had certain built-in requirements, many of which influenced his playwriting before he even took up his quill and parchment to begin. In the first place, a sixteenth-century dramatist always had the talents and characteristics of the company's actors in the back of his mind. He didn't have to write roles for superstar actors who would be flown in from Los Angeles and New York City. The cast for any play was always the same—the permanent members and employees of the acting company —and unless he wrote a play with roles that they could perform, it would never see the light of day. Shakespeare was fortunate to be writing for a company of extremely talented actors.

The playwright also had to compensate for minimal scenery and the lack of a lighting system. Shakespeare transformed this limitation into an advantage, writing some of his most beautiful poetry to paint the set. Has there ever been anything to equal Romeo's evocative heralding of the dawn? "Look, love," he says to Juliet, "what envious streaks Do lace the severing clouds in yonder east. Night's candles are burnt out, and jocund day Stands tiptoe on the misty mountain tops."

The playwright's stagecraft was also influenced by the necessity of role-doubling. He had to construct the play carefully so that two characters being played by the same actor would never have to be onstage at the same time. A playwright who insisted that his play was a sacred and untouchable work of art wouldn't last long in the sixteenth-century theater.

The contracted poet did much more than provide his company with two or three plays a year. It was a common practice for a company to dig up old plays, brush them off and dress them in up-to-date material, and perform them again—and the playwright was expected to write new scenes or make alterations in these revival plays. He also had to compose prologues and epilogues to be stuck on to plays that were either being adapted for Court performance or being revived after a period of neglect. And finally, the playwright wrote lyrics for songs in the plays; the Hecate songs in Acts 2 and 4 of *Macbeth* are an example of this.

But the one thing that was definitely *not* part of a playwright's job description was preparing his plays for publication. Acting companies were violently against the printing of plays. In an age when there were no copyright laws, publishing a popular play meant that rival acting companies could get hold of it and perform it without the fear of legal consequences. An acting company was usually only willing to let a play go to the printer if it was hopelessly out-of-date (and unrevivable) or a total failure. One playwright excused the fact that his plays hadn't been printed by blaming his acting company, "who think it against their peculiar profit to have them come in print."

Most staff playwrights didn't seem to be bothered by this. Shakespeare's body of plays wasn't published in any permanent form until seven years after he had died. The man who took over Shakespeare's position as ordinary poet for the King's Men, John Fletcher, was equally indifferent. One playwright declared that "it was never any great ambition in me, to be in this kind voluminously read." This same playwright had also lost several of his plays because he wrote them on scraps of paper in local eating houses or taverns—which says a lot about how seriously he took the whole business.

To most people within the theater business, it seemed pointless to preserve such a transient form of entertainment as the stage play. A play wasn't a literary text, but a passing event—splendid and quickly-vanishing.

The general reading public felt the same way. A clear and unquestioned distinction was made between "real" literature and mere stage-plays, which were on a par with broadside ballads and other forms of cheap printed material. As he was setting up the famous Bodleian Library at Oxford, the nobleman Sir Thomas Bodley excluded plays from his grand collection. Classifying them with almanacs and other riffraff, he called them "baggage books," of "very unworthy matters" not fit for his shelves.

For a public inclined to judge a book by its cover, plays were bound to be left off library shelves. Plays in Shakespeare's time were produced in cheap single editions called quartos (pieces of paper folded twice, with no binding), sharing bookstall space with equally cheap items such as joke books and penny-pamphlets. Like newspapers or comic books today, their very appearance suggested that they were intended to be read and discarded. The more substantial folio format, much bigger and formidably permanent-looking, was reserved for the ancient classics, modern sermons, ponderous geographies, or books by England's rulers—the types of writing that were considered *worthwhile* additions to England's stock of literature.

It was the upgrading of plays in the book market that began to soften the anti-playwright prejudice. This process began in 1616 with the publication of the *Works* of Ben Jonson (a colleague and rival of Shakespeare) in a Folio edition. It was the first time a playwright had ever given his plays the grandiose title of "works" and the first time plays had been published in folio. This edition, and the Folio publication of Shakespeare's plays seven years later, did much to improve the inferior status of the playwrights and their plays. Folios proclaimed a new and improved standing for the playwright as a serious writer worthy of respect. With the packaging and labeling of plays as real books, professional status for the playwright was on its way.

WITH PATIENT EARS

BOTH IN THE old-fashioned morality and mystery plays of the Middle Ages and in the popular informal plays put on by the traveling actors in the early 1500s, audiences were always being pulled into the play. Characters addressed them from the stage, made them the butt of jokes, walked through their midst, and included them as equal participants in the performance.

As drama became professionalized in the 1580s and 1590s, the audience began to play an even greater role, not merely in the performance of a given play but in the survival and success of the theater. An acting company's success depended on attracting audiences to a play and pleasing them once they'd gotten there. The people of London could make or break the fate of a play by attending or staying away; because they held the power of the pennies, they had an indirect voice in what kinds of plays were written and performed in the public theaters. A play that was unpopular with an audience might close after a few performances.

Who was this all-important audience? The other players in the theatrical enterprise spanned the social classes: in general, the actors were from the lower artisan classes; the theater managers, and some of the playwrights, were from the middle classes; and the patrons and officials were from the noble, upper classes. Which one of these categories did the audience fit into?

The answer is, all of them. Thanks to the cheap admission fee, no one was excluded from the theater. Even the humblest alehouse tapster (like Francis the drawer in *Henry IV Part I*) could walk through the door of that public theater for a single penny. Those who were concerned with greater comfort or eager for greater prestige could shell out another penny or two to sit in the gallery section, sometimes on cushioned seats.

The basic entry fee of a penny was within the reach of most people. The average worker brought home about seven shillings a week; a shilling was equal to twelve pennies; and so seeing a play cost one eighty-fourth of the average person's weekly earnings. To get an idea of the relative prices, consider that today a $6 movie ticket is one eighty-fourth of $500 in weekly earnings ($25,000 a year), and a Broadway ticket would require nearly $4000 a week ($208,000 a year) to achieve the same ratio!

Theater wasn't just inexpensive relative to today's prices; even in the sixteenth century, it was the cheapest way to have fun, aside from going to the bearbaiting. Spending an afternoon in an alehouse and drinking the standard quart of ale would set you back four pennies. If you wanted to try the new fad of smoking tobacco, you could expect to pay three pennies for a ridiculously small pipe. Gambling was expensive (depending on how good you were); "whoring", or visiting a brothel, was a minimum of six pennies; and going out to dinner, a less controversial pastime, could cost up to twenty pennies. By these standards, a play in the public theater—chock-full of action, spectacle, and adventure—was without a doubt the best bargain in town.

Because plays were so affordable, accessible, and fun, they drew people from a wide range of social classes. Young noblemen studying at the Inns of Court, prosperous merchants and traders, well-to-do lawyers and doctors, grocers and glovemakers and booksellers and bakers and their families, enthusiastic teenage apprentices, poor peddlers, humble household servants, and menial workers—all crowded in through the same two doors before separating to go upstairs to the galleries or straight through to the yard. As one critic observed, "the common people which resort to the theaters [are] but an assembly of tailors, tinkers, cordwainers, sailors, old men, young men, women, boys, girls, and such like. . . ."

It was very much a democratic gathering, remarkably so considering the undemocratic and status-conscious nature of sixteenth-century London. Inside the public theater, the social distinctions that kept everyone in his or her place in the real world simply melted away.

It was precisely this aspect of the theater that disturbed its critics; they feared that young people would begin to talk back to their elders, or that inferior classes would rise up against their betters as a result of their brief but heady experience of democracy in the public theaters. For where democracy flourished, these people reasoned, could danger be far behind? Theaters were ideal places, in the eyes of such fearful observers, for "contrivers of treason and other idle and dangerous persons to meet together."

Of course the size of the crowds that went to the theater was nothing like the huge numbers that fill the Super Bowl or Madison Square Garden today. The Globe and the Rose probably drew about 1250 people apiece daily, about half of their capacity. The audiences were always bigger for the first performance of a new play and on the public holidays of Easter, Christmas, and Whitsunday; indeed, the actors always looked forward to the larger and more celebratory holiday crowds. The number of regular playgoers, however, hovered somewhere between twelve percent and twenty percent of London's population—far fewer people than go to the movies today. In a six-day performance week in the late 1590s, probably around fifteen thousand people went to plays put on by two or three main acting companies.

The fact was that most Londoners *didn't* go to plays at the public theaters. There were several reasons for this. One of them was the hour of the performances—usually two o'clock. Free time was hard for working people to find, and it was hardly possible to take off from work in the middle of an afternoon for a two-hour performance a mile away through the fields or all the way across the river. This is why holiday crowds were so big—holidays gave workers the leisure time to go. There was also a sizable contingent of Puritans who stayed away because of their religious conviction that a play was not a place for upright citizens but a nasty sewer "whereunto all the filth doth run." Some people may not have had the inclination; and, of course, there were the few who didn't have the means to afford even the penny admission.

But if those who came to the theaters represented a minority, it was certainly a vocal minority. Their behavior was much more enthusiastic, alive, and responsive than that of the average member of a modern audience; Shakespeare's audience was a boisterous crowd.

While in the theater, one had to keep an eye out for the pickpockets in the audience and maintain a safe distance from the exuberant apprentices. Fistfights only occasionally broke out; one entire audience erupted into an angry riot when they realized that they had been duped by a man who had promised them a nonexistent play and then made off with their money—"the common people when they saw themselves deluded, revenged themselves upon the hangings, curtains, stools, walls, and whatsoever came in their way very outrageously," one reporter commented.

Barring understandable reactions like this, things rarely got so out of hand. After all, Elizabethans had paid good money to get in to see the play, and it was unlikely that they would spend their time talking to each other, fighting, or ignoring it. Of course audiences were far more used to listening to the spoken word than we are today. Years of relying on word of mouth as the only source of news, information, and entertainment—whether it was village gossip, preachers' sermons, or fireside stories—made them much more sensitive to the importance of good listening.

However, just to insure their cooperation, the actors would often begin the play with a prologue begging the audience to be silent. The Prologue to *Henry V* bids them "gently to hear, kindly to judge, our play." The Chorus to *Romeo and Juliet* tells the audience that "if you with patient ears attend [listen], What here shall miss, our toil shall strive to mend."

The audience would leave no doubt in anyone's mind as to their reactions to the performance. When they liked what they saw, they laughed loudly and long; as a contemporary observer noted, "In the theaters they generally take up a wonderful laughter, and shout altogether with one voice, when they see some notable cozenage [deception] practiced." And they hissed and booed unabashedly if the play didn't please them. Some spectators got so involved with what was happening onstage that they practically participated themselves; one observer reported the perturbed members of an audience "mounting the stage, and making more bloody catastrophe amongst themselves than the players did."

In the absence of any newspapers or magazines, the audience members *were* the theater critics, for better or worse. Plays were talked about in taverns over a quart of ale, on the walk across London Bridge from the Globe, during the work day, and in the theaters themselves. Despite what Hamlet says jokingly about the "groundlings, who for the most part are capable of nothing but inexplicable dumb shows and noise," Shakespeare understood full well that he was writing for a literate and perceptive audience who had their wits about them. In a big bustling city like London you couldn't survive unless you were alert and streetwise.

Different theaters attracted different audiences. The Red Bull, where Worcester's Men played, drew the rowdies and lovers of spectacles, noise, and clowning around. An indoor theater like Blackfriars, within the city walls, attracted a more select clientele.

But the Globe drew the most diverse crowd, a patchwork assembled from all occupations, ages, and social classes. People from many different backgrounds came to see and enjoy the plays of Shakespeare; for two or three magical hours, their workaday divisions were forgotten.

Without such an audience, Shakespeare would have had no one to write for, the actors would have had no one to act for—and the plays would have ended up on someone's bookshelf.

CHAPTER 10

FROM PAGE TO STAGE: PRODUCING A PLAY IN THE SIXTEENTH CENTURY

IF YOU COULD somehow watch a new play being produced in the late decades of the sixteenth century, from the very first step all the way through an afternoon's performance in one of the popular outdoor theaters, you would probably be baffled by some unfamiliar things but also surprised at how much you actually recognized.

Imagine an aspiring sixteenth-century playwright reading his recent play, or an outline of it, to an acting company one afternoon after their two o'clock performance. He waits anxiously as the actors finish their quarts of ale, put down their mugs, and deliver their verdict. If they like it, they will buy it right then and there, paying the author six or seven pounds for his effort. If they like some of what they see but aren't completely enamored of it all, they might advance him part of the total payment and suggest some revisions for him to think about as he finishes the play. And of course they might also reject it flat out, telling him to try again when he's got something that's worth their time.

Once the playwright has finished the first draft and delivered his "foul papers" (the messy, blotted parchment he's written the play on) to the company, the company scribe makes the "fair copy" (which means that it's legible!). It is sent straightaway to the Revels Office to be approved and stamped by the Master of Revels. This office, which has been in existence for several decades, is the single biggest hurdle a company has to negotiate in the process of putting on a play. Originally set up to supervise, choose, and organize all entertainment performed for England's monarch at Court, by the 1580s it has become the extremely powerful department through which government regulation (a nice word for censorship) of all dramatic activities is carried out. Not only does the Master of Revels have the sole authority to license plays and theaters (the average fee, essentially a tax, is between five and ten shillings), and to enforce the closing of the theaters during certain Church seasons or in the time of plague epidemics, but he is also the person responsible for censoring unsuitable materials from all plays. In 1589 he was given permission (with several other high-placed officials) to inspect play manuscripts and "strike out such part and matters as they shall find unfit and undecent to be handled in plays, both for divinity and state." Anything thought to undermine the orthodoxy of the Church ("divinity") or the governing of the commonwealth ("state") is off-limits to dramatists.

Indeed, things get worse early in the reign of King James, when onstage profanity is decreed illegal and punishable. The act of 1606 "to Restrain Abuses of Players" prohibits actors from jokingly or irreverently using the names of God, Jesus, or the Holy Ghost; playwrights are sent scurrying to revise "Good God" to "Great Jove" and "Heaven" to "the heavens." And so Rosalind in *As You Like It* swears "By my troth, and in good earnest, and so God mend me, and by all pretty oaths that are not dangerous. . . ."

If the Master of Revels receives any play that contains political criticism of government policies (domestic or foreign) or religious criticism of the established Church of England, he will demand that the company cut out or alter the seditious or abusive material. The actors disobey his instructions at their peril. At the very least they will have to pay a fine of up to ten pounds, but the penalties could be far worse. The Office of Revels has no qualms about stopping an illegal performance of an unlicensed play or closing a theater down for a long period of time, and on occasion its officials have been known to throw the offending playwright and actors into prison.

Once the Master of Revels has stamped the playbook

with the official stamp and sent it back to the company and the play's author has deleted the offending material, then the playbook goes to the book-keeper, who takes the heavily-edited, sliced-up, scrawled-on manuscript and writes each of the parts out on long scrolls—by hand, of course. Then the parts are distributed as the company has decided. For casting, like everything else, is a collective decision made by the actors. The acting company that Shakespeare brings to life in *A Midsummer Night's Dream* illustrates this perfectly as the players hand out parts for their upcoming performance. Bottom declares, "Name what part I am for, and proceed," to which Quince replies "You, Nick Bottom, are set down for Pyramus." Another player, Flute, protests that he can't play Thisbe, the woman's part, because he is growing a beard; Snug makes a special request for the lion's part, since, he says, he has trouble memorizing lines but can roar without rehearsal.

Of course, the company uses a lot of common sense in casting. For example, the role of a youthful and romantic swain won't be given to a comically ugly actor; nor will a part that requires a lot of singing be handed to someone who can't carry a tune.

While all this is going on, the book-keeper is keeping a careful watch over the revised and edited playbook; as the only complete copy of the play, it is extremely valuable. He never lets "the Book"—bound in a protective dustcover or wrapper, with the all-important license from the Master of Revels stamped inside—out of his sight and takes great care to lock it up in one of the trunks or coffers in the dressing room each afternoon before he leaves. During the day he carries it around with him, making notes in the lefthand margin about props, or sound cues, or any sort of stage directions he'll need to make during the performance. In the margin next to the second act of a new play, for example, he'll write "Flourish" to remind himself to be sure the trumpeter blows on cue; for another scene he'll scrawl "a bed brought in" and look around for the stagehand who is responsible for the bed.

The book-keeper doubles as the prompter, standing backstage to remind forgetful actors of their lines. As the guardian of the playbook offstage and the guardian of order onstage, he fulfills the functions of both librarian and stage manager. Indeed, a contemporary writer urges the book-keeper to look to his task: "I pray you hold the book well." Quince demonstrates how a good prompter operates in *A Midsummer Night's Dream*. He hisses out the correct pronunciation and timing to Bottom and then fumes about his clumsiness: "You speak all your part at once, cues and all." And he still has the energy to give another actor a tongue-lashing: "Pyramus, enter: Your cue is past."

The text of the play, cut and patched, is finally ready. What happens next? Unlike their twentieth-century successors, these Shakespearean actors don't have time to go into a long period of rehearsal, crafting every line to perfection under the seasoned eye of a director. If anyone guides the actors through the play, explaining his sense of how it should be performed, it may be the playwright himself. A German visitor commented on this practice: "So far as the actors are concerned they, as I have noticed in England, are daily instructed, as it were in a school, so that even the most eminent actors have to allow themselves to be taught their places by the dramatists, and this gives life and ornament to a well-written play. . . ."

Rehearsal itself isn't really an issue, it appears, simply because there is never time for it to become one. The average time span between the day a company receives a new play from a playwright and the first performance is about two weeks. Whether the company rehearses as the comical players do in *A Midsummer Night's Dream*, "by moonlight" in a forest clearing, where "This green plot shall be our stage, this hawthorn brake our tiring-house," or on the stage of the Globe in the remaining hour or two of daylight after that afternoon's performance, not much time can be spent working out the details.

But, like everything else in the theater, the few rehearsals that do take place are a collaborative effort. Bottom and Quince and Company again provide a delightful illustration of this. They all agree on the length and form of a prologue to introduce their play. They discuss the possible effects of their presentation on the ladies in the audience, and they resolve the problems that come up in the course of the rehearsal by mutual consent. For example, when they realize that the play's action requires a wall, Bottom says, "Some man or other must present [represent] Wall. And let him have some plaster, or some loam, or some roughcast about him, to signify wall."

While the actors are running around onstage trying to pull the play together in two weeks, the stationer or printer they take their business to is busy printing up playbills to advertise "A New Play, to be played at the Globe on Bankside the Tuesday next." The hired men post these signs all over town to lure audiences to their theater. Competition with the other forms of popular entertainment is heated indeed, and a less-than-scrupulous actor might feel perfectly within his rights to post his sign on top of an ad for the bearbaiting at the nearby arena. But this isn't really necessary, for a new play is guaranteed to draw big crowds, even if its title and author aren't announced ahead of time. Everyone is always curious to see what the Lord Chamberlain's Men, or the Lord Admiral's Men, have come up with this time.

Opening day arrives almost before anyone can turn around. Up goes the company's silken flag on the pole above the playhouse. Backstage the book-keeper hangs the "plot," a big piece of thick paper pasted on cardboard that dangles from a nail in the tiring-room. It is crucial to a smooth-running performance, for it contains all the esssential information about which actor is playing which parts, when actors enter and exit, what props they should be carrying, at what point specific sound effects are needed, and other necessary stage business.

As the actors scan this plot for last-minute reminders, the audiences flock in. The gatherers, or ticket-takers, make sure that no one tries to sneak in without paying his penny. The fruit and nut sellers, having laid in an extra supply for the bigger and more enthusiastic opening day crowds, wander about the theater hawking their wares. There is a general hubbub as apprentices jostle one another to sit near their friends or an attractive girl, bricklayers happily rub elbows with perfumed ladies, and jealous playwrights stand, quill in hand, ready to borrow a catchy phrase or two.

It is a pleasure just to glance around the physical building of the theater, to see the stage, with its sturdy wooden pillars painted to look like marble; the cover over the stage, called the "heavens," painted blue and gold to resemble the sky; the straw scattered on the stage floor—all in all, a splendid frame for the stage action.

As the flourish of the trumpet and the beat of the drum waft out over the heads of the groundlings, the crowd grows quiet and settles in for "the two hours' traffic of our stage," as Shakespeare refers to it in his Prologue to *Romeo and Juliet*. (It is still a mystery how a four-hour play like *Hamlet* could be played in two hours.) Over that time there's plenty of action to hold the attention of the most impatient apprentice. There is dancing and singing; there are processions, tournaments, battles, betrothals, and lots more—all as run-of-the-mill in an Elizabethan theater as car chases, bedroom scenes, and shoot-outs are in today's adventure movies.

The costumes are a stunning component of the spectacle, colorful and lavish, richly embroidered with pearls and golden thread, and made of the finest materials. They are a company's most important possession, and the single biggest expenditure in the production budget, along with the playbooks. One theater owner's "Inventory of Apparel" includes one short cloak of black satin, one peach-colored satin doublet, one blue taffeta suit, and a blue robe with sleeves. No expense is spared in collecting the most beautiful garments. Luckily, most of the costumes actually turn out to be less expensive than they look. Many costumes, in fact, are cast-offs from rich nobles, bought secondhand from their servants. As a foreign tourist observes, "It is the English usage for eminent lords or knights at their decease to bequeath and leave almost the best of their clothes to their serving men which it is unseemly for the latter to wear, so that they offer them then for sale for a small sum to the actors."

But a good play is more than just a pretty picture; it requires good acting as well. And the audience at the Globe sees plenty of that. The actors in Shakespeare's company are the cream of the crop—talented, versatile entertainers who combine the legs and lungs of an Olympic athlete, the vocal chords of a rock star, the quick wit of a stand-up comic, and the memory of a computer.

The audience listens, rapt, to the actors' stirring delivery of their lines—in a somewhat more artificial style than a modern audience might be comfortable with, and at a decibel level high enough to compete with the cries of the watermen on the river, the creaking of coach wheels rolling by, and the suburban bustle of Southwark.

But although their speech might be more rhetorical or formalized, it is lively and natural. We have only to look at the evidence of Shakespeare's plays to understand that his actors couldn't be anything *but* natural and life-like. And indeed, Shakespeare shows what his conception of good acting is when he has Hamlet instruct the Players in the essentials of the art of performing. Hamlet counsels them to speak nimbly but with feeling, to gesture gently and to remember above all that the purpose of acting is —and always will be—"to hold . . . the mirror up to nature."

If the actors have succeeded, time has been suspended for the afternoon. The sun slants across the English autumn sky as the audience tumbles out of the gates of the Globe and scatters slowly in different directions. Some head east across Maiden Lane, planning to take the cheap route into the city by walking across London Bridge. Those whose wallets are fatter stroll a few hundred yards north along Horseshoe Alley to the riverbank of the Thames to catch a water-taxi back across to London. And some, who have no more pressing business than enjoying themselves, and who can afford to see a play and drink a quart of ale in the same afternoon, adjourn to a nearby tavern. But wherever they're going, no doubt all would agree that it's been a fine, fun-filled afternoon at the Globe.

CHAPTER 11

SOURCES AND RESOURCES

SHAKESPEARE'S READING LIST

POUNDS OF FLESH in Venice; ambitious king-killers in Scotland; star-crossed lovers in Verona; daughterly ingratitude in ancient Britain; whimsical courtships in the Forest of Arden; sultry love and stern politics in ancient Egypt—Shakespeare's imagination appears to have cornered the market on exciting, inventive plotmaking. It seems there's no story he hasn't thought of. But how could all of these intriguing plots and stirring adventures possibly come from a single brain?

The answer is simple—they didn't. When it came to plots, Shakespeare was a borrower, not an inventor. It is astonishing to realize that not a single one of the stories in his plays was his own creation. Rather than growing his plots himself, he plucked them from the plentiful orchards of other authors. Some had good English names like Thomas Lodge, George Whetstone, and Raphael Holinshed, while others hailed from the Continent—Giraldo Cinthio (Italy), Jorge de Montemayor (Portugal), and Plautus (ancient Rome).

The list of sources Shakespeare probably used reads like the roll call of a sixteenth-century United Nations: French philosophy, Spanish romance, Scottish chronicle, Italian novella, Greek tragedy, Roman comedy, English poetry, and much, much more. Ancient or modern, prosaic or poetic, sacred or profane, nothing escaped Shakespeare's roving eye.

And there was plenty for that roving eye to light on in sixteenth-century London, thanks to the happy combination of the Renaissance zest for learning (which created literary wealth) and the new high-technology of the printing press (which helped spread it). London in Shakespeare's day was absolutely brimming over with things to read—the massive 3000-page chronicles of England, Scotland, and Ireland, compiled by Holinshed and his colleagues; adventure stories and exotic tales from Italy, France, and Spain; hair-raising eyewitness travel accounts written by daring explorers; pleasant pastoral romances of prose writers; and scores of translations of foreign works, past and present.

But of all the books on the market, the ancient Greek and Latin classics were far and away the Elizabethan favorites. Recently revitalized by the Renaissance, they were on sale both in their original languages and re-packaged in popular translations—and Elizabethan readers just couldn't get enough of them. Arthur Golding's rendering of Ovid's epic poem *The Metamorphoses* was a best-seller; also popular was Plutarch's *Lives of Famous Greeks and Romans*, as translated into English by Thomas North. The names of such long-dead dramatists as Euripides, Plautus, Terence, and Seneca lived as household words in many an educated Elizabethan home. Anyone who *could* read in Shakespeare's day *did* read, eagerly and avidly—for in an age not blessed with radio or television, reading was the best way to become educated about the world.

Shakespeare had to read selectively, with a collector's eye for useful detail; as a busy, highly-pressured playwright, he couldn't afford to do otherwise. And yet the range of his reading was remarkably wide. It's mind-boggling to contemplate the number of folio pages Shakespeare must have thumbed through in a single year, looking for plots, names, characters, speeches, or whatever the immediate situation called for.

Yet before we start suspecting Shakespeare of plagiarism, we'd better take a look at what everyone else was doing in the literary world. Although this business of outright lifting from other writers' work might seem dubious to us, it wasn't unusual in Shakespeare's time. Without copyright laws to protect an author's works, the business of writing and publishing was truly a "free trade" affair, and everyone's works were salable commodities. Furthermore, the authors' originality just wasn't an issue; in fact, they were openly encouraged to imitate certain writing styles and literary models, especially, but not exclusively, the classical ones. The upshot of all this was that sixteenth-century authors and playwrights regularly raided both their predecessors and their colleagues, without giving it a second thought; one contemporary of Shakespeare's boasts proudly, "I have so written, as I have read."

In his far-flung borrowing, then, Shakespeare was a product of his times; and yet in this, as in so much else, he flew high above his contemporaries. Shakespeare's ultimate source was the broad spirit of his age, which he drew on in his own unique fashion. The great literary works available in the Elizabethan time mingled in his mind with cheap ballads and penny-pamphlets on sale in Paul's Churchyard, with tavern jokes, church sermons, and the constant influx of new information about foreign lands. All of this jostled up against the phrases and sounds of the everyday work and play of tanners, alehouse keepers, sailors, merchants, constables, nobles, and foreigners in London. Shakespeare imbibed the rich Elizabethan atmosphere as he walked the streets of London, and it was this atmosphere that he converted magically into theater.

HIT AND MYTH

SHAKESPEARE HAD A stock repertoire of allusions to various well-known figures from Greek and Roman mythology; Circe, Cupid, Phaëthon, Diana, Orpheus, Hercules, and Jason were among them. In *The Comedy of Errors*, for example, the Duke comments on the strange goings-on in Ephesus: "I think you all have drunk of Circe's cup," referring to the sorceress who transformed men into beasts. The fat little love god Cupid, who turned seeing humans into blind lovers, is another familiar figure, especially in the comedies. Most of the hundreds of references to him are playful, as when Rosalind passionately condemns (in *As You Like It*) "that same wicked bastard of Venus that was begot of thought, conceived of spleen, and born of madness, that blind rascally boy that abuses everyone's eyes because his own are out, let him be judge how deep I am in love." The precocious boy Phaëton, who fell to the earth from the sky while trying to drive the chariot of his father the sun god, was the standard symbol of misguided—or misguiding—ambition. In *King Henry VI Part 3*, the would-be king, the Duke of York, is compared to Phaëton: "Now Phaëton hath tumbled from his car And made an evening at the noontide prick." The Greek hero Jason was well-known; in *The Merchant of Venice*, Gratiano celebrates his and Bassanio's success in wooing Nerissa and Portia by crowing, "We are the Jasons, we have won the fleece."

Shakespeare didn't just throw these in to impress the audience with his knowledge. He used them in appropriate contexts, to illustrate a theme, drive home a point, or give a deeper meaning to the passage. In *The Two Gentlemen of Verona*, the disguised Julia underlines the theme of her beloved Proteus' treachery when she tells Silvia about her role in the Pentecostal pageant, where "I did play a lamentable part: Madam, 'twas Ariadne passioning For Theseus' perjury and unjust flight," referring to the desertion of Ariadne by her lover, the hero Theseus.

Shakespeare often used myths as joke material. Again Rosalind in *As You Like It* supplies us with an example, mocking the notion that men have ever died for love: "Leander, he would have lived many a fair year though Hero had turned nun, if it had not been for a hot midsummer night; for, good youth, he went but forth to wash him in the Hellespont (River) and being taken with the cramp was drowned . . ."

Sometimes Shakespeare's characters refer to well-known stories and legends to explain their behavior to others or rationalize it to themselves. In *The Merry Wives of Windsor*, for example, Pistol refuses to carry Falstaff's letter to Mistress Page by invoking the spirit of an infamous go-between in the Trojan War: "Shall I Sir Pandarus of Troy become, And by my side wear steel?" Later in the play, Falstaff rationalizes his ridiculous disguise as Herne the

Hunter by summoning Jove, who often appeared in animal shapes to woo mortals: "Remember, Jove, thou wast a bull for thy Europa; love set on thy horns . . . You were also, Jupiter, a swan for the love of Leda. O omnipotent Love!"

BIBLICAL BREEZES

THE GREEK AND ROMAN classics weren't the only ancient works that appeared on the landscape of Shakespeare's plays; alongside these pagan works lived a classic of another kind—the Bible. All in all, Shakespeare refered to forty-two books of the Bible and mentioned fifty-five biblical names. He also had several passages from the Book of Common Prayer, used in the church services of his day.

Just as the classics infused the Elizabethan atmosphere, so phrases from the prayer book and biblical stories were an intimate part of daily life. Remember that this was an age when going to church was required by law and religion played a prominent role in everyday affairs.

Most of Shakespeare's biblical allusions were probably familiar to his audiences. Although modern audiences often miss the point of these references or require footnotes in order to understand them, even the faintest biblical echoes would have been picked up by the church-going ears of most Elizabethans. In *The Taming of the Shrew*, for example, when Hortensio exclaims "From all such devils, good Lord deliver us!" Shakespeare's audience undoubtedly recognized the refrain from the litany in the prayer book they used each Sunday: "From all evil and mischief, from sin, from the crafts and assaults of the Devil . . . Good Lord, deliver us."

Often, as with the classics, Shakespeare twisted biblical or religious references to suit his humorous purposes. Hamlet's reference to "these pickers and stealers" comes from the catechism in the Book of Common Prayer, "To keep my hands from picking and stealing." In *A Mid-*

summer Night's Dream, Shakespeare has Bottom unconsciously distort a verse from 1 Corinthians, "The eye hath not seen, and the ear hath not heard, neither have entered into the heart of man . . ." when he emerges from his dream to say, "The eye of man hath not heard, the ear of man hath not seen, man's hand is not able to taste, his tongue to conceive, nor his heart to report. . . ." The humor of these exchanges is too often lost on us today, but these witty allusions are all examples of how richly Shakespeare threaded the resonances of contemporary language into his plays.

Some of Shakespeare's most famous lines are flavored with biblical verse. Compare Portia's "The quality of mercy is not strained. It droppeth as the gentle rain from heaven Upon the place beneath" in *The Merchant of Venice* with this verse from Ecclesiastes: "O how fair a thing is mercy in the time of anguish and trouble? it is like a cloud of rain that cometh in the time of drought." Petruchio's claim to his wife in *The Taming of the Shrew,* which begins "She is my goods, my chattels; she is my house, My household stuff, my field, my barn, My horse, my ox, my ass, my anything," comes straight from the tenth commandment, "Thou shalt not covet thy neighbor's house . . . nor his ox, nor his ass, nor anything that is his."

Ironically, it is Shakespeare's version of these lines rather than the Bible's that has lingered in the minds of most people. This is partly because Shakespeare placed them in the mouths of unforgettable characters in equally unforgettable dramatic situations. By bringing them to life in the theater, he insured that they will live forever, constantly resurrected on the stage.

SHAKESPEARE'S LAB

THERE WERE MANY other sources from all over the world that Shakespeare drew on for his plots, sources representing scores of different cultures, centuries, genres, and languages. The Italian Giraldo Cinthio's *Hecatommithi*, a collection of prose tales, provided a plot for *Othello;* the ideas in the essays of the French philosopher Michel de Montaigne are represented in *Hamlet;* and Giovanni Fiorentino's *Il Pecorone* ("The Dunce") is re-created in *The Merchant of Venice.*

The variety of this material alone is impressive and has intrigued professors and scholars for decades. But even more amazing is what Shakespeare did with his sources. No matter how dull the material he started with, his finished product was always an exciting, funny, or gripping drama.

This is because Shakespeare approached his sources not as a scholar but as a playwright. Although he had plenty of facts at hand, his goal was dramatic truth. Everything he read, everything his absorbent mind took in, was shaped and molded to the needs of the theater. The question at the back of his mind as he flipped through Samuel Harsnett's *Declaration of Egregious Popish Impostures*, or Thomas Lodge's *Rosalynde*, or Raphael Holinshed's *Chronicles*, was always the same: what will work on the stage?

In the process of answering this question, Shakespeare often took extraordinary liberties with his sources—changing names, settings, and centuries; rearranging events; compressing or extending time; and cutting and inventing characters. He made tragedy out of biography, comedy out of pastoral, and "pastoral-comical, historical-pastoral, tragical-historical, tragical-comical-historical-pastoral" (as Polonius might have said) out of everything.

To comprehend how amazing his transformations were, just imagine *Romeo and Juliet* without the nonstop patter of the Nurse; *As You Like It* without Touchstone's wit and Audrey's country simplicity; or *Henry IV Part 1* without the fiery prominence of Hotspur. All of these colorful characters were either nonexistent or very minor figures in the sources Shakespeare borrowed from. From the historian Raphael Holinshed's brief comment in the story of Richard II that the Duke of York "communed with the Duke of Lancaster," Shakespeare fashioned the powerful scene between York and Bolingbroke in Act 2 of *Richard II*. Here, the playwright brings family relationships, power games, and conflicting loyalties to a dramatic climax—all from a historian's short reference.

TRAGICAL-POETICAL

IMAGINE SHAKESPEARE COMING home at the end of an afternoon after a performance at the Globe and a pint of beer at the alehouse. He returns with a load of books under his arm and an idea in his head: to write a tragedy about young lovers who are done in by forces beyond their control. Although he's vaguely familiar with Arthur Brooke's narrative poem on such a couple, *The Tragicall History of Romeus and Juliet* (itself based on a French source), his friends have told him not to bother reading it, as it's terribly long and tedious. But Shakespeare sits down and begins to leaf through it anyway, since he knows from past experience that every source, no matter how unpromising it seems, has something to offer.

He is quickly dismayed by the moralizing tone of Brooke's opening remarks, which censure the love of the unwed couple. For already Shakespeare is completely sympathetic to the plight of Romeo and Juliet. As he makes his way through more than three thousand lines of sing-song poetry, he jots down a few of Brooke's meticulous details on upper-class life—the feuding, the church customs— knowing that, although they seem dead on the page, they will revive when he puts them on his stage.

He also realizes that the story Brooke tells is too slow-paced for his dramatic purposes. Instead of nine months Shakespeare gives the young lovers four and a half days, turning the story into a tragedy of missed opportunities and crossed purposes. While he's at it, he chops a few years off Juliet's age, just to heighten the pathos a bit more. As he continues to flip through the pages, his eye is caught by Brooke's brief two-line reference to a character called "Mercutio, A courtier that each where [everywhere] was highly had in price For he was courteous of his speech and pleasant of device." "Hmmm . . ." muses our poet, "there's got to be something I can do with him." He thinks about it awhile, taking a few paces around the room, finally deciding to turn him into Romeo's witty and fiery friend and foil. To show early on how the pointless feud between the families causes the shedding of innocent blood, he then kills off Mercutio halfway through the play.

He rummages around in his imagination and comes up with a lovable, talkative, treacherous nurse for Juliet. And then, seasoning the play with a pinch of servant comedy, a dash or two of swordfighting, and some of the most beautiful poetic language ever written, Shakespeare decides that *Romeo and Juliet* is finally complete. The wooden, tedious narrative poem has become a powerful, unforgettable tragedy of star-crossed lovers.

TRAGICAL-HISTORICAL

SUPPOSE THAT INSTEAD of a tragic love story, Shakespeare is interested in writing a historical play to compliment the new king of England, James I. He remembers seeing a story about the Scottish nobleman Macbeth in Holinshed's *Chronicles*, his much-used historical source. The playwright has come to rely on Holinshed for his painstaking detail, his long and balanced sentences, his simple, powerful metaphors, and even his moralizing comments in the margins. In fact, by the end of his career, Shakespeare will have used Holinshed for almost one quarter of his plays.

Since James I is reputedly descended from the character Banquo, who figures prominently in the Macbeth story, Shakespeare now opens the massive three-volume folio to volume 2, the *History of Scotland*. Immediately he finds the reference to "Banquo, the Thane of Lochaber, of whom the House of the Stuarts is descended, the which by order of lineage hath now for a long time enjoyed the crown of Scotland even till these our days. . . ." He reads with mounting excitement about an encounter that the victorious Macbeth and Banquo have with "three women in strange and wild apparel, resembling creatures of an elder [ancient] world," knowing that sinister witches will go over extremely well with his audience. An ambitious wife for Macbeth—yes, that will be fine; so far, so good.

Then he arrives at the account of Macbeth's plot to murder the king, and suddenly everything falls apart with the statement that Macbeth, "communicating his purposed intent with his trusty friends, *amongst whom Ban-*

quo was the chiefest," killed the king. This last phrase is troublesome: it simply will not do for an ancestor of King James to be an accomplice to murder. Shakespeare buries his head in his hands for a minute and then decides to read through the rest of the story, just to see what happens. It is full of great stage material—ambiguous prophecies from the witches, Macbeth's slaughter of Macduff's wife and children, and the final dramatic confrontation between Macbeth and Macduff, which ends with Holinshed's statement, "he [Macduff] stepped unto him and slew him in the place."

All of that will be fine with just a little Shakespearean retouching. But this business of James's ancestor Banquo as a conspirator in the murder of the king is sticky. What can Shakespeare do? Absentmindedly he flicks back through a few pages of the *History of Scotland* and begins to read the story of the nobleman Donwald and his murder of King Duff. Though Donwald has a grievance against the king, he is reluctant to kill him and does so because his ambitious wife eggs him on: "thus being the more kindled in wrath by the words of his wife, [he] determined to follow her advice in the execution of so heinous an act."

Together the couple gets the king's guards drunk and then arranges to have the king's throat cut while he sleeps in their castle. When the murder is discovered, the treacherous Donwald, pretending to be shocked and horrified, kills the guardians of the chamber in supposed revenge. The murder is followed by all sorts of monstrous portents and unnatural signs—clouds, wild winds and tempests, and, worst of all, the horses of Lothian, beautiful and swift, eating their own flesh.

Shakespeare throws his quill up in the air joyfully: here is the answer to his problem! He can simply fuse the story of Macbeth's murder of Duncan (and Banquo) with the story of Donwald's murder of King Duff, perhaps blackening Macbeth's character even more by having him actually do the murdering himself. By turning Donwald into Macbeth, Shakespeare can save Banquo's reputation. And with that problem out of the way, the playwright can concentrate on creating the sinister vapors of terror and violence that swirl around the play. *Macbeth* is well on its way.

TRAGICAL-PLUTARCHAL

AFTER RELYING ON the English chroniclers for several of his history plays, Shakespeare turns to a different sort of historical source, the more psychologically oriented biographies of Brutus, Coriolanus, and Mark Antony, written by the Greek Plutarch and translated by Thomas North. North's Plutarch is perfectly suited to Shakespeare's needs: Plutarch provides him with the inherently dramatic contradictions within characters and with illustrative little stories, while North supplies him with much of the gorgeous language.

A striking example of the way Shakespeare transforms Plutarch's words—in this instance into a masterpiece of sensual expression—is the famous description by Enobarbus of Cleopatra on her barge in *Antony and Cleopatra*. Imagine Shakespeare reading Plutarch's prosaic description of the barge in North's translation: "the poop whereof was gold, the sails of purple, and the oars of silver, which kept stroke in rowing after the sound of the music of flutes, citherns, viols, and other such instruments." Note how Shakespeare's fine hand transforms these lines for Enobarbus to speak on the stage. "The poop was beaten gold; Purple the sails, and so perfumèd that The winds were lovesick with them. The oars were silver, Which to the tune of flutes kept stroke, and made The water which they beat to follow faster, As amorous of their strokes." How gorgeously Shakespeare takes the cold facts of the historian and heats them up with perfumed sails, lovesick winds, silver oars caressing the water "as amorous of their strokes." Now we cannot only *see* Cleopatra, we can taste her, smell her, and feel her exotic presence. In this one example, we can actually understand the process of Shakespeare's great mind.

CHAPTER 12

English as a Foreign Language

Shakespeare's Language

Shakespeare's words have been uttered in many nations and in many languages during the last four hundred years: Shylock can ask "Hath not a Jew eyes?" in Swahili, and Juliet can exclaim "O Romeo, Romeo, wherefore art thou Romeo?" in Serbo-Croatian. Certainly good translations preserve the vividness of Shakespeare's characters and the universality of his themes—but no matter how good they are, they cannot convey the quintessence of Shakespeare's greatness. The flavor or spirit of a language is almost always lost in any translation; here that loss is incalculably great—for Shakespeare the dramatist is inseparable from Shakespeare the poet of Elizabethan language.

Words are the core of what Shakespeare and his theater are all about. It is through language that he paints the set and creates mood, emotion, and atmosphere. And it is through language that he breathes life into his characters. Shakespeare moves us with the same rhetoric and rhythms that have moved audiences for centuries.

LENDING HIM OUR EARS

SHAKESPEARE'S LANGUAGE, WHEN spoken, both entertains and stirs audiences. The principles of word-patterning, or language arranged for effect, are gathered together under a term that has fallen into disgrace in our time—"rhetoric."

In the sixteenth century, however, the term didn't imply insincerity; it was simply what divided ordinary talk from poetic language. Rhetoric was the arrangement of words in certain artificial or unlifelike patterns, called figures and tropes, to achieve results of beauty or power. As a contemporary writer put it, rhetoric was "a novelty of language evidently (and yet not absurdly) estranged from the ordinary habit and manner of our daily talk and writing. . . ." Rhetorical devices dressed up plain everyday language in rich, sumptuous clothes that rarely failed to have an impact.

Most Elizabethan writers thought that rhetoric was a useful, natural, even preferable way to express feelings and emotion; the more rhetorical a work, the more elegant and persuasive it was considered. Scores of handbooks and tracts were written on the subject of rhetoric. Schoolboys struggled to master hundreds of rhetorical figures with such unpronounceable Greek names as "hendiadys," "polyptoton," and "bdelygmia." Rhetorical studies employed many technical terms to describe things that might go unnoticed today. Some have a familiar ring to them, such as "allegory," "alliteration," and "repetition."

Others have far more intimidating names. "Hyperbole," for example, was the Greek name for exaggeration, such as that with which Doll Tearsheet comforts Falstaff in *Henry IV Part 2:* "Thou art as valorous as Hector of Troy, worth five of Agamemnon, and ten times better than the Nine Worthies." "Anaphora" was repetition at the beginning of several consecutive sentences—as in Petruchio's indignant questioning from *The Taming of the Shrew:*

Have I not in my time heard lions roar?
Have I not heard the sea, puffed up with winds,
Rage like an angry boar chafèd with sweat?

Have I not heard great ordnance in the field,
And heaven's artillery thunder in the skies?
Have I not in a pitchèd battle heard
Loud 'larums, neighing steeds, and trumpets' clang?

And "anastrophe" was simply an unusual word order in a
sentence—a Shakespearean favorite, as this jigsaw puzzle
of a sentence from *The Tempest* illustrates: " . . . at pick'd
leisure, Which shall be shortly, single I'll resolve you, Which
to you shall seem probable, of every These happen'd ac-
cidents."

Even these few examples amply demonstrate that
Shakespeare knew his rhetoric. In some of his earlier plays,
he seems to be enthralled with rhetoric for its own sake;
these plays could be chapters in sixteenth-century rhetoric
textbooks. *Richard III*, for example, is filled with elaborate
and formal rhetorical devices. Shakespeare wraps up the
remarkable scene in which the devilish Duke of Gloucester
wooes Anne with a flourish of "stichomythia," an extremely
stylized device in which speakers alternate single lines of
poetry:

ANNE	I would I knew thy heart.
RICHARD	'Tis figured in my tongue.
ANNE	I fear me both are false.
RICHARD	Then never was man true.
ANNE	Well, well, put up your sword.
RICHARD	Say, then, my peace is made.
ANNE	That shalt thou know hereafter.
RICHARD	But shall I live in hope?
ANNE	All men, I hope, live so.
RICHARD	Vouchsafe to wear this ring.
ANNE	To take is not to give.

Throughout the plays Shakespeare's characters use
rhetoric to argue, debate, persuade, and exchange witty
statements. No play is immune from rhetorical contagion
—and as we watch the characters play off each other's
words, we may find ourselves infected with enthusiasm
for these word-patterns. For there's just no getting away
from it.

In *Titus Andronicus*, for example, Demetrius sets out

a persuasive little syllogism justifying the rape of Lavinia to Aaron:

> She is a woman, therefore may be
> wooed;
> She is a woman, therefore may be
> won;
> She is Lavinia, therefore must be
> loved.

On a lighter note, Julia and Lucetta have an absolutely delightful debate about Julia's various suitors in *The Two Gentlemen of Verona*, including Proteus:

JULIA   And wouldst thou have me cast my love on him?
LUCETTA   Ay, if you thought your love not cast away.
JULIA   Why, he of all the rest hath never moved me.
LUCETTA   Yet he of all the rest I think best loves ye.
JULIA   His little speaking shows his love but small.
LUCETTA   Fire that's closest kept burns most of all.
JULIA   They do not love that do not show their love.
LUCETTA   O, they love least that let men know their love.

That master of mercurial rhetoric, *Much Ado*'s Benedick, establishes himself as a merciless show-off as he subverts a conversation between Don Pedro and Claudio about Claudio's love for Hero:

CLAUDIO   That I love her, I feel.
DON PEDRO   That she is worthy, I know.
BENEDICK   That I neither feel how she
should be loved nor know how she should be worthy is the opinion that fire cannot melt out of me. I will die in it at the stake.

In addition to more formal rhetorical devices, Shakespeare frequently resorted to simple wordplay, with an emphasis on punning. Although Shakespeare has come under fire for his frequent punning (Samuel Johnson said it held "some malignant power over his mind"), puns in his time were signs of stylistic elegance and were good tools for argument, not the debased and silly form of humor some people think they are today. Shakespeare was addicted to witty wordplay: *Love's Labor's Lost* has an estimated two hundred puns, and the average is around eighty per play.

There are puns on words that sound the same, such as Touchstone's pun in *As You Like It* on "goats" and "Goths," which were pronounced alike in Shakespeare's day, or Falstaff's effort in *Henry IV Part I*, when he tells Hal, "were it not *here* apparent that thou art *heir* apparent. . . ." Hamlet, one of Shakespeare's champion punners, rebuffs Claudius' attempt to call him "son" by responding, "I am too much in the sun." And Cassius makes a revealing joke about Julius Caesar's preeminence when he says, "Now is it Rome indeed, and room enough, When there is in it but one only man!"

There are also puns on words that have more than one meaning. Portia plays on two meanings of "will" when she says, "so is the *will* of a living daughter curbed by the *will* of a dead father." And Pistol refers both to his departure and his future livelihood when he punningly proclaims in *Henry V*, "To England will I steal, and there I'll steal."

Shakespeare's characters sometimes pun in what we might consider the most inappropriate circumstances— which must have tickled his audience. Lady Macbeth, about to carry out her dastardly crime, declares "I'll *gild* the faces of the grooms withal, For it must seem their *guilt*." Defying Richard II, the dying John of Gaunt puns on his name— "Gaunt am I for the grave, gaunt as a grave." And the great Mark Antony, lamenting beside the dead body of Caesar, finds time for a pun: "O world, thou wast the forest to this *hart*, And this indeed, O world, the *heart* of thee!" Even in death Shakespeare finds room for a pun.

FROM GOOD TO VERSE

SHAKESPEARE WROTE HIS plays largely in blank verse—un-rhymed iambic pentameter of five beats per line. Although writing a play in poetry may seem unnatural to us, it was the common method in Shakespeare's time. For one thing, the rhythm of the poetry made memorization easier (as many modern actors will attest); with the number of roles an actor had to keep in his head at once, easy memorization was a priority. And verse was a subtle way to manipulate the emotions of the audience with its flowing yet insistent current.

But the most important purpose of verse was a dramatic one: through it Shakespeare delineated character and unfolded subtler meanings. He took a much less bombastic approach than many of his contemporaries, preferring music to thunder—but oh, the variety of the music he plays! Sometimes his poetry is a baroque air of magic and fantasy, like the four-beat verses of the fairies in *A Midsummer Night's Dream*. Other times it raps out a stern military march—the kind of verse-music Coriolanus is most at home with. And in such plays as *Othello*, *Hamlet*, and *Lear*, Shakespeare composes music of tragic intensity, with powerful rhythms and gentle but relentless waves of sound that carry the verse forward—as in Othello's final speech, "Soft you; a word or two before you go."

Of course Shakespeare didn't allow verse to monopolize rhythm. Even when he wrote in prose, he had an unfailing ear for the sounds of words and used prose rhythms on the stage just as effectively as those of verse. *As You Like It* is almost entirely in prose: indeed, Jaques abandons Orlando's company when the young swain unintentionally speaks a line of iambic pentameter, declaring, "Nay, then, God b' wi' [be with] you, an [if] you talk in blank verse." Lear goes mad in prose, Benedick and Beatrice fall in love to the intoxicating rhythms of their own witty prose, and Juliet's Nurse patters her delightful prose way through *Romeo and Juliet*. Hamlet signifies a change of mood by slipping from verse into more comfortable prose, and Othello deteriorates from dignified verse into an almost incoherent babbling as he capitulates to his jealous frenzy—"noses, ears, and lips. Is 't possible? Confess—handkerchief!—O devil!" Prose, like verse, is a many-splendored thing in Shakespeare's skilled hands.

CROSSING THE BORDER

EVEN THOUGH SHAKESPEARE's language may be the most effective stage language ever created, it can also be the single biggest hurdle for modern readers and audiences. His vocabulary is sometimes incomprehensible, his word order strangely convoluted, and his grammatical usage unlike anything we've ever heard. Many of us might want to say to Shakespeare the words Hermione utters to Leontes in *The Winter's Tale*—"Sir, You speak a language that I understand not." Much of his language, we might suspect, wouldn't make it past the eagle eye of a modern-day English teacher. For initially, Shakespeare's plays appear to be full of grammatical mistakes and bizarre usages.

For example, he frequently uses double negatives. In *As You Like It*, Celia cries, "I pray you, bear with me; I *cannot* go *no* further." Subject and verb don't always agree: in *Julius Caesar*, Cassius says to Antony "The *posture* of your blows *are* yet unknown," and Falstaff quizzes a young servant in *Henry IV Part 2* "*Is* there not *wars*? Is there not employment?" Adjectives often follow their nouns instead of coming before them: Claudio in *Measure for Measure* wonders "whether that the *body public* be A horse whereon the governor doth ride," and Othello speaks of "*antres vast* and *deserts idle*." Shakespeare sometimes even ends his sentences with prepositions, as in *Richard III* when Clarence tells of his dream: "Methoughts I saw a thousand fearful wracks; Ten thousand men that fishes gnawed *upon*."

There seems to be a great deal of carelessness in the greatest poetry of the English language. But before we convict our hapless playwright on charges of disturbing the grammatical peace, we might first take a whiff of the linguistic atmosphere in which he was writing. The order of the day, when it came to language, was *dis*order. Despite the regular and sensible linguistic model of Latin, English grammar and syntax were sprawling in all directions, free of any straitjacketing notions of correctness. Nouns didn't need to match their verbs, and a word might be spelled three different ways within a single paragraph. Word order was a complete free-for-all: objects could precede verbs, adjectives could follow nouns, and questions could be asked simply by reversing the verb (Macbeth asks Banquo, "Ride you this afternoon?"). Ellipsis, in which a subject or a verb is left out and supplied by the mind of the reader, was common. The general guideline was that energy and color in language were much more interesting than logic and agreement.

The language of Shakespeare's time was branching out in wild profusion, growing richer and more varied as the country opened its eyes and its doors to the great world beyond its own shores. The sixteenth century was an age of *linguistic* as well as global and intellectual expansion. The growth of international trade, the revival of Greek and Latin works, and the influx of information about other countries all had their effect on the language of Elizabethan England.

In fact, the use of words from other languages was a controversial topic of the day. Many linguistic patriots were outraged by the importation of foreign words, although there were thousands of Greek, French, Saxon and Latin words already in the English vocabulary. They condemned them as unpatriotic contaminations of English and argued that only words that bore the all-important "Made In England" stamp should be allowed into the country. One pamphleteer asserted "that our own tongue should be written clean and pure, unmixed and unmangled with borrowing of other tongues." He was not alone. "The more monosyllables you use, the truer Englishman you shall seem," counselled another. These writers made fun of their colleagues who frequently borrowed foreign words, ridiculing them in sentences they composed: "I being a scholasticall panion obtestate your sublimity to extol mine infirmity."

Still, there were plenty of moderates to speak in defense of an open-door policy for verbal immigrants. One writer thought it perfectly all right to "augment our English tongue" with words from "Greek, Latin, or any other tongue." An open-minded writer pointed out that such Latin-based words as "conduct," "function," "figurative," and "indignity" had become staples of the English language and were therefore acceptable; in the next breath, though, he warned against the suspiciously new-fangled "audacious," "egregious," and "compatible," which time has since proved enduring. Still another considered the immense numbers of borrowed foreign terms an asset: "Seeing then we borrow (and that not shamefully) from the Dutch, the Breton, the Roman, the Dane, the French, Italian, and Spaniard, how can our stock be other than exceeding plentiful?" And a contemporary of Shakespeare's who was an actor and playwright praised playwrights for their role in improving the language: "Our English tongue . . . is now by this secondary means of playing, continually refined, every writer striving in himself to add a new flourish unto it; so that in the process, from the most rude and unpolished tongue, it is grown to a most perfect and composed language." In the end, of course, as they always do, linguistic conservatives and protectionists failed to stem the ·tide of change. And so foreign words flowed steadily into England both from the shores of Greco-Roman antiquity and those of the modern-day Continent.

Shakespeare, ever the man of his times, had his share of foreign words and phrases. Sometimes, as Benedick says of Claudio in *Much Ado About Nothing*, "his words are a very fantastical banquet, just so many strange dishes." Latinisms abound: Cordelia in *Lear* bids "All blest secrets . . . Be *aidant* and *remediate* In the good man's distress." Agamemnon distinguishes himself as the stud of Latinisms in *Troilus and Cressida* by using four Latin-derived words within fifteen lines: "conflux," "tortive," "protractive," and "persistive." (None of these words caught on!)

Shakespeare often used Latin words that we recognize today—but in their literal or original meanings. When Macbeth shouts at Banquo's ghost, "Thou hast no *speculation* in those eyes Which thou dost glare with," he means that Banquo lacks the power of seeing, not that he is failing to consider an investment in the stock market. When Parolles refers to "an advertisement to a proper maid in Florence" in *All's Well That Ends Well*, he is saying that he has sent her a warning, not a suggestion that she buy cosmetics or rug-cleaner. Similarly, an "accident" in Shakespeare is usually just an "occurrence," and *Hamlet*'s "extravagant" ghost is one who wanders out of bounds, not a big spender.

Latin wasn't the only lender. Shakespeare took from Portuguese as well, using the word *crusado*, a gold coin; and from French he borrowed *oeillades*, meaning "looks of love." Italian was well represented, especially in *The Taming of the Shrew*. Hortensio says to Petruchio, "I shall be your *ben venuto* [welcome]," and Lucio cries, "*Basta* [enough], content thee, for I have it full." Mercutio mocks Italian fencing terms in *Romeo and Juliet:* "Ah, the immortal *passado*! The *punto reverso*! The hay!" for Mercutio can't abide people who use pretentious foreign phrases— "The pox of such antic, lisping, affecting phantasimes, these new tuners of accent."

In general Shakespeare applied a light hand to the use of foreign words, ridiculing those, like Don Armado, Holofernes, and Sir Nathaniel in *Love's Labor's Lost*, who use them in excess. He was much more interested in seeing how far his native language could be stretched. If the existing language didn't provide him with quite what he needed, he could either resculpt an old word or invent a new one altogether.

Shakespeare played the variations in his native tongue to their full advantage. He nonchalantly switched around parts of speech as the circumstances require. Verbs play the roles of nouns: Anne accuses the evil Duke of Gloucester in *Richard III* of making earth into a living hell and filling it "with cursing cries and deep *exclaims*." And nouns magically become verbs: Iago declares to Othello, "O, 'tis the spite of hell, the fiend's arch-mock, To *lip* a wanton in a secure couch." Edgar laments of Lear, "He *childed* as I *fathered*." And Menenius commands the Tribunes in *Coriolanus*, "Go, you that banished him: A mile before his tent fall down and *knee* The way into his mercy." And within a single sentence Sir Hugh Evans demonstrates how a noun can be both a verb and an adjective, solemnly promising Slender in *The Merry Wives of Windsor*, "I will *description* the matter to you, if you be *capacity* of it."

Among Shakespeare's most important tools in changing one part of speech to another were prefixes and suffixes. "Be-" is useful for turning a noun into a verb— Prospero in *The Tempest* boasts, "I have *bedimmed* The noontide sun;" and Albany rebukes Goneril in *King Lear*, "*Bemonster* not thy feature." It can also make intransitive verbs transitive, as when Puck says in *A Midsummer Night's Dream*, "the wolf *behowls* the moon." Another Shakespearean favorite is "en-," as when the Prologue to Act 4 of

Henry V tells us that the King shows no worry over "How dread an army hath *enrounded* him," and Iago plots to "make the net That shall *enmesh* them all." Salerio imagines how the treacherous rocks might wreck his ships and "*Enrobe* the roaring waters with my silks."

Suffixes were equally versatile instruments: "-ly" and "-y," for example, turn nouns into adjectives, as when Autolycus asks, "But what talk we of these *traitorly* rascals?" (*The Winter's Tale*) or the Doctor in *Macbeth* refers to Lady Macbeth's "*slumbery* agitation." And often Shakespeare combined good old native Anglo-Saxon prefixes or suffixes with elaborate Latin roots to create such hybrid words as "increaseful," "exteriorly," "unseminared," "entreatments," and this whopper from *Othello*, "exsufflicate." Armado gets off a double whammy when he orders Moth to "give *enlargement* to the swain, bring him *festinately* hither."

When he ran out of steam with prefixes and suffixes, there was always compounding to play with. Shakespeare must have entertained himself for hours making up word combinations, joining adjectives and nouns, adverbs and nouns, participles and prepositions—all with the help of the ever-adaptable hyphen.

Shakespeare's compounds come in all sorts of flavors. There are noun compounds, such as "thick-lips," "brazen-face," and "fat-guts." Cleopatra calls herself "marble-constant," and Cordelia invokes the pity of the gods on her "child-changed father." Tormented by jealousy, Othello bids farewell to "The spirit-stirring drum, th' ear-piercing fife."

There are verb compounds, too; King Henry V brushes aside the prudish opinions of "all find-faults" as he prepares to kiss his Kate; Rosalind warns Orlando against being a "pathetical break-promise" in *As You Like It;* and in *Love's Labor's Lost* Berowne reels off a list of abusive compounds as he grumbles that "Some carry-tale, some please-man, some slight zany, Some mumble-news . . . Told our intents before."

There are compounds made with adverbs—Imogen prepares for her "hence-going" in *Cymbeline*, while Malcolm refers to Macduff's "here-approach" in *Macbeth;* and there are compounds made with adjectives, such as "childish-foolish," "heady-rash," and "rocky-hard." The lowly preposition isn't forgotten; Prince Hal, speaking to his father, calls himself "your unthought-of Harry." Sometimes there are even compounds of compounds, in such phrases as "the always-wind-obeying deep" from *The Comedy of Errors* and "a world-without-end bargain" in *Love's Labor's Lost*. Often Shakespeare lets loose with an especially vivid compound, such as the insult Thersites hurls at Ajax in *Troilus and Cressida*, "thou mongrel beef-witted lord," or Armado's dismissal of Costard as "that unlettered small-knowing soul" in *Love's Labor's Lost*.

If either of the two "-fixes" or compounding didn't provide what he needed, Shakespeare might very well have made up a word. He usually did this for comic purposes. One of the funniest examples of his linguistic inventiveness is the scene in *All's Well* where the soldiers blindfold and kidnap Parolles to trick him into betraying Bertram. As the accompanying lords gabble on, they come up with such gems of nonsense as "Throca movousus, cargo, cargo, cargo" and "Oscorbidulchos volivorco." If this is funny to read, it is that much more hilarious to hear.

Shakespeare's inventiveness and versatility seem to have had no bounds. Besides his extraordinary range of foreign importation and native production, he drew on technical terms of coinage, law, sailing, falconry, and medicine, among others. He also had an incredible repertoire of terms of abuse, vulgarity, and profanity.

If all this is true, one might ask, why is he so hard to understand today? The simple answer is that language changes; just as it grew and expanded in Shakespeare's time, so it has developed through the centuries, and many words that served a need then have fallen out of use, replaced by more relevant or functional words. This happens in every age. An Elizabethan who came to the twentieth century would be as mystified by our words "Reebok," "rayon," and "user-friendly" as we are by Shakespeare's "chopine," "kecksy," and "to slubber" (a kind of shoe, a wild plant, and to treat carelessly). Shakespeare, like any good dramatist, filled his plays with contemporary vocabulary, words that reflected the daily lives and immediate concerns of his audience.

But in fact, these archaic words aren't the real trouble-makers; it's easy enough to keep an eye out for them, for they are like red flags directing us to footnotes or dictionaries. More dangerous are the words that seem familiar

—ones we think we recognize but that mean something different now than they did then. For example, when a Shakespearean character says he'll do something "*presently*" he means immediately, not "whenever I get around to it." When Nym in *The Merry Wives of Windsor* worries, "I love not the *humor* of it," he isn't talking about a bad joke, but about the general tone or tenor of the situation. When Hamlet says to his friends, "I'll make a ghost of him that lets me," he means "stops me" rather than "allows me." Polonius' complaint that Hamlet is "*Still* harping on my daughter" doesn't mean quite what we think it does either; "still" means "always" in Shakespeare's English. And when Friar Lawrence says that the letter he sent to Romeo was "not *nice*," he isn't implying that it insulted the youth but that it was not trivial or insignificant.

Even characters within Shakespeare's plays sometimes have trouble with meanings; after all, Costard in *Love's Labor's Lost* thinks that "remuneration" means three farthings. And the rebel Jack Cade in *Henry VI Part 2* may speak for many a hapless modern student in his indictment of Lord Say: "It will be proved to thy face," he says accusingly, "that thou hast men about thee that usually talk of a noun and a verb and such abominable words as no Christian ear can endure to hear."

Shakespeare's audience might have cheered Cade on here; certainly not everyone understood every word they heard. But it's highly unlikely that they worried too much about it. These people were listeners and spectators, not scholars and readers. They were intent on absorbing the sounds, the rhythms, and the gist of the language. That's how we should approach it, too, whether reading a play in a quiet room or watching Shakespeare come to life, again and again, in the hustle and bustle of the living theater.

CHAPTER 13

SHAKESPEARE ALIVE?

GLOBE-TROTTER

In 1982, AN "off year," there were well over one million visitors to Shakespeare's native Stratford in England, most of them foreigners. The United States topped the list, with the United Kingdom a close second. But native English speakers weren't the only pilgrims to pay homage at Shakespeare's shrine. Visitors also came from Iraq, Iran, Burma, Algeria, Vietnam, Borneo, Haiti, and Costa Rica, among others; there was even one each from Estonia, Ethiopia, Madagascar and Mongolia.

Although Shakespeare may have made his home in Stratford, he has obviously found a home in every corner of the world since then. Even during his lifetime, his plays were performed by Catholic recusants in the north of England, on a ship off of Sierra Leone, and in the cities of Elbing and Gdansk in eastern Europe. In the subsequent four centuries Shakespeare's plays seem to have gone everywhere else as well; each nation has annexed him and made him its own by translating, adapting, and performing his plays.

Only the Bible has been translated into more languages than Shakespeare. Among others, he can be found in ancient Latin, modern Greek, Assamese, Chinese, Turkish, Yiddish, Bengali, Gujarati, Swahili, and at least twenty-eight of the languages of the modern-day Soviet Union. The Germans were already busy translating him in the early 1600s; on the other hand, the first complete translation of Shakespeare in Serbo-Croatian wasn't finished until 1963.

His track record of stage performance is no less impressive. Shakespeare has been glimpsed in a lunatic asylum in Greece, in a village of mud huts in Zanzibar, and on the ramparts of a ruined fifteenth-century fort overlooking the Straits of Bosphorus in Turkey. A French actress got so carried away while performing the role of Kate in *The Taming of the Shrew* that she fell into the orchestra pit. Never mind that at the first genuine performance of *Othello* in Italy, given at Milan in 1845, the audience laughed so hard that the show had to be stopped (they misunderstood the opening scene and thought it was a farce): the Italians adore Shakespeare. A Japanese acting company risked the wrath of the Tokyo police in 1901 when it deliberately performed *Julius Caesar* a month after the assassination of a prominent political leader. And most recently, Shakespeare crossed the Great Wall into China for that nation's first-ever Shakespeare Festival in Peking, where *A Midsummer Night's Dream* was performed by a troupe of coal miners, and *King Lear* was set in the darkness and oppression of feudal China.

Foreigners the world over have been eloquent witnesses to Shakespeare's power to move and stir his audiences. After seeing *Hamlet* in 1866, the dashing Italian general Garibaldi declared ruefully, "That Shakespeare is a great magician; he kept me awake all night." The German political philosopher, Karl Marx, commented in the nineteenth century that Launce and his dog (from *The Two Gentlemen of Verona*) were more valuable than all German comedies put together. A Frenchman declared that Shakespeare is "part and parcel of our literary consciousness." One observer at the brand-new China Shakespeare Festival commented that "the Chinese love Shakespeare so much that in a few years time they will say the bard was Chinese."

He might just as well have said Indian, or Japanese, or Polish. Every nation pats itself on the back for keeping Shakespeare alive; and every nation finds itself in Shakespeare. A German will look at Hamlet and see the mirror of the German soul; a native of India will make Hamlet an Indian, like the writer who scrawled, "What are we Indians, but pale Hamlets, sick with too much thinking and chattering?" A provincial Scottish troupe in the eighteenth century reached an impasse when every actor insisted on playing Hamlet, and only Hamlet—the company settled it by abandoning the play.

To some, Shakespeare is a provider of endless delight and entertainment; the empress of Russia, Catherine the Great, translated and reworked *The Merry Wives of Windsor* and *Timon of Athens* along Russian lines. To others, Shakespeare is a source of inspiration in times of hardship or turmoil. The French performed his plays during the German occupation of Paris in World War II, when English books were banned. The Armenians, engaged in a struggle for political autonomy, are said to have taken courage from the struggles of King Lear, Macbeth, Shylock, and Othello. And in 1916, though they were in the middle of World War I, the people of Yugoslavia took time out to organize a ceremony for the three hundredth anniversary of Shakespeare's death, basing their celebration on the same premise that our observer in China stated— that Shakespeare truly belongs to all nations.

TRANSATLANTIC SHAKESPEARE

PERHAPS HE DOES, but Americans would like to believe that he is just a little more at home in the United States than anywhere else. Shakespeare has made frequent cameo appearances in the chronicles of American history, and he's meant many different things to people at various times in the life of the republic. Early American citizens loved him for his tales of swashbuckling and romance; early American statesmen looked to him for examples of political wisdom and moral courage. He also provided journalists and cartoonists with endless material to use in their commentaries on the state of the union.

The first presidents were lovers of Shakespeare. George Washington's boyhood home contained six volumes of Shakespeare's plays, and several signers of the Declaration of Independence owned Shakespeare volumes. John Adams got up at four o'clock on a winter morning to answer a letter about *Hamlet* and to "commune with a lover and worthy representative of Shakespeare upon the glories of this immortal bard." Abraham Lincoln carried a copy of *Macbeth* (his favorite) with him as he rode the law circuits in Illinois. Later, when he was president, a copy of Shakespeare sat on the White House desk (along with the Bible and the U.S. Statutes). Art, religion, and society—what else did one need for a full understanding of the achievement and genius of humankind but these three books?

Both sides enlisted Shakespeare's help in the American Revolution. Writers revised and revamped Hamlet's famous question to dramatize the conflicting impulses within the rebelling colony. A Tory loyalist lambasted the rebels by asking,

> To sign or not to sign!—That is the question:
> Whether 't were better for an honest man
> To sign—and so be safe . . .

or to risk the consequences of loyalty by refusing to sign the oath of rebellion against Britain. A Boston newspaper pondered the taxation question similarly:

> Be taxt or not be taxt—that is the question.
> Whether 'tis nobler in our minds to suffer
> The sleights and cunning of deceitful statesmen
> Or to petition 'gainst illegal taxes
> And by opposing, end them?

Once war had actually broken out, Shakespeare appeared behind the lines of both the British and the rebel armies. Clinton's Thespians, a group of British officers under the command of General Clinton during the occupation of New York, put on productions of *Richard III*, *Macbeth*, and Garrick's *Catherine and Petruchio* (a shortened version of *The Taming of the Shrew*) to while away the time. And dispirited American soldiers in New Hampshire, discouraged by the feeling that their sacrifices and suffering for their new country weren't being appreciated, found companionship and solace in Shakespeare's *Coriolanus*, another story of ingratitude for military service.

In fact, makeshift military productions were the only entertainment going during the Revolution; in 1774, in the interests of economizing, the Continental Congress closed down the theater and other wartime extravagances such as horse racing, cockfighting, and gambling. Up to that time, Shakespeare had been a familiar and popular playwright on the American stages of New York, Boston, Philadelphia, Richmond, and Charleston.

Shakespeare had made his first transatlantic crossing in 1752, when a group of actors arrived from England to perform *The Merchant of Venice* in Williamsburg, Virginia, (preferring this hospitable southern city to the rocky moral terrain of Puritan New England). No doubt the playwright would have felt right at home in the theater conditions in early America—enthusiastic audiences, unpredictable theater arrangements, and gritty opposition from the New England Puritan faction. In addition, the colonial audiences were as responsive as any to be found at the Globe in the 1590s. For example, when the emperor and empress of the Cherokee Indians saw a performance of *Othello* in 1752, they were so startled by the stage swordplay that the empress ordered her attendants to go stop the actors before they killed each other. Things in America weren't so different from what they had been in Shakespeare's London, where spectators would sometimes climb up on stage and make more ruckus than the actors!

Although the United States won its political independence in 1776, theatrical independence was a longer time in coming. The American stage tended to mimic whatever was going on in London; the famous English actor David Garrick's huge success with *Richard III* was a surefire guarantee that it would be popular in America. Moreover, many English actors crossed over to tour in the ex-colonies, either because they hadn't been able to make it on the London stage or because they hoped for financial gain. Such imported actors as the flamboyant G. F. Cooke, the fiery Edmund Kean, and the elegant and eloquent William Charles Macready were tremendously popular with American audiences (although Edmund Kean was never forgiven for refusing to perform for a Boston audience he considered too small, and Macready was plagued by anti-British prejudices).

Gradually, though, America began to develop an acting

tradition of its own, led by such native-born actors as J. H. Hackett, the first major American actor to perform in England; the towering Edwin Forrest, whose rivalry with the British Macready culminated in a bloody riot in New York City that left thirty-one people dead; the great nineteenth-century actress Charlotte Cushman, who dazzled London with her performance as Romeo; and Edwin Booth, the best-loved actor of nineteenth-century America, most famous for his quiet and graceful Hamlet.

While city audiences were oohing and aahing English productions and actors were refining Shakespeare on stately stages in wealthy old cities, out on the frontier people were just having a good old time. Rough, rugged, and rowdy themselves, they responded heartily to Shakespeare's melodrama, spectacle, bloodshed, and oratory; plays that exemplified these virtues—*Richard III*, *Hamlet*, *Othello*, and *Julius Caesar*—were performed over and over again in saloons and mining camps, in billiard halls and village halls, and on Mississippi riverboats and wagon trains plodding West. And in the 1840s, a band of Seminole Indians gave a new twist to frontier Shakespeare: they attacked a traveling company in Florida, appropriated their costumes, and were later taken into custody wearing the costumes of *Othello*, *Hamlet*, and *Julius Caesar*!

Frontier people especially loved Shakespeare's rhetoric —the force and power of shouted passages, the grandeur of accumulated phrases, the patterns of the speeches. They weren't put off by his vocabulary because they themselves used a lot of tall talk and often created words with suffixes and prefixes—"bodacious,""monstropolous," and "exflunctificate." They weren't alone in this; speechmaking had been a way of life in American politics even before Patrick Henry uttered his famous one-liner, "Give me liberty or give me death!" Oratory was practically a national pastime and made Americans all the more receptive to Shakespeare on the stage. The American poet Walt Whitman used to ride down Broadway in the old omnibuses declaiming passages from *Julius Caesar* or *Richard III* to bemused passersby.

That Shakespeare has lived through many of the crises and triumphs of American history is indisputable; his place in *the* national consciousness is assured. Once, long ago, before America had even become a nation, the playwright even saved someone's life: in 1764, an officer missed an Indian ambush because he was floating down the river in a canoe at the time—reading *Antony and Cleopatra*!

VERSIONS AND REVERSIONS

IF SHAKESPEARE CROSSES national borders with the ease of a man on a flying trapeze, he also traverses the boundaries of genre with equal aplomb. Through the centuries his plays have been made into operas, ballets, films, novels, poems, and musicals—not to mention a spate of burlesques and parodies. Like Falstaff in *Henry IV Part 2*, Shakespeare is not only witty in himself, but the cause that wit is in other men.

Hundreds of composers and librettists have created operas out of Shakespeare's plays. Although separated by nearly three hundred years, both Henry Purcell (in 1692) and Benjamin Britten (in 1960) have "operatized" *A Midsummer Night's Dream*. *Hamlet*, *Macbeth*, *The Tempest*, and *Romeo and Juliet* are all now operas as well as plays. Some of the greatest composers of every generation find themselves challenged and inspired by Shakespeare. The Italian composer Verdi, having already composed the operas of *Macbeth* and *Falstaff*, capped his career with perhaps his greatest achievement, *Otello*, in which the Moor's tragedy is heightened and intensified by the majesty of Verdi's music.

Ballets, too, abound: *Romeo and Juliet* and *A Midsummer Night's Dream* seem to be the most popular of these. The choreographer George Balanchine took on the latter; Kenneth MacMillan the former. Mendelssohn, Tchaikovsky, and Prokofiev are but a few of the composers to have written music for Shakespearean ballets.

Shakespeare and the stage musical have also enjoyed a long and happy partnership. There was a 1976 musical called *Rockababy Hamlet*, a rock version of *Othello* called *Catch My Soul*, and a Tony award-winning musical of *The Two Gentlemen of Verona* with a distinctly black and Puerto Rican flavor. In 1939, the jazz greats Louis Armstrong and Benny Goodman created *Swingin' the Dream*, a black musical adaptation of *A Midsummer Night's Dream*, with Louis Armstrong as Bottom the Fireman, Moms Mabley as Quince the Midwife, and Butterfly McQueen as Puck in a wild midsummer night's romp down in New Orleans. Cole Porter's *Kiss Me Kate* is a justly famous musical version of *The Taming of the Shrew*. Songwriters Rodgers and Hart came up with *The Boys From Syracuse*, an immensely popular version of *The Comedy of Errors*. And everyone knows of *West Side Story*, the Broadway hit in which Romeo and Juliet became Tony and Maria, the Montagues and the Capulets became the Jets and the Sharks, and Verona became a community of Puerto Rican and Italian immigrants in New York City.

Playwrights, too, have had fun with Shakespeare's plays, creating extra characters, changing the plot, or focusing on one aspect of a play. The best-known of these spinoffs is probably Tom Stoppard's *Rosencrantz and Guildenstern Are Dead*, in which Hamlet's two friends, who have only minor roles in Shakespeare's play, become central characters around whom the tragedy is acted out. Stoppard is very clever at this sort of thing; he also wrote a fifteen-minute version of *Hamlet* to be performed on double-decker buses in London.

Shakespeare has always been an obvious target for writers of parody and burlesque, who take his well-known plays and characters and comically distort them, usually adding in a heavy measure of social and political satire. These enjoyed a heyday in the nineteenth century. Such titles as *A Thin Slice of Ham-let!*, *As You Lump It*, and *Antony and Cleopatra; or His-story and Her-story in a Modern Nilo-meter* are indications of the irreverent approach of these parodists. As the prologue to an 1856 burlesque of *The Winter's Tale* announces, "I'm here as the Chorus. The fact is, this play, As written by Shakespeare, won't do in our day."

One of the funnier American ones, *Much Ado About a Merchant of Venice*, is set in the New York City of the 1860s, and of course tells us more about life in the city at that time—the immigrant population, the prominence of Wall Street, legal corruption, political machines—than it does about Shakespeare's play. Antonio and Shylock are financiers on Wall Street; Nerissa is Portia's Irish maid; and Portia disguises herself as a "Philadelphia lawyer."

Puns and topical remarks are the order of the day: "He jests at scars that never felt a wound" (from *Romeo and Juliet*) becomes "He jests at cigars who never learned to smoke." Shylock's grievances against Antonio center on the stock market:

> Many's the time, sir, when we've chanced to meet,
> He's treated me most shameful on the street.
> Told me that stocks were up when they were
> down;
> Made me the laughing stocks of all the town.

And the message on the casket that Bassanio chooses to win Portia advises him, "You've chosen well, your wife is no virago; Get married soon, and don't go to Chicago."

In recent decades, filmmakers have joined the long line of Shakespeare borrowers, capitalizing on the cinematic nature of Shakespeare's stagecraft: no curtains, no rigid act division, and a progression of rapidly-switching scenes. Movies of his plays began with the silent film, which is hard to believe given that Shakespeare's language is so central to his work. Sarah Bernhardt was in silent-film excerpts playing Hamlet, and a 1920 German film of *Hamlet*, based on a number of sources, unveiled its hero at the end as a woman! With the introduction of sound in 1927, Shakespearean filmmaking took a big step forward; Hollywood can now boast that some of the biggest movie stars of our time have starred in these films— Marlon Brando, Charlton Heston, Richard Burton, and Elizabeth Taylor.

Hollywood has no monopoly on Shakespearean films; they circle the globe: a Czech puppet film of *A Midsummer Night's Dream; Ophelia*, a French adaptation of *Hamlet;* and Japanese interpretations of *Macbeth* and *King Lear* — *Throne of Blood* and *Ran*, by the director Akira Kurosawa. Orson Welles filmed *Othello* and concocted a Falstaffian brew called *Chimes at Midnight;* and the great British actor and director Laurence Olivier made famous movie versions of *Henry V*, *Richard III*, and *Hamlet*, which more people are estimated to have seen in the last thirty years than have seen the plays in the four hundred years since Shakespeare's birth.

Perversions on
the English Stage

SHAKESPEARE'S PLAYS HAVE also traveled through centuries of stage presentation, each age interpreting him in accord with what was both popular and possible. The results have sometimes been horrendous, sometimes quite successful, but always interesting in what they tell us about the tastes of the time and what they show us about Shakespeare's seemingly endless capacity to adapt and survive.

In England, after nearly twenty years of life without theater under Puritan rule, the English stage was brought back when the monarchy was restored in the 1660s. Unfortunately, the rage for "restoration" extended to Shakespeare's plays, too, often with disastrous effects. To the sophisticated and elegant new Court, the stage tactics and dramatic techniques of the Globe seemed dreadfully primitive and wholly unsuitable to the glitter of the Restoration stage. Rather than regarding Shakespeare as supreme and his work as sacred, they considered the plays "a heap of jewels, unstrung and unpolished," and greatly in need of stringing.

Unburdened by four centuries of literary history, theater managers and actors set about bringing Shakespeare up to snuff for their purposes by making the plays heroic, balanced, grammatically "correct"—in other words, modern. Nahum Tate has gone down in history (or infamy) as the adaptor who gave *King Lear* a happy ending and made Edgar and Cordelia fall in love and get married. Even Tate had doubts about the happy ending "till I found it well-receiv'd by my audience."

Now that women were permitted to act, Shakespeare was expanded to accommodate these new players. The poet John Dryden collaborated with theater manager (and alleged godson of Shakespeare, if not the illegitimate son he hinted he might be) William Davenant to create a truly horrific perversion of *The Tempest*, in which Miranda has a sister Dorinda, Ariel a sweetheart, and Caliban a sister who's as monstrous as he is. The play is full of the bawdy suggestive jokes that were fashionable at the time, and the entire production strangles the spirited life right out of Shakespeare.

Although we scorn these adaptations as acts of vandalism at the shrine of Shakespeare's plays, they were immensely popular with audiences, and in fact succeeded in driving the real Shakespeare into hiding for centuries. Shakespeare "improved"—cut, rewritten, adapted, and embellished—continued to be quite the fashionable thing throughout the eighteenth century. Adapting fever was still running high; even the great tragic actor of the age, David Garrick, wasn't immune to it. In addition to his condensed version of *The Taming of the Shrew*, he also tried his hand at *Romeo and Juliet*, altering the ending to reunite the lovers before they died.

Many profit-thirsty theater managers of the eighteenth century thought it perfectly reasonable to spice up Shakespeare with light entertainment—songs, dances, and interludes between acts or even during the course of the play. An advertisement for *Romeo and Juliet* gave equal billing to "the Nautical Drama (founded on the popular ballad) called *Black Eyed Susan*" and promised "A Masquerade and Dance" in Act 1 as well as "the Funeral Procession of Juliet, and a Solemn Dirge" in Act 5. It was also a common practice to introduce a flashy afterpiece at the play's end, which might include musical farce, acrobatic feats, hornpipe dances, pantomime, even a man who could catch a peacock feather level on his forehead!

All these additions were designed to feed the public's appetite for spectacle. The eighteenth century preferred to consume its Shakespeare with as much visual excitement as possible, and the theater managers, equipped with innovations like painted scenery and artificial lighting, were only too happy to oblige. But critics felt differently. "Three fourths of every audience," grumbled one, "are more capable of enjoying sound and show, than solid sense and poetical imagination."

The nineteenth century gave mixed signals about its Shakespeare. On the one hand, there was a worthy movement afoot to restore Shakespeare's original texts, to do away with the botched and butchered versions of seventeenth- and eighteenth-century adaptors. But on the other hand, it was the age of blockbuster effects, of unparalleled scenic splendor designed according to the strictest principles of historical authenticity—and the real Shakespeare too often got lost beneath all the hoopla. For example, one actor-manager, Charles Kean, rummaged through books of English history and medieval heraldry and then added to *Richard II* an extravagant pageant for Bolingbroke's entry into London, a scene that employed five or six hundred extras onstage.

Such an approach gave new meaning to Shakespeare's reference in *Romeo and Juliet* to the "two hours' traffic of our stage." Sometimes audiences had to wait nearly an hour between scenes while the elaborate sets were bullied into place. And, not surprisingly, Shakespeare's poetry was swamped by the weighty scenery and magnificent visual effects.

But although he may have been buried alive, Shakespeare somehow managed to survive as the ponderous nineteenth-century sets tottered their way into well-deserved oblivion. And long after the names of Nahum Tate, David Garrick, and Charles Kean have been forgotten, the name of the poet who was the cause of all this effort lives on, as it has continued to live for nearly four centuries.

AND TODAY?

SHAKESPEARE HAS BEEN just as successful on the modern stage as he was in the Globe. His plays have attracted such American actors as Meryl Streep, Raul Julia, Martin Sheen, Kevin Kline, James Earl Jones, and Elizabeth McGovern, all of whom have graced the stage in New York Shakespeare Festival productions.

As in previous ages, the staging of Shakespeare in the twentieth century reflects the tenor of the times. Orson Welles depicted Julius Caesar as a fascist dictator in 1937; Hamlet appeared as an inspiring man of action in a 1945 production given for American G.I.'s. The 1960s saw a burlesque version of *Macbeth* making fun of American politics, called *Macbird;* and in a production by Jewish senior citizens in a Brooklyn old folks home, an eighty-two-year-old Romeo turned to a seventy-year-old Juliet and asked, "You Jewish?"

There have been all-black, all-male, and all-female stagings of Shakespeare. The first recorded black acting company in America opened in lower Manhattan with *Richard III* in 1821. Over a century later, in 1936, Orson Welles produced his "voodoo" *Macbeth* at the Lafayette Theater in Harlem with a cast of one hundred blacks. Set in Haiti, with real witch doctors, jungle drums, and cackling voodoo priestesses, it was an eerie spectacle and a huge hit. In 1979, the New York Shakespeare Festival assembled an all-black company that performed *Julius Caesar* and *Coriolanus*. *As You Like It* was staged in the late 1960s with an all-male cast in modern dress. Recently, *The Taming of the Shrew* was performed by a cast of women in an interpretation intended to highlight what they saw as the play's now-outmoded expressions of chauvinism. And in 1986, at the Belasco Theater on Broadway, a company of Afro-American, Hispanic, and Asian-American actors performed Shakespeare's plays for New York City high-school students, under the auspices of the New York Shakespeare Festival.

In our century, when the director has taken on a much greater role in interpreting and guiding a play, there are as many different approaches to Shakespeare's work as there are people to think them up. Hamlet may be an adolescent in the grip of an unresolved Oedipal complex or a resolute man of action; *The Comedy of Errors* takes place in Edwardian England on one stage and in the American West among cowhands and ranchers on another stage. Whatever the interpretation, it seems that Shakespeare's plays are so expansive and flexible that they can accommodate any race, creed, color, gender, or directorial approach. Not all versions work equally well, but together they illustrate how one writer's plays can mean such very different things to different people.

SHAKESPEARE ALIVE!

THE REAL MYSTERY is *why*.

How is it that Shakespeare can continue to entertain, inspire, and instruct people all around the world? Is it the themes he addresses? Is it that the human dilemmas he explores transcend specific centuries and particular civilizations? As a British soldier wrote from the trenches in World War I, "There is no hardship or terror or doubt that happens out here that Shakespeare does not touch on or give advice for"; a copy of *Henry V* was found on his body when he died. The terrible randomness of suffering, the conflict of justice and mercy, the nature of power and the individual, life within a family, the transforming magic of love—Shakespeare works and reworks these themes in all of his plays. Such concerns don't go away; they are an eternal part of the human condition. Is *this* what keeps Shakespeare alive?

Or does it have something to do with the wide range of his sources? Shakespeare plundered legends and stories from many cultures, and in rewriting them for the theater gave them new and enduring life. And, of course, he himself became a source that subsequent artists would quarry, using him as he used his predecessors, as a springboard for their own creativity. Is *this* what keeps Shakespeare alive?

Perhaps it's the language his characters speak. Although some of Shakespeare's vocabulary has become archaic and his syntax and grammar obsolete, the rhythms of his lines and the sounds of his words retain their extraordinary power and remarkable emotional expressiveness. As one fan enthused in the late 1700s, "In his native tongue he shall roll the genuine passions of nature." Is *this* what keeps Shakespeare alive?

Maybe it's his astonishing characters, so full of vitality that they practically jump off the page. Each of them seems to have a life elsewhere, which the play glimpses only momentarily. And yet so real and vibrant are they that one Victorian author was inspired to invent biographies of the childhoods of Rosalind, Celia, Portia, Desdemona, and all of Shakespeare's heroines, leading up to the point where the plays begin.

But though they may seem to have lives elsewhere, they *truly* come to life only on the stage. Shakespeare's characters are creatures of the theater; they exist not to be dissected and psychoanalyzed but to be performed. Falstaff couldn't exist without an audience to show off for and a stage to prance and play on; Cleopatra craves a theater for her melodramatic histrionics; and where would Richard III be if he couldn't confide in us?

This insistent vitality isn't just expressed by major characters like Falstaff, Cleopatra, Hamlet, Rosalind, or Richard; Shakespeare breathes life into even the most insignificant of his stage creatures—the spear carriers, the servants, the children, and the minor courtiers. Think of the prisoner Barnardine in *Measure for Measure*, who throws a monkey wrench into the duke's plot by refusing to die at the convenient time; the Capulets' servant Peter in *Romeo and Juliet*, who grieves profoundly at Juliet's supposed death; and the nameless servant of Gloucester in *King Lear* who runs to fetch flax and egg whites to soothe his blinded master's bleeding face.

All of Shakespeare's characters, from talkative Hamlet to the lowliest one-line speaker, are both *of* life and larger than life. And they will continue to hold on to that life as long as they have a theater somewhere. Is *this* what keeps Shakespeare alive?

The answer to the question, of course, is all of the above. Shakespeare's universal themes and human concerns, his rhythmic language and great stories, as well as his lively theatrical characters, are all part of what keeps Shakespeare alive.

And yet, centuries of change might easily have killed him off. Our language and vocabulary, as well as our world view and our understanding of religion; the rights accorded to women and minorities; our standard of living; our understanding of the ways and values of other nations; the behavior of the family; the way our theaters are organized, equipped, and run; the tastes and preferences of the audience—all these things are drastically different from what Shakespeare knew in sixteenth-century England.

In spite of these changes he continues to speak to us —from the wings of the theater. The comic effect of the scene in *Love's Labor's Lost* where each of the four young men eavesdrop on the next, till they are four deep listening to each other's confessions of love, is difficult for us to visualize as readers. Likewise, the cold-blooded cruelty of Goneril and Regan comes across in all its horrific barbarity only when we *see* the blinding of old Gloucester carried out in front of our eyes. The funny business of the

frightened jester Trinculo creeping under the long gaber-
dine of the monster Caliban in *The Tempest* is less vivid
when it's not seen onstage. And the utter comedy of Falstaff's cowardice in the theater renders pointless all armchair analyses of his personality by critics. As a German
poet said early in the twentieth century, "the true readers
of Shakespeare and also those in whom Shakespeare is
truly alive are those who carry within them a stage."

No doubt Shakespeare would be astonished to discover
that his plays are still being performed, let alone read, and
are widely hailed as the greatest dramatic works of all
time. After all, he dashed them off, two a year, with little
thought beyond the next day's takings at the Globe, and
whether or not they would be enough to pay the rent.
They were temporary, transient pieces of entertainment,
conceived and written to satisfy the particular tastes of a
particular audience in a particular time and place, and
definitely *not* sacred works of art to be enshrined.

This is the paradox of it all: the quickly-vanishing me-
dium for which Shakespeare wrote—the theater—is precisely what keeps him alive and well today. In adapting
his sources, his language, his characters for the stage, he
transformed them into something immortal. The plays,
the dramatic events that thrilled and delighted Elizabethan audiences nearly four hundred years ago, live on
in the twentieth century, re-created every time an actor
steps up to the footlights and begins to utter the lines of
Hamlet. For as long as the theater continues, and as long
as actors, directors, and producers remain committed to
putting the works of the world's greatest playwright on
the stage where they belong—so, too, will Shakespeare
stay alive.

BIBLIOGRAPHY

(in order of appearance)

CHAPTER 1: DAILY LIFE

GIVE US THIS DAY OUR DAILY BREAD

Thomas, Keith, *Religion and the Decline of Magic* (1971), Chapter 1

Wrightson, Keith, and Levine, David, *Poverty and Piety in an English Village* (1979)

Wrightson, Keith, *English Society 1580–1680* (1982)

Clark, Alice, *The Working Life of Women in the Seventeenth Century* (1919, reprint 1968)

Appleby, Andrew, *Famine in Tudor and Stuart England* (1978)

[p. 5] in Appleby, op. cit.

[p. 5–6] the High Sheriff of Somerset, in Clark, op. cit.

HITTING THE ROAD

Lee, Sidney, and Onions, C. T., *Life in Shakespeare's England* (1917)

Beier, A. L., "Vagrants and the Social Order in Elizabethan England," *Past and Present* 64 (1974)

Slack, P., "Vagrants and Vagrancy in England," *Economic History Review*, second series xxvii (1974)

[p. 7] Stubbes, Philip, *Anatomy of Abuses*, (1583) ed. F. J. Furnivall, (New Shakespere Society 1877–82) Series VI, nos. 4, 6, 12

THE CITY THAT NEVER SLEEPS

Stow, John, *Survey of London* (1603), ed. C. L. Kingsford (1908)

Hudson, K., *The Woman's Place in Society* (1970)

Drummond, J. C., and Wilbraham, A., *The Englishman's Food* (1957)

Appleby, A., "Diet in Sixteenth Century England: sources, problems, and possibilities," in *Health, Medicine, and Mortality in Sixteenth Century England*, ed. C. Webster (1979)

Harrison, William, *Description of England* (1577, 1587, ed. G. Edelen, 1968)

Clark, Peter, *The English Alehouse* (1983)

Richardson, A. E., and Eberlein, H. D., *The English Inn, Past and Present* (1968)—good pictures

Forbes, T. R., "By What Disease or Casualty: The Changing Face of Death in London," in *Health, Medicine, and Mortality in Sixteenth Century England*, ed. C. Webster (1979)

Thomas, K., op. cit.

Wolf, A., *A History of Science, Technology, and Philosophy in the Sixteenth and Seventeenth Centuries* (1950)

Draper, J. W., *The Humors and Shakespeare's Characters* (1945)

Stone, Lawrence, "The Educational Revolution in England," *Past and Present* 28 (1964)

Briggs, Julia *This Stage-Play World* (1983)

Wright, L. B., *Middle-Class Culture in Elizabethan England* (1958)

Spufford, Margaret, *Small Books and Pleasant Histories* (1981)

Meyer, A. O., *England and the Catholic Church under Queen Elizabeth* (1967 edn.)

Chew, Samuel, *The Crescent and the Rose* (1937)

Harrison, G. B., *The Elizabethan Journals* (1955), for 28 February 1596

Lee and Onions, op. cit.

Rye, W. B., op. cit.

ADDITIONAL RECOMMENDATIONS

Hurstfield, J., and Smith, A.G.R., *Elizabethan People* (1972)—an anthology of contemporary writings on the age

Wilson, John Dover, *Life in Shakespeare's England* (1968)—contemporary writings

CHAPTER 2: THE RENAISSANCE

GENERAL

Briggs, Julia, *This Stage-Play World* (1983)

Rowse, A. L., *The Elizabethan Renaissance* (1972)

Neale, J. E. Neale, *Essays in Elizabethan History* (1958)

THE BESTSELLER LIST

Einstein, L., *The Italian Renaissance in England* (1902)

Rowse, A. L., op. cit.

Stone, op. cit. on education

WHICH WAY IS UP?

Wolf, A., op. cit.

Miller, H. H., *Captains of Devon* (1985)

[p. 20] Samuel Purchas, quoted in Miller, op. cit.

Hakluyt, Richard, *Voyages and Discoveries*, J. Beeching ed. (1972)

Dodd, A. H., "Mr. Myddelton the Merchant of Tower Street", in S. T. Bindoff, J. Hurstfield, C. H. Williams, ed., *Elizabethan Government and Society: Essays Presented to Sir John Neale* (1961)

Chew, Samuel, op. cit.

A MIGHTY FORTRESS

Meyer, A. O., *England and the Catholic Church under Elizabeth* (1967)

[p. 23] in Meyer, op. cit.

McGrath, Patrick, *Papists and Puritans Under Elizabeth I* (1967)

Collinson, Patrick, *The Elizabethan Puritan Movement* (1967)

Smith, Lacy Baldwin, *Elizabeth Tudor, Portrait of a Queen* (1975)

[p. 24] the deposition of Henry Barrow, in "The Egerton Papers," *Camden Society Publications* #12 (1840)

Pritchard, Arnold, *Catholic Loyalism in England* (1979)

[p. 25] quoted in "The Egerton Papers," op. cit.

[p. 25] quoted in Meyer, op. cit.

Morris, J. Allen, *Richard Topcliffe: "A Most Humble Pursuivant of Her Majesty"* (1964)

Stenton, D. M., *The Englishwoman in History* (1957)

[p. 26] in Thomas, Keith, "Age and Authority in Early Modern England," *Proceedings of the British Academy* 62 (1976)

A MOST EXCELLENT AND PERFECT ORDER?

Briggs, op. cit.

Fletcher, A., and Stevenson, J., *Order and Disorder in Early Modern England* (1985)

[p. 27] "Homily on Obedience," quoted in A. F. Kinney, *Elizabethan Backgrounds* (1975) (three quotations)

[p. 28] Act of Apparel, in *Camden Society Publications* #12 (1840)

[p. 28] Stubbes, Philip, op. cit.

Tillyard, E. M. W., *The Elizabethan World Picture* (1943)

Thomas, Keith, *Man and the Natural World* (1983)

James, Mervyn, "English Politics and the Concept of Honor," in *Society, Politics, and Culture* (1986)

[p. 31] Sir Thomas Elyot, "Book Named the Governor," in Kinney, op. cit.

CHAPTER 3: SUPERSTITION AND THE SUPERNATURAL

Sullivan, George, *Sports Superstitions* (1978), for anecdote about the black cat at the baseball game

Thomas, Keith, *Religion and the Decline of Magic* (1971)

[p. 33] Scot, Reginald, *The Discovery of Witchcraft*, ed. Montague Summers (1930) [p. 33] in Thomas, K., op. cit.

Hill, Christopher, "Plebeian Irreligion in Seventeenth Century England," in *Studien uber die Revolution*, ed. M. Kossok (1969)

[p. 33] Hill, op. cit.

[p. 34] in Dickens, A. G., *Lollards and Protestants in the Diocese of York, 1509–1558* (1959)

Monter, E. W., *Ritual, Myth, and Magic in Early Modern Europe* (1984)

[p. 35] Thomas, op. cit.

Scot, op. cit.

STAR-STRUCK

Allen, D. C., *The Star-Crossed Renaissance* (1941)

Sondheim, M., "Shakespeare and the Astrology of His Time," *Journal of the Warburg Institute* ii (1939)

Stone, W. B., "Shakespeare and the Sad Augurs," *Journal of English and Germanic Philology* lii (1953)

Tillyard, op. cit.

Briggs, K. M., *The Anatomy of Puck* (1959)

[p. 36] Digges, Leonard, *Prognostication . . . for ever* (Old Ashmolean Reprint, 1926)

Rowse, A. L., *The Elizabethan Renaissance* (1972)

[p. 39] Digges, op. cit.

GHOST-BUSTED

Thomas, op. cit.

[p. 39] Nashe, Thomas, "The Terrors of the Night," in *The Unfortunate Traveller and Other Works*, ed. J. B. Steane (1971)

Stoll, E. E., "The Objectivity of Ghosts in Shakespeare," *Proceedings of the Modern Language Association* xxii (1907)

FAIRY-TAILED

Briggs, K. M., *The Anatomy of Puck* (1959)

Latham, M. W., *The Elizabethan Fairies* (1930)

Packer, Alison, *Fairies in Legends and in the Arts* (1980)

[p. 41] Scot, op. cit.

SPELL-BOUND

Scot, Reginald, *The Discovery of Witchcraft*, ed. Montague Summers (1930)

Thomas, op. cit.

[p. 43] Scot, op. cit.

Ewen, C. L. *Witchcraft and Demonianism* (1933)

[p. 43] Ewen, op. cit.

[p. 44] Scot, op. cit.

Kittredge, *Witchcraft in Old and New England* (1956)

[p. 45] episode in Ewen, op. cit.

[p. 45] episode in Kittredge, op. cit.

[p. 46] remedy in Scot, op. cit.

HOUSE CALLS

Thomas, op. cit.

Rowse, op. cit.

[p. 47] Kittredge, op. cit. for headache remedy #1 and warts solution

[p. 47] Scot, op. cit. for headache remedy #2

[p. 47] Scot, op. cit.

CHAPTER 4: FOREIGNERS
AND IMMIGRANTS

Hunter, G. K., "Elizabethans and Foreigners," in *Dramatic Identities and Cultural Tradition* (1978) [p. 48] Rye, W. B., *England as seen by Foreigners* (1865), Emanuel van Meteren's comment

[p. 48–9] John Stow, in F. M. Wilson, *They Came as Strangers* (1959)

[p. 49] Rathgeb, Duke of Wurtemburg's secretary, quoted in F. M. Wilson, *Strange Island: Britain through Foreign Eyes 1395–1940* (1955)

Meyer, op. cit.

[p. 50] Lady Russell, quoted in D. M. Stenton, *The Englishwoman in History* (1957)

Duffy, M., *The Englishman and the Foreigner* (1986)

[p. 51] Nashe, Thomas, *Pierce Penniless His Supplication to the Devil*, in Steane, op. cit.

[p. 52] quoted in Georgiana Hill, op. cit. (1896)

TURNING TURK

Chew, Samuel, op. cit.

[p. 53] Richard Knolles, *The Generall Historie of the Turkes*, in Chew, op. cit.

Horniker, A. L., "William Harborne and Anglo-Turkish Relations", *Journal of Modern History* xiv (3) (1942)

Baumer, F. L. "England, the Turks, and the Common Corps of Christendom," *American Historical Review* 1 (1944–5)

[p. 53] in Baumer, op. cit.

OUT OF AFRICA

Little, K., *Negroes in Britain* (1972)

Miller, W. E., *Notes and Queries* 8 (1961), "Negroes in Elizabethan London"

Jones, Eldred, ibid., on evidence of Africans in Elizabethan England

[p. 54] Jones, op. cit

Tokson, Elliot, *The Popular Image of the Black Man in English Drama* (1982) [p. 56] Scot, Reginald, op. cit.

Jones, Eldred, *The Elizabethan Image of Africa* (1971)

George, K., "The Civilized West Looks at Primitive Africa," *Isis* 49 (1958)

[p. 57] John Lok, quoted in Hakluyt, *Voyages and Discoveries*, op. cit.

Chew, op. cit.

JOINING THE JEWS

Roth, Cecil, *The History of the Jews in England* (1941)

Wolf, Lucien, "Jews in Tudor England," *Essays in Jewish History* (1934)

——— "Jews in Elizabethan England," *Transactions of the Jewish Historical Society of England* xi (1926), including the quotation from the Spanish prisoner on Jews' observance of rites in London

Sisson, C. J., "A Colony of Jews in Shakespeare's England," *Essays and Studies* xxiii (1938)

Cunningham, W., *Alien Immigrants to England* (1894 repr. 1969)

[p. 58–9] Wolf, "Jews in Elizabethan England," op. cit.

Katz, D., *Philosemitism and the Re-admission of the Jews to England* 1603–1655 (1982), chapter one

Times Literary Supplement, May 12, 1950, letter from E. A. B. Barnard on Lopez' manor house near Stratford

Harrison, G. B., *The Elizabethan Journals* (1955) for 1594

Camden, William, *The Historie of Elizabeth Queen of England* (1630)

ARMADAS AND ARMADOS

Neale, J. E., *Queen Elizabeth* (1934)

Duffy, op. cit.

Meyer, A. O., op. cit.

Maltby, W. S., *The Black Legend in England: The Development of Anti-Spanish Sentiment* (1971)

[p. 63] in Maltby, op. cit.

DUTCH TREAT, PETTY FRANCE

Cunningham, W., *Alien Immigrants to England* (1894 repr. 1969)

[p. 64] in Meyer, A. O., op. cit.

Duffy, M., op. cit.

Nicolson, C., *Strangers to England: Immigration to England 1100–1952* (1974)

[p. 65] in Nicolson, op. cit.

[p. 65] John Stow, quoted in F. M. Wilson, *They Came As Strangers* (1959)

Tretiak, A., "The Anti-Alien Riots in England," *Review of English Studies* v (1929)

CHAPTER 5: QUEEN ELIZABETH AND THE STATUS OF WOMEN

WOMEN'S STUDIES

Mahl, M., and Koon, H., *The Female Spectator: English Women Writers Before 1800* (1977)

Hill, Georgiana, *Women in English Life* (1896)

[p. 69] Hill, op. cit.

Phillips, M., and Tomkinson, W. S., *English Women in Life and Letters* (1926)

Hogrefe, P., *Women of Action in Tudor England* (1977)

[p. 70] Nicholas Udall, headmaster of Eton, in Hill, op. cit.

Camden, Carroll, *The Elizabethan Woman* (1952)

[p. 70] Richard Mulcaster, quoted in Camden, op. cit.

[p. 70] quoted in Camden, ibid.

Notestein, W. "The English Woman 1580–1650", in *Studies in Social History*, ed. J. H. Plumb (1955)

[p. 71] in Notestein, op. cit.

Jardine, Lisa, *Still Harping on Daughters* (1983)

Stenton, D. M., *The Englishwoman in History* (1957)

[p. 71] quoted in Stenton, op. cit. (all)

WOMEN'S WORK

Clark, Alice, *The Working Life of Women in the Seventeenth Century* (1919 repr. 1968)

[p. 72] Sir Anthony Fitzherbert, *Book of Husbandry*, quoted in Clark, op. cit.

[p. 72–3] Emmanuel Van Meteren in W. B. Rye, *England as Seen by Foreigners (1865)*

SECOND-CLASS

Houlbrooke, Ralph, *The English Family 1450–1700* (1984)

[p. 73] in Stenton, op. cit.

[p. 74] van Meteren, in Rye, op. cit.

Hogrefe, op. cit.

[p. 74] T. E., *The Lawes Resolution of Women's Rights*, quoted in Stenton, op. cit. (three quotations)

[p. 75] Camden, op. cit. (two quotations)

Stubbes, Philip, op. cit.

[p. 75] Stubbes, op. cit.

Henderson, K., and McManus, M., *Half Humankind: Contexts and Texts of the Controversy About Women in England, 1540–1640* (1985)

[p. 77] Joseph Swetnam, "The Arraignment of lewd, idle, forward, and unconstant women . . . ," (1615) in Henderson and McManus, op. cit. (two quotations)

[p. 77] Esther Sowernam, "Esther hath hanged Haman," (1617) in Henderson and McManus, op. cit. (two quotations)

MEANWHILE, BACK ON THE THRONE . . .

Neale, J. E., *Queen Elizabeth* (1934)

Heisch, A., "Queen Elizabeth and the Persistence of Patriarchy", *Feminist Review* 4 (1980)

Smith, Lacy Baldwin, *Elizabeth Tudor* (1975)

[p. 78] Rowse, A. L., *The Elizabethan Renaissance* (1972), quoting J. E. Neale, *Elizabeth I and her Parliaments*

Levine, Joseph, *Elizabeth I* (1969)

[p. 79] John Aylmer, quoted in Levine, op. cit.

[p. 79] quoted in Neale, op. cit.

[p. 80] John Knox, quoted in Neale, op. cit.

[p. 81] Neale, op. cit.

[p. 81] quoted in Levine, op. cit.

MacCaffrey, W. T., "Place and Patronage in Elizabethan Politics," in *Elizabethan Government and Society*, ed. Bindoff, et al. (1961)

[p. 82] Rye, op. cit.

Jardine, op. cit.

Strong, Roy, *The Cult of Elizabeth* (1977)

[p. 83] Neale op. cit.

[p. 83] quoted in Levine, op. cit.

CHAPTER 6: FAMILY LIFE

GENERAL

Houlbrooke, Ralph, *The English Family 1450–1700* (1984)

Stone, Lawrence, *The Family, Sex, and Marriage in England 1500–1800* (1977)

Wrightson, *English Society 1580–1680* (1982)

DEATH COMES A'KNOCKING'

Schofield, R. and Wrigley, E. A., "Infant and Child Mortality" in *Health, Medicine and Mortality in Sixteenth Century England*, ed. C. Webster (1979)

Forbes, Thomas, "By What Disease or Casualty: The Changing Face of Death in London", in ibid.

IN THE NURSE'S ARMS

Maclaren, D., "Marital Fertility and Lactation 1570–1720," in *Women in English Society 1500–1800*, ed. M. Prior (1985)

[p. 88] quoted in Maclaren, op. cit.

A FIRM BUT LOVING HAND

[p. 88] quoted in Wrightson, op. cit.

[p. 89] in Mahl and Koon, *The Female Spectator*

[p. 89] Mistress Dorothy Leigh, "The Mother's Blessing," quoted in Stenton, op. cit. (1957)

Thomas, K., "Age and Authority in Early Modern England," *Proceedings of the British Academy* 62 (1976)

HALFWAY HOUSE

Smith, S. R., "The London Apprentices," *Past and Present* 61 (1973)

OUT FROM UNDER

[p. 92] in Stone, op. cit.

THE PARTY'S OVER

Meads, D. M., *The Diary of Lady Margaret Hoby* (1930)

[p. 95] in Notestein, op. cit.

[p. 96] quoted in Houlbrooke, op. cit.

Hair, P.E.H., "Bridal Pregnancy," in *Population Studies* 24 (1970)

Quaife, G. E., *Wanton Wenches and Wayward Wives* (1969)

Wrightson, K., and Levine, D., "The Social Context of Illegitimacy in Early Modern England," in *Bastardy and Its Comparative History*, ed. P. Laslett, K. Oosterveen, and R. M. Smith (1980)

Macfarlane, A., "Illegitimacy and Illegitimates in English history" in ibid.

[p. 98] Stubbes, op. cit.

THE DYNAMIC DUO

[p. 100] Sir Thomas Hoby, in Meads, op. cit.

[p. 100] the Earl of Shrewsbury to his wife Bess (of Hardwick) quoted in Hogrefe, *Women of Action in Tudor England* (1977)

Todd, B. J. "The Remarrying Widow: a stereotype reconsidered" in Prior, M. op. cit. (1985)

CHAPTER 7: THE THEATRE IS BORN

THE WORLD BEFORE THE THEATRE

Bradbrook, M. C., *The Rise of the Common Player* (1964)

Bevington, D. M., *From Mankind to Marlowe* (1962)

[p. 108] Heywood, Thomas, *Apology for Actors* (1612) (Scholars' Facsimiles and Reprints, 1941)

[p. 108] in Bevington, op. cit.

Bradbrook, op. cit.

Gurr, Andrew, *The Shakespearean Stage, 1574–1642* (1980 edn.)

Schoenbaum, S., *William Shakespeare: A Compact Documentary Life* (1977)

Hosley, Richard, "Playhouses," in J. Leeds Barroll, Alexander Leggatt, Richard Hosley, and Alvin Kernan, *The Revels History of Drama in English*, Vol. 3, 1576–1613 (1975)

THE PLOT HEARD ROUND THE WORLD

Gurr, op. cit.

Hosley, op. cit.

Bevington, D. M., *Action is Eloquence* (1984)

Beckerman, *Shakespeare at the Globe* (1962)

[p. 112] Thomas Platter (1599), in F. M. Wilson, *Strange Island* (1955)

[p. 112] Paul Hentzner, *Travels*, quoted in A. Cohn, *Shakespeare in Germany in the Sixteenth and Seventeenth Centuries* (1865)

BATTLE LINES DRAWN

Chambers, E. K., The Elizabethan Stage (1923). 4 volumes

[p. 114] Chambers, op. cit., vol. 4

Gurr, op. cit.

Barroll, "Social and Literary Context," in *The Revels History*

[p. 115] in W. C. Hazlitt, *The English Drama and Stage Under the Tudor and Stuart Princes, 1543–1664* (1869)

Harbage, Alfred, *Shakespeare's Audience* (1941)

[p. 116] Stubbes, Philip, *Anatomy of Abuses*; the Reverend Mr. Spark, in the introduction to Gosson, *School of Abuse* (Arber English Reprint, 1868)

[p. 116] the Reverend Willcocks' sermon, 1577, quoted in ibid.

[p. 116–117] Gosson, Stephen, *Plays Confuted in Five Actions* (1582, reprinted in Hazlitt, op. cit.); ibid.; Gosson, *School of Abuse*, op. cit.; Stubbes, op. cit.; ibid.; *The Second and Third Blast of Retreat from Plays and Theater* (1580, reprinted in Hazlitt op. cit.)

[p. 117] sermon by John Stockwood, in introduction to Gosson's *School of Abuse*, op. cit.

[p. 118] Gosson, *Plays Confuted in Five Actions*, op. cit.

[p. 119] ibid.

[p. 119] Fynes Moryson, quoted in Gurr, *The Shakespearean Stage*

[p. 119] quoted in Bradbrook, *The Rise of the Common Player*

CHAPTER 8: THE ACTING COMPANIES

ORIGINS

Bevington, D. M., *From Mankind to Marlowe* (1962)

Bradbrook, M. C., op. cit.

DOUBLE TROUBLE

Leggatt, A., "Companies and Actors" in Barroll et al., op. cit.

[p. 123] Chambers, op. cit. Vol. 4

[p. 123] ibid.

[p. 124] ibid.

Gurr, op. cit.

Murray, J. T., *English Dramatic Companies 1558–1642* (1910)

Leggatt, op. cit.

Baldwin, T. W., *The Organization and Personnel of the Shakespearean Company* (1927)

[p. 125] John Stow, *Annales*, quoted in Bradbrook, op. cit.

Bradbrook, op. cit.

Gurr, op. cit.

Leggatt, in Barroll, op. cit.

[p. 126] Sir E. K. Chambers, op. cit. Volume 2; ibid.

[p. 126] ibid.

A RUNG ON THE LADDER

Gurr, op. cit.

Baldwin, op. cit.

Thomson, P. W., *Shakespeare's Theatre* (1983)

Bentley, G. E., op. cit.

Jamieson, M., "Shakespeare's Celibate Stage," in *The Seventeenth Century Stage*, ed. G. E. Bentley (1968)

[p. 128] Thomas Coryat, quoted in Jamieson, op. cit.

DOUBLE THE FUN

[p. 129] Thomas Platter, quoted in Harbage, op. cit.

Chambers, op. cit. Vol. 2 and 4

Beckerman, op. cit.

Leggatt, in Barroll, op. cit.

Thomson, op. cit.

[p. 131] quoted in Schoenbaum, op. cit.

GLOBAL DIMENSIONS

Baldwin, op. cit.

Gurr, op. cit.

Leggatt, op. cit.

Beckerman, op. cit.

Beckerman, op. cit.

Gurr, op. cit.

[p. 135] Cohn, A., op. cit.

Brennecke, E., *Shakespeare in Germany 1590–1700* (1964)

[p. 135] Moryson, quoted in Gurr, op. cit.

CHAPTER 9: PLAYWRIGHT AND AUDIENCE

WIELDING THE PEN

Bentley, G. E., *The Profession of the Dramatist in Shakespeare's Time* (1971)

[p. 136] Foakes, R., *Henslowe's Diary* (1977+)

Baldwin, op. cit.

Gurr, op. cit.

[p. 139] Thomas Heywood, preface to *The English Traveller*, quoted in Arthur Brown, "The Printing of Books," *Shakespeare Survey* 17 (1964)

[p. 139] ibid.

Bevington, D. M., *Action Is Eloquence* (1984)

WITH PATIENT EARS

Bevington, D. M., *From Mankind to Marlowe* (1962)

Gurr, op. cit.

Harbage, *Shakespeare's Audience* (1941)

Barroll, "Social and Literary Context," in Barroll, et al., op. cit.

[p. 142] Gosson, op. cit.

[p. 143] quoted in Harbage, op. cit.

[p. 143] Henry Crosse, 1603, quoted in Harbage

Bradbrook, op. cit.

[p. 144] Harbage, op. cit.

[p. 144] Gosson, op. cit.

Weimann, Robert, *Shakespeare and the Popular Tradition in the Theatre* (1978)

CHAPTER 10: PRODUCING A PLAY

Baldwin, op. cit.

Greg, W. W., *Dramatic Documents*

Gurr, op. cit.

Bentley, *The Profession of the Dramatist in Shakespeare's Time* (1971)

Barroll, "Social and Literary Context," in Barroll et al., op. cit.

[p. 147] in Barroll, op. cit.

Harbage, *Theatre for Shakespeare* (1955)

[p. 149] Nashe, "Summer's Last Will and Testament" in Steane, op. cit.

Armstrong, W. A., "Actors and Theatres," *Shakespeare Survey* 17 (1964)

Klein, David, "Did Shakespeare Produce His Own Plays?",
    Modern Language Review lvii (1962)

[p. 149] in Klein, op. cit.

Leggatt, in Barroll, et al., op. cit.

Dessen, Allen, *Elizabethan Drama and the Viewer's Eye* (1977)

Bevington, D. M., *Action is Eloquence* (1984)

Foakes, op. cit.

[p. 151] Thomas Platter, quoted in Gurr

Marker, Lise-Lone, "Nature and Decorum in the Theory of
    Elizabethan Acting," in *The Elizabethan Theatre* 2, ed. Gal-
    loway (1970)

Gurr, Andrew, "Elizabethan Action," *Studies in Philology* lxiii
    (1966)

Hunter, G. K., "Flatcaps and Bluecoats: Visual Signals on the
    Elizabethan Stage," *Essays and Studies* n.s. 3 (1980)

Weimann, op. cit.

CHAPTER 11: SOURCES AND RESOURCES

SHAKESPEARE'S READING LIST

Bullough, G., *Narrative and Dramatic Sources of Shakespeare*
    (1957), several volumes

Muir, K., *Shakespeare's Sources* (1977)

Hunter, G. K., "Seneca and the Elizabethans", in *Dramatic
    Identities and Cultural Tradition* (1978)

Jones, Emrys, *The Origins of Shakespeare* (1977)

Hunter, G. K., "Shakespeare's Reading," in K. Muir, and S.
    Schoenbaum, *A New Companion to Shakespeare Studies*
    (1971)

Wilson, F. P. "Shakespeare's Reading," *Shakespeare Survey* 3
    (1950)

Doran, Madeline, *Endeavors of Art* (1956)

Thomson, J.A.K., *Shakespeare and the Classics* (1966 [1952])

Spencer, T.J.B., "Shakespeare and Elizabethan Romans," *Shakespeare Survey* 10 (1957)

Walker, A., "The Reading of an Elizabethan," *Review of English Studies* viii (1932)

[p. 155] quoted in Walker, op. cit.

Thomson, op. cit.

Smith, B. R., "Seneca on the Renaissance Stage," *Renaissance Drama* 9 (1978)

Root, R. K., *Classical Mythology in Shakespeare* (1965 [1903])

Thomson, op. cit.

Doran, op. cit.

BIBLICAL BREEZES

Noble, R., *Shakespeare's Biblical Knowledge* (1935)

Milward, P., *Biblical Influences in Shakespeare's Great Tragedies* (1987)

TRAGICAL-POETICAL

Bullough, op. cit. (used in all subsequent sections)

Muir, op. cit.

Brooke, A., *The Tragicall History of Romeus and Juliet* (1562)

TRAGICAL-HISTORICAL

Smallwood, R. L., "Shakespeare's Use of History," in *The Cambridge Companion to Shakespeare Studies*, ed. S. Wells (1986)

Hosley, R., *Shakespeare's Holinshed* (1968)

TRAGICAL-PLUTARCHAL

Hunter, G. K., op. cit.

Spencer, T.J.B., *Shakespeare's Plutarch* (1964)

CHAPTER 12: ENGLISH AS A FOREIGN LANGUAGE

LENDING HIM OUR EARS

Brook, G. L., *The Language of Shakespeare* (1976)

Ewbank, Inga-Stina, "Shakespeare and the Arts of Language," in *The Cambridge Companion to Shakespeare Studies*, ed. Wells (1986)

Joseph, Sister Miriam, *Shakespeare's Use of the Arts of Language* (1947)

————,*Rhetoric in Shakespeare's Time* (1962)

Blake, N. F., *Shakespeare's Language: An Introduction* (1983)

Hussey, S. S., *The Literary Language of Shakespeare* (1982)

[p. 165] George Puttenham, *The Arte of English Poesie* in *English Critical Essays*, ed. G. G. Smith (1904), Vol. 1

Vickers, B., "Shakespeare's Use of Rhetoric," in K. Muir and S. Schoenbaum, *A New Companion to Shakespeare Studies* (1971)

Wilson, F. P., "Shakespeare and the Diction of Common Life," in *Shakespearian and Other Studies*, ed. Helen Gardner, (1969)

Mahood, M. M., *Shakespeare's Wordplay* (1965)

Byrne, Muriel St. Clare, "The Foundations of the Elizabethan Language," *Shakespeare Survey* 17 (1964)

FROM GOOD TO VERSE

Abbott, E. A., *A Shakespearian Grammar* (1966 [1870])

Brook, op. cit.

Blake, op. cit.

Doran, *Shakespeare's Dramatic Language* (1976)

CROSSING THE BORDER

Abbott, op. cit.

Blake, op. cit.

Brook, op. cit.

Quirk, R., "Shakespeare and the English Language," in Muir and Schoenbaum, op. cit.

Willcock, G. D., "Shakespeare and Elizabethan English," *Shakespeare Survey* 7 (1954)

[p. 171] all quotations from Elizabethan authors—John Cheke, George Gascoigne, Thomas Wilson, and Thomas Elyot—in Sir William Craigie, *The Critique of Pure English from Caxton to Smollett* (1946)

[p. 172] Richard Carew, "The Excellency of the English Tongue," in G. G. Smith, op. cit.

[p. 172] Thomas Heywood, *Apology for Actors* (1612)

Brook, op. cit.

Ewbank, op. cit.

Blake, op. cit.

Onions, C. T., *A Shakespeare Glossary* (1919; revised R. D. Eagleson, 1986)

Wilson, F. P., op. cit.

CHAPTER 13: SHAKESPEARE ALIVE?

GLOBE-TROTTER

——— *Annual Report and Statement of Accounts for the Year ended 31 December 1982*, Shakespeare Birthplace Trust

Brown, I., *This Shakespeare Industry* (1939)

Zbierski, H., "Shakespeare in Poland," *Theatre Review* 2 (1960)

National Library, Calcutta, *Shakespeare in India* (1964)

Samarin, R., and Nikolyukin, A., *Shakespeare in the Soviet Union* (1966)

Klajn, H., "Shakespeare in Yugoslavia," *Shakespeare Quarterly* 5 (1954)

Sideris, Joannis, "Shakespeare in Greece," *Theatre Review* 6, no. 2 (1964)

Harwood, Gina, "Shylock in Zanzibar," *Spectator*, June 1, 1934

And, Metin, "Shakespeare in Turkey," *Theatre Review* 6, no. 2 (1964)

Fluchère, Henri, "Shakespeare in France 1900–1948," *Shakespeare Survey* 2 (1949)

Fernando, Guido, "Shakespeare in Italy," *Shakespeare Association Bulletin* 5 (1930)

Kawatake, Toshio, "Shakespeare in the Japanese Theatre," *Theatre Review* 2 (1960)

Kynge, J., "Shakespeare in China," *Plays and Players* (1986)

[p. 178] quoted in Fernando, op. cit.

Gibian, George, "Shakespeare in Soviet Russia," *Russian Review* 11 (1952) for Karl Marx comment

[p. 178] Fluchère, op. cit.

[p. 178] quoted in Kynge, op. cit.

[p. 179] quoted from R. G. Shahani, *Shakespeare Through Eastern Eyes* (1932), in J. P. Mishra, *Shakespeare's Impact on Hindi Literature* (1936)

Sisson, C. J., *Shakespeare in India*, 1926

Conklin, P., *A History of Hamlet Criticism* (1947)

Simmons, E. J., *English Literature and Culture in Russia*, (1964)

Fluchère, op. cit.

Alexander, E., "Shakespeare's Plays in Armenia," *Shakespeare Quarterly* 9 (1958)

TRANSATLANTIC SHAKESPEARE

Falk, Robert, "Shakespeare in America to 1900," *Shakespeare Survey* 18 (1967)

Willoughby, E. E., "The Reading of Shakespeare in Colonial America," *Papers of the Bibliographical Society of America* xxxi (1937)

Dunn, E. C., *Shakespeare in America* (1939)

[p. 180] quoted in Dunn, op. cit.

Berkelman, R., "Lincoln's Interest in Shakespeare," *Shakespeare Quarterly* 2 (1951)

[p. 180] quoted in Moses C. Tyler, *The Literary History of the American Revolution* (1900), Vol. 2

[p. 180] quoted in Dunn, op. cit.

Shattuck, C. H., *Shakespeare on the American Stage* (1976)

Gale, C., *Shakespeare on the American Stage in the Eighteenth Century* (1948)

VERSIONS AND REVERSIONS

Dean, W., "Shakespeare in the Opera House," *Shakespeare Survey* 18 (1965)

Hill, E., *Shakespeare in Sable* (1984)

Cohn, R., *Modern Shakespeare Offshoots* (1976)

Wells, Stanley, ed., *Nineteenth Century Shakespeare Burlesques* (1978), in five volumes

[p. 184] in Wells, op. cit.

[p. 185] John Brougham, *Much Ado About a Merchant of Venice* (1868) in Wells, op. cit.

Manvell, R., *Shakespeare and the Film* (1979)

Morris, P., *Shakespeare on Film* (1972)

PERVERSIONS ON THE ENGLISH STAGE

Odell, G. C., *Shakespeare from Betterton to Irving* (1935), two volumes

[p. 186] Nahum Tate, preface to his *King Lear* (1678)

Spencer, H., *Shakespeare Improved: Restoration Versions* (1927)

[p. 186] Tate, op. cit.

Johnson, Charles, *Love in a Forest* (1723)

[p. 187] from the Hiram Stead Collection, New York Public Library

Nalley, Sara, "Shakespeare on the Charleston Stage, 1764–1799," in *Shakespeare in the South*, ed. Kolin (1983)

[p. 187] quoted in Odell, op. cit. Vol. 1

David, Richard, *Shakespeare in the Theatre* (1978)

Sprague, A. C., *Shakespearian Players and Performances* (1953)

AND TODAY?

Babula, W., *Shakespeare in Production 1935–78* (1981)

Cohn, R. op. cit.

———, "International Round-up" in *Shakespeare Survey* 18 (1965)

Hill, E., op. cit.

———, *London Theatre Record* Vol. 5, Issue 5, Feb. 27–Mar. 12 for *Shrew* reviews

Lawrence, W. J., *Actresses in Male Shakespearean Roles* (1901)

SHAKESPEARE ALIVE!

[p. 190] quoted in Lucy Collison-Morley, *Shakespeare in Italy* (1916, repr. 1967)

[p. 190] Morgann, M., *An Essay on the Dramatic Character of Sir John Falstaff* (1777), ed. W. A. Gill (1969)

Clarke, M. C., *The Girlhood of Shakespeare's Heroines* (1880)

Trader, G. H., *Shakespeare's Daughters* (1910)

[p. 192] Hugo von Hofmannsthal, 1905, quoted in *Shakespeare in Europe*, ed. O. LeWinter (1963)